BECOMING BROTHERS

Howard Waskow & Arthur Waskow

THE FREE PRESS
A Division of Macmillan, Inc.
NEW YORK

Maxwell Macmillan Canada
TORONTO

Maxwell Macmillan International
NEW YORK OXFORD SINGAPORE SYDNEY

The Free Press
A Division of Macmillan, Inc.
866 Third Avenue, New York, NY 10022

Maxwell Macmillan Canada, Inc.
1200 Eglinton Avenue East
Suite 200
Don Mills, Ontario M3C 3N1

Macmillan, Inc. is part of the Maxwell Communication
Group of Companies.

Printed in the United States of America

printing number
1 2 3 4 5 6 7 8 9 10

Library of Congress Cataloging-in-Publication Data

Waskow, Howard.
  Becoming brothers / Howard Waskow and Arthur Waskow.
    p. cm.
  ISBN 0-02-933997-9
  1. Brothers—United States—Psychology—Case studies.
  2. Brothers—United States—Biography. 3. Waskow, Arthur I.
  4. Waskow, Howard. I. Waskow, Arthur I. II. Title.
  BF723.S43W37 1993
  306.875'2'0922—dc20
  [B]   93–16701
                                                         CIP

For Grey,
who never stopped believing

— Howard

For Phyllis Ocean Berman,
my beloved, my *bashert*:
who helped me to open my heart
in walking this life-path
and shaping these words

— Arthur Ocean Waskow

And to the promise of:
Dan, Debi, Saul, Ilan,
Ben, Morgan, and Ursula;
David, Shoshana, Michael,
Joshua, and Morissa

Contents

	Introduction	1
1.	Beginnings	11
2.	Otts	23
3.	Older	35
4.	In the Neighborhood	43
5.	Behind the Door	63
6.	Call Me Ishmael	79
7.	Inside the Family	89
8.	The Heart of the Matter	111
9.	Letting Go	143
10.	To Wrestle a Brother	163
11.	Life after Death	171
12.	Face to Face	193
13.	Last Word	209
	Acknowledgments	217

Introduction

WE'RE BROTHERS. Two American Jewish men, the only siblings in a family from Baltimore. Arthur, now in Philadelphia, is a leader in the movement for Jewish renewal; Howard is a Gestalt therapist in Oregon. Both of us are already well into our fifties, Arthur three years the older. Gray-bearded and balding, both of us; thick around the waist, slope shouldered, large like bears.

Fifty years ago, posed side by side in well-pressed shirts, we sit, flanked by our parents, on the battered concrete steps of the row house we spent our childhoods in. In this photograph Arthur is thin and dark; Howard, round-cheeked and relatively fair. We look content. The two of us are shielded by the concentric circles of our family and our Jewish neighborhood, which in turn are overseen by the enlightened benevolence of FDR, whose portrait hangs in half the houses on our block. So cared for and protected, we are turned away from the pogroms of Eastern Europe that had threatened our grandparents; turned away from poverty, away from the Depression and the concentration camps. We are aimed toward education, security, success. Progress is our watchword.

1

Forty years ago, we are well along our ordered way. The Eisenhower years are just beginning. Now our photographs show us in sports coats, slacks, and shirts and ties; we are, of course, shaven clean and neatly coiffed. Both of us—Arthur in college, Howard in high school—are student journalists; but because of that focus on security, we prepare ourselves to teach in public high school, as our father does. Our furthest imaginings stretch only to professorships.

Thirty years ago, 1963, everything is changing, and about to change yet more. The civil rights movement has begun. Howard is demonstrating in the streets of Philadelphia with the Congress of Racial Equality; he wears a button insisting "FREEDOM NOW." Arthur has been arrested, the first of several times, in a walk-in at the amusement park in Baltimore where we used to dance at high school proms. The Cuban missile crisis has come and gone and left its mark. John Kennedy has sent fifteen thousand "advisers" to South Vietnam.

Both of us have been married for several years, by 1963, and both of us have been studying toward Ph.D.s, Arthur in American history, Howard in American literature. But also both of us are exploring something new, heading off the track so carefully prepared. Arthur has put aside his thesis (on race riots) to work in Washington, D.C., for a liberal congressman. Meanwhile, Howard's about to head out West—leaving the homey Middle Atlantic states and his teaching job at Penn for a small liberal arts college in Portland, Oregon named Reed. It is not named for the Portland journalist who wrote *Ten Days That Shook the World*, but many people think it is, because for years its students have been wearing sweatshirts proclaiming "free thought! free love!"— long before the Berkeley Free Speech Movement, now still a year away.

Twenty years ago, everything *has* changed. Nixon and Kissinger are still spilling bombs on Hanoi, but Watergate is heating up. Howard is divorced, and Arthur nearly so. Both of us now wear long hair and full black beards, Arthur's extending almost to his waist. Arthur is well established as an intellectual leader of the New Left; he's a fellow of the Institute for Policy Studies, a writer on disarmament, a planner of mobilizations against the war in Vietnam. Howard, after years of struggling to liberalize the curriculum at Reed, which had turned out not to be so free, has resigned his tenured job, led a local "new politics" organization, helped to found an intentional community focused on education, written on politics for an underground newspaper, and is about to begin a "small is beautiful" restaurant with the feminist and radical economist with whom he lives.

All this time, from the late 1930s to the early 1970s, our relationship was civil. Except for a few incidents, we appeared to get along. We sat without complaint for formal photographs; each of us was best man at the other's wedding. We were the Waskow Brothers, the pride and promise of our family.

But, as in the relationships of many siblings, beneath this civil surface, something else was happening. Had been happening all along. Something quite uncivil, quite improper.

Something that, finally, fully showed itself, when both of us were closing in on forty, in the summer of 1972. Arthur and his wife, Irene, are visiting Howard and his partner, Millie, at a friend's cabin on the Oregon coast, at Manzanita. It is meant to be a friendly visit—time out from the hard work all of us do, time for relaxed connection. Despite the fall of LBJ, despite the killings at Kent State, despite all our massive demonstrations, the war in Vietnam is still not over, but this is a refuge, an idyllic spot. To the north, Neahkahnie Mountain rises, its rugged cliff face dotted with scrubby evergreens bent away from the ocean by the wind. Far south, a beach stretches in a long and gentle curve, the waves are scallops on the shore.

In the living room of this cabin, however, instead of loving connection, peace and amity, suddenly there's enmity. The talk is of politics. Or maybe of religion. Or maybe of—of what, we don't recall. What we do recall is this exchange:

"Ah, bullshit!" Arthur spits, in answer to something Howard says. He flings the word at Howard in a tone of casual contempt.

Howard's response surprises Arthur, and Howard too. It slides forth quiet, cold, and deadly as a knife. "I really may have to kill you some day after all," Howard says. Arthur blinks and looks afraid.

The masks held so long in place slide instantly away. We are two right-thinking liberal men, two workers for harmony and peace, but in us, between us, rage and hatred burn. No outward sign since we were adolescents, but now—when we have become fathers and men of the world respected in our separate communities—the ugly secret's out. Actually we are Cain and Abel, Ishmael and Isaac, Jacob and Esau, Joseph and his brothers—we have fear, disdain, and murder in our hearts.

Years later, Arthur would say it was the "after all" that scared him—the long-held rage that it implied. In the moment, he just blinks; then raises his eyebrows, purses his lips, and leaves the cabin without a word, going for a long walk with Irene on the beach. On his return, he sits on a couch across from Howard, bends forward toward him, and begins: "I've been talking to Irene . . . I need to talk with you . . . I felt afraid of you, really afraid—as if you might really hurt me."

"Good," Howard replies, leaning back on his chair, his hands clasped behind his head. "Good. Because that's the way I've always felt when you say 'Bullshit!' to me that way—as if really you want to kill me, wipe me out. Good. I'm glad that finally *you* know how it feels."

• • •

How did we come to this murderous place? Why are so many brothers, so many sisters too, fearful of and angry at each other? Why this warfare between siblings?

Why so between the two of us? We were raised, after all, to be allies. "Be close to your brother!" our mother would insist. She might be washing dishes while we dried, or ironing as we did our lessons at the kitchen table, or working at the fringes of the crocheted bedspread as we sat next to her, learning how to comb the tangles out, and suddenly she would glance at the one of us who happened to be there. She was short and thin, and all of her would concentrate into this moment. Her voice would be urgent and her eyes would burn: "Be close to your brother above all! Some day you'll need each other!"

Her mother and her mother's sister had fallen into an angry silence of twenty years, about what we did not know. And our mother had been separated for years from her sister, not once but several times, though by the end they were somewhat reconciled.

The last time, their falling out was over us: over the beards and long hair that we grew; over our radical politics; over Arthur's new-found Jewishness; over Howard's seeking for community; over our divorces. It was over our becoming other than what we had been raised to be, that's what it came to. Tante Freda couldn't bear it, our mother defended us, and so they fought unto a bitter silence.

Thus were we warned: "Be close to your brother above all!"

In the service of this maxim, we were raised to be not only allies but alike. We were educated at the same schools (but for one) from kindergarten all the way through college; we made similar grades and partook of the same extracurricular activities. For half a dozen summers, we went to the same Jewish day camp, where both of us wrote for the weekly newspaper and were pinched by the same counselor for, literally, getting out of line, and where we learned songs that we chorused at family celebrations. Later, both of us studied American culture, eventually with an eye toward teaching it in college. Both of us married young; both of us were social activists; both of us divorced and tried to deal with being part-time parents. Later yet, both of us left the academic world and wrenched ourselves into new forms: institutes for action research, utopian educational experiments, collectives and communities. We improvised whatever served our purposes. Much later, both of us remarried, within three months of one another. Our voices on the telephone, we're told, are all but identical.

Then why, being so raised and so alike, were we so distant in our hearts? Why, though we put on a decent, civil face, were we, like so many other siblings, furiously angry at each other?

For a number of reasons, as we've come to understand.

We were similar, but from the start we also were different in crucial ways. First was the simple accident of history: Arthur was born first, the most defining single fact of our identities. Also, of course, we were made different by genetics, and not only in complexion and body type. Arthur was quick to walk and talk, Howard slow both afoot and verbally.

Arthur was volatile: intense, rebellious, imaginative, sarcastic; a loner, and at times suddenly and explosively angry, seemingly

with little cause. Howard was relatively placid, humorous, theatrical, slow to anger, "well rounded," accommodating in spirit
and tone. Arthur almost never cried; Howard did, even on occasions when no one else seemed to feel the necessity for tears.
Was this difference only a matter of temperament, as the family
assumed? Perhaps; but if so, why were we full of rage at one another?

Over the years, this question nagged at us. Gradually, we've
come to see that our wariness and anger, and our differences in
personality, had a lot to do with our family's way of being—its beliefs, its style and tone—and also with the roles that it assigned
us, which we elaborated. This basic fact about our lives—that our
identities had been profoundly influenced by our family—we did
not altogether grasp until we were well into writing this book.

We wrestled for position and acceptance. Is there room on
earth for me? Where do I fit? This issue we first meet in the family. What was at stake between us brothers—what is at stake between most siblings—was emotional survival. Given each other's
presence, was there room to be?

Sometimes it seemed that there was not. That is how we arrived—killers in spirit, both of us—at that moment in the cabin
on the Oregon coast.

How did we come away from there, to the place where we
thought that we could collaborate on a book? Step by step toward
one another during two decades, beginning even before our con-
frontation in the cabin. Looking back, we see ourselves approach
each other awkwardly: a question here, a thoughtful gesture
there, a confidence revealed, a half-formed understanding passed
along, an angry exchange in which a basic truth reveals itself. A
series of verbal approaches, from 1971 to 1975. Then a ten-year
plateau, followed in these more recent years by actions taken in
concert. Words, then cooperative work, and now this further
work of writing.

In the largest of these steps toward one another, we cooperated to help our mother die. Joining forces against hospital regu-
lations and machines, we put aside our differences—and used
them—in her support. It was the closest we had ever been.

During the ensuing year, Arthur, acting on his own, published an account of his experience of her death. But soon we were again furthering our connection, at each other's weddings. After the second wedding, Arthur's, we considered going even further. Both of us had written books, Arthur many of them, but for the first time we talked about collaborating. What a joint book would be about, we were not exactly sure. Something about growing up together yet becoming different. Maybe something about how both of us had made new careers for ourselves—Arthur rooting his politics in spirituality, Howard shifting his focus from literature to issues of relationship and self. Probably, we thought, our subject would become clearer to us as we went along. It would be an experiment, this book, an exploration.

Our project became even more intriguing than we had guessed. As we looked for the roots of our different perspectives on the world—Arthur's political, Howard's personal; Arthur's spiritual, Howard's psychological; Arthur's Jewish, Howard's humanist—we were led deep into our family's past.

Talking from across the continent in letters and by telephone, risking the loss of defenses we had depended on most of our lives, we came hesitatingly upon some questions: about the times we had lived in, about the neighborhood where we grew up, about what it had been like to be part of our family—the whole family, including aunts and uncles and grandparents, even ones who had died before our births. We seemed to have had quite different experiences of our surroundings and, for that matter, of our mother and our father. How had this similar and different history defined our personalities, our work, and our relationships with our present families?

This research into our past and into one another has yielded an intimate record, an "inside report" from two participants at different stations, of how our family worked. It's a story in which people bleed and die. They die of addiction, of abortion, of a "shameful" disease passed down through the generations like the curse in a Greek tragedy; they die of suicide. Also it's a story about three generations of determined striving: about a family reaching not toward material wealth but toward the vision of a decent existence in a just society; about people overcoming painful circumstance to make their lives anew.

It's a mixed history, like the histories of most families. Odd as our family has seemed even to us when we penetrate its surfaces, breaking its mystifying code— "God, we've been living inside a Faulkner novel!" we'd exclaim, discovering yet another secret— we have come to see that our family is also ordinary. "Ordinary" in the sense that it shares its deepest truths with other families: the truths of courage and deceit, authority and rebellion, hopefulness and limitation, of suffering and death and creativity. The family patterns we've uncovered and the complicated feelings we find within ourselves—finally these are simply human. If you're allowed to see and hear what *really* happened, you learn that other families are not unlike your own, however odd your own might seem.

If the particular goes deep enough, it's general. For millennia, storytellers have been chronicling this truth. Sophocles, the writer of Genesis, Shakespeare, the Brontes, Chekhov, Tolstoy, Woolf, Flaubert, Joyce, O'Neill, Faulkner, Morrison, Wideman— to read them is to see that the most extreme passions burn and the most grievous wounds are inflicted in families grand and small. Cain and Abel are not "other": if they are writ large, it is to encourage us to pay attention, thereby to see ourselves in them.

Our grandparents tried to flee their past; our own hope was to use our history to turn the current of our lives. But because both of us believe that the personal can be fruitfully public and political, we hoped that our venture with one another would prove to be of use to others too. A life well understood and described is in its nature interesting, we thought, even if it is not the life of someone widely known. Perhaps yet more could be learned, we told ourselves, from a comparative study of the lives of two brothers in their middle age.

After five years of talk and writing and revision, it seems to us that what we've done has implications beyond what we'd thought of at the start. Implications for the emerging men's movement, in which men let go their usual armor, learn to speak and work with one another, attempt to make a "brotherhood." Relevance also for all people interested in family matters—not only family therapists, but sisters, brothers, and parents who are cut off from one another in anger, resignation, and despair, and who yearn for understanding and release.

The stubborn difficulty of our own situation as brothers became apparent to us even as we attempted to meet each other in this writing. What was, what is the other one's reality? It is hard to see clearly through a long-distorted lens; hard to see fresh. Hard to listen openly and speak with honesty. Yet this is the necessary work of intimate relationship: among men, between siblings, between parents and children, between friends and lovers and spouses, among members of a community. To know the other and allow one's own self to be known.

Within our present selves as writers, we've been forced to recognize, we carry the same problematic qualities we remember from our childhood. We've been dismissive, indirect, curt, stiff-necked, peremptory, too accommodating. Seeing ourselves writing and revising—observing our different pictures of reality, our different styles, even our different methods of composing—we can read our lives not only from the past into the present but also in reverse.

Collaboration on a book is rare because the nature of the enterprise of writing—reaching toward readers across a gap of time and space—seems to call for a particular perception and a particular voice. When writers do collaborate, typically they construct a single voice. Their separate selves are meant to disappear, lest they distract.

Our own task has been different. We needed to make a book with room for both our voices. For twenty years we'd created structures to contain and express our philosophies and politics. Could we find a literary form to suit our need?

At first, in place of our old war of words, we laid out separate essays side by side. But as we learned each other better and took each other more into account, our writings spoke more deeply back and forth. Eventually all our chapters, and their ordering, were profoundly affected by our different ways of being sons and brothers.

What is this shape that has finally emerged? A struggle for expression played out on the page. An inquiry or exploration in which we grapple with the nature of our beings. A memoir and commentary in two voices intertwined. A dialogue: testimony and response from each to each, toward something new.

1
Beginnings

by Howard

WHERE TO BEGIN? To me, the answer is immediate and obvious: on Cottage Avenue in Baltimore, where we grew up. Our common place, our common history. How could anyone hope to understand about us without having some sense of Cottage Avenue, which embodied the spirit of our age?

To Arthur—to Otts, as I've called him since at ten I stopped calling him "Ottie"—the answer mightn't be so obvious. He might start with now, who we have become, then circle back; he's passionately interested, these days, in spirals. Or even, a dedicated futurist, he might want to begin by imagining us twenty years from now, when we'll be on our way toward eighty. Or he might start with an idea—about the nature of brotherhood, for instance—rather than with images of lived experience, physical reality.

But we've assigned Chapter 1 to me. Otts says, "It's only fair. I was older, so I talked first; now it should be your turn. You should get to establish your voice first. So why don't you do the beginning of the book?" I don't completely trust this notion, but the reversal's fine with me. "Fair" or not, I *want* to be the one who starts, who sets the scene. And to me the scene's historical: start with our native ground.

Baltimore around the time of World War II was the sixth largest city in the United States, Otts and I were proud to learn at P.S. No. 59. It was a port of great significance, we understood, and the Bethlehem Steel Works, at nearby Sparrows Point, contributed greatly to the struggle of the Allies against the unholy Axis of Germany, Japan, and Italy.

But to us Baltimore was the blocks of row houses with white marble steps that we saw from the streetcar windows as we traveled occasionally to downtown. It was the Orioles before they made the major leagues; in the glorious summer of 1944, they won the International League pennant. It was the two editions of the *Sun* that were delivered daily to our porch—far superior, even the *Evening Sun*, to the despicable William Randolph Hearst's *News-Post*. Baltimore was vaudeville at the Hippodrome on Howard Street. It was Augusts with temperature and humidity both over ninety degrees. It was street vendors, A-rabs we called them, whipping their plodding horses, calling out their wares. "Water—milyun! water—milyun!" It breaks mournfully in the middle, a blues song of the street. Forty-five years later, I can hear it yet more clearly than at first.

Baltimore was not New York. There was a given in our lives, an assumption so deep that it was rarely acknowledged, that we lived on the far outskirts of The City, as natives we encountered called it. We were sixth, but New York was FIRST. It had the tallest building in the world, the Empire State, and *three* major-league baseball teams. America was first among the nations; it had never lost a war. And New York was first in America. It was undeniable.

Since we did not visit New York till we were sixteen, it was not exactly a place for us. We knew it only by way of stories in the *Sun*, newsreel images, anecdotes from the grandparents who had stopped on the Lower East Side for a while before heading south.

This New York of our imaginations included the vast expanse of Yankee Stadium, easily three times the size of Oriole Park, which burned down in '44. Babe Ruth had been a boy from Baltimore, but the House That Ruth Built was in the Bronx. There the peerless DiMaggio, returned to his natural element after four long years in khaki, glided in newsreel black-and-white in center field. Our New York included also a picture decades old but powerfully present to us—scores of women crammed into stifling sweatshops, sewing sixteen hours a day to make a single dollar. And it included FDR's shining glass dream, the United Nations. There the Babel we had heard about in Shaarei Zion Sunday School was to be transformed into universal peace. We watched flickering clips of the interpreters bent earnestly over their microphones, laboring toward the promised end.

Otts was enthralled by the United Nations; I, by DiMaggio. World federalism, Otts believed, was the only route to social harmony; DiMaggio, I thought, was harmony itself. And genius, courage, and human decency.

Brought by our school to compete in the Columbia University contests for high-school journalists, finally we made it to New York in our senior years. Having walked amidst the skyscrapers and watched the rosy-cheeked girls circle the rink at Rockefeller Center, we wrote awestruck postcards home. For really we didn't live even in sixth-place Baltimore. Our everyday life from birth onward, with brief exceptions, had been spent in one house on one street in a Jewish district in northwest Baltimore that amounted to a kind of village.

Baltimore was on the outskirts of New York; and our village, on the outskirts of Baltimore's downtown. Only to satisfy unusual needs did we make the trip downtown: to shop with our mother— Honey, she instructed us to call her—for a pair of shoes, or a bar mitzvah suit at Hamburger's; to be tested by old Dr. Robinson the eye doctor; to watch the Orioles; to do research for a term paper at the central building of the Enoch Pratt Free Library. Almost everything else we needed was within comfortable walking distance, a six-block radius of home: Branch No. 16 of the library, P.S. No. 59, woods for hiking in, our pediatrician Dr. Glick, the corner lot for basketball, the Avalon movie theater, and two long blocks of stores. We had easy access to a mixed assortment of resources that stretched farther than the eye could see.

Home was a narrow row house that sat high above a steep, twisting side street called Cottage Avenue. It was eight houses from the corner, one among a long line of houses so close to identical that at night, when I was small, I had to count to make sure which one was ours. By day the front porch number—3645—was big enough to see even from the sidewalk at the bottom of three flights of stairs.

Grandma had searched out the house on Cottage Avenue while her husband, Avraham, lay dying in a tuberculosis sanitarium. After she had taken herself and three children through a series of moves from one rental to another, "3645" was meant to be security, finally a place to stay.

At Cottage Avenue, everyone pitched in to make ends meet. Tante Freda, just fourteen, quit school and lied about her age to get a job; twelve-year-old Honey cooked and cleaned and sewed. Only the ten year old who became our Uncle Dave was not productive; he had had St. Vitus Dance and still was sickly.

Later Grandma sold the house to Honey and Dad, though toward the end of the war she returned to occupy the upstairs apartment, where she remained for years, to take care of us after Honey got tuberculosis too. A specialist said that Honey would live only a year, but in fact she lived for forty more.

Honey and Dad were together at Cottage Avenue for sixty years in all, until she died in 1985. By the end, the house was a gallery for photographs, a repository for documents, a museum for objects and furniture. When old friends and neighbors came to sit with us after Honey's funeral, people who had not been to Cottage Avenue for a generation, they were touched to find it just the same as it had been.

It was a complex organism pinned in time. In the entry hall, a blue ceramic swan perched upon a Zenith console television set defunct for decades. In the living room, on a finely made mahogany end table, next to one of a matched pair of delicate loveseats, was a silver lighter that had not lit a cigarette in thirty years. On the mantelpiece above the imitation fireplace were porcelain statuettes of Chinese ladies and birds, from the antique shops of Charles Street. Around and about, filling every space, were photographs of members of the family and gifts from birthdays and Chanukahs of long ago. A mobile made in Israel drifted in the warm air shimmying above the iron radiator.

One of the photographs hung above Dad's desk, a portrait of him from 1950, taken by Uncle Dave, who later killed himself, and hand-colored by his wife Rosie. Dad's suit is tinted a garish blue, unlike anything he ever wore, and his expression also is far from characteristic—too serious, his teacher's look perhaps.

Atop the bookcase, placed so as to face the entry hall, was a photograph of Otts in the early 1960s. In a flaming orange sweater, he sits at a table looking angrily determined. His beard, which later reached from his Tevye cap in tangles nearly to his belt, here is neatly trimmed.

Lower down on this bookcase, enclosed in a delicate gold frame, was a small brown wedding photograph of Grandma and Avraham, whose name was given to Arthur as his Hebrew one. The year is 1907. Grandma, in a fine lace blouse and long dark skirt, stands regally by her seated husband, whose mustachioed face seems grave and aloof. Still farther down on the bookcase are two more wedding pictures, individual black-and-white portraits of Irene and Betty, who had been our wives.

On the sewing table near the bookshelves—in the drawers of which we found, still there, the material that Honey had fashioned into costumes for us so long ago, then disassembled to save for another Halloween—stood a photograph of Otts and me with Dad's father, Pop, taken in 1949. The occasion, probably, was my bar mitzvah. I sit next to Pop, who's softly smiling, only his curling white forelock covering his baldness. Otts looms above us in a padded-shouldered suit.

Otts and I grin at the camera, saying "cheese." We are the precious fruit of all these generations. I am in my last year of junior high; Otts is a senior in high school. Our orderly careers, our lovely family lives stretch out before us. Already our successes seem assured. We've been constructed for the solid fifties, coming up; the 1960s are not within imagining.

Near the sewing table, on the record player cabinet, was the most recent photograph: a portrait of Honey and Dad made just a year before she died. Honey, in a gray herringbone dress, open at the neck for breathing room, her necklace of amber beads highlighting it, manages a little smile. Her eyes are lively still but show some pain; the skin under them is dark. She is pushing herself, sitting for this photograph: she knows it is their last. Behind her, a head taller, Dad is natty in a green shirt, brown suit, and light gray tie. His moustache, reddish-brown when we were kids, is fully white, and bushier than when he was a teacher. His eyes and smile are warm.

Around this fixed point our house, the neighborhood had "turned," as realtors used to say. Transmogrified from all-but-solid Jewish to all-but-solid Black: from ghetto to ghetto in a generation. Decades after their friends, fearful of even stepping from their cars, had stopped coming over for Sunday night canasta games, Honey and Dad had remained just where they were, eventually becoming the only whites for blocks around. After a burglary, they put bars and heavy wire screens on all the doors and windows. Merely to take the garbage to the cans out back, they had to negotiate four separate locks. But they continued to insist that they could live contentedly with Blacks. "Why not? They're decent people," Honey would say. "They asked after Grandma when the ambulance took her to the nursing home." When there were no more break-ins, Otts and I figured that the burglars had been put off by all the iron bars, but after Honey died, we learned from the neighbors that the word had gone out on the street: "Don't mess with the white folks' house. They're good people, and they stayed." Honey and Dad, a legend in the neighborhood: The Ones Who Stayed.

The only Blacks who came to Cottage Avenue when we were kids were maids. "Colored girls" or simply "girls," they were called, or "Negroes"—or, in other houses, *"schvarzers."* Black garbagemen came too, riding on the backs of trucks, but they were only passing through. Before Honey got sick, our maid, Sarah, came once a week to help with heavy cleaning; after, she came twice. So did maids come to almost all the other houses on our block, though the residents themselves were far from wealthy.

It was a neighborhood of refugees, who had fled from pogroms or poverty. Grandma had left home at age nineteen, never again to see her parents, after having nearly been ridden down by Cossacks in a narrow Polish street. Pop had left Russia before he could be conscripted into twenty years of service in the army of the czar. In our generation Hitler was seen not as an anomaly but as the most recent in an endless line of murderous tyrants. Pharaohs, czars, kaisers, Stalins, Hitlers: they were all more or less the same.

On our whole long block there were only two or three gentile families, who stood out by virtue of their wreaths at Christmastime and their flags on national holidays. We let each other be. More numerous were the Orthodox families, whose men wore yarmulkes and walked daily to one or another synagogue, and whose women got their chickens from the ritual chicken killer in his basement off the alley just around the corner, where passing by we could not avoid the stench of feathers and the final squawks.

The majority of the neighborhood, like our parents and grandparents, were upright but not pious Jews. They sought a safe place against the buffetings of fortune, and their lives were focused toward their children and grandchildren—toward progress, the promise of the future.

When Otts and I lived on Cottage Avenue, from the late 1930s to the mid-1950s, there were only one or two children per family, a product of Depression planning. But when Honey was a child there, she was one of many. Children were everywhere. To make extra money—in Grandma's case, simply to support her family— many in the neighborhood raised foster children sent by the Hebrew Orphans Asylum. Grandma took a dozen, who slept four to a room upstairs. Honey, doing her part, would arrange the smaller kids in the bathtub four at once and work on down the line: all ears, all necks, all chests, and so on until the toes.

Dad himself had been a foster child on Cottage Avenue. After his mother had died of an illegal abortion when he was six, his father, Pop, finding himself unable to raise five boys alone, had put Dad and his two younger brothers into the Orphans Asylum. When Dad was fifteen, the three of them had moved into the Shapiros' up the block. In this way Dad and Honey—both "half-orphans," in the phrase of the time—had found each other. In his second year of teachers' college, Dad rented out a room at Grandma's—and lived at "3645" until he was seventy-eight.

The people of Cottage Avenue worked hard; they saved; they lived modest, prudent lives. The closest to an outlaw on our block was Sam the Bookie, two houses up. The men went off each morning, Sam included, to their separate jobs. The women shopped, and cooked, and washed their clothes by hand, and ironed, and scrubbed floors on their knees, and fed their children lunch and met them with cookies after school. Honey soothed her cracked and bleeding hands with Jergen's Lotion.

Doors were seldom locked on Cottage Avenue, even when we went downtown. They opened easily to a knock, a ring, a call. On holidays the women brought sweet cakes and *mandel brot* to one another. They helped each other out with recipes, medical advice, and family counseling. Mrs. Luntz, who lived next door above the Glassmans, came almost every day to talk with Honey over coffee and a cigarette. And together with their sisters, cousins, aunts all over Jewish northwest Baltimore, the women sustained the Co-op, as it was called, a social club and credit union, off-limits to men, which lent money to its members. Tante Freda—who also lived with us as need demanded, together with her son, Allen—was a bookkeeper for the city and kept ledgers for the Co-op too, laboring late at the kitchen table.

Cottage Avenue was a community within the community that was our village. Alliances passed on through the generations. Grandma and Mrs. Shapiro, who had been Dad's foster mother, were best friends. Mrs. Shapiro's daughter, Lil Schunick, who lived with her while her husband, our dentist, was away at war, was Honey's best friend. And Lil's only child, Little Howard, and I, Big Howard, were best friends too.

These friends, these neighbors, maintained a certain privacy—the family unit functioned inside a kind of tent—but they were involved in one another's lives. When they were young, Grandma and Mrs. Shapiro would rise at 4:00 A.M. to walk to the fish market and back, ten miles, to get the freshest catch. On the way they plotted a conspiracy. To save Mrs. Shapiro the expense of buying the separate set of dishes required by Orthodox Jewish law for Passover use, they'd simply exchange their everyday sets for the duration of Passover week. No one—Mr. Shapiro in particular, who was a stickler on such matters—would be the wiser.

When Grandma was sixty-four, thirty years after Avraham had died, her good friend Mrs. Gimpelman, who lived two houses down from us, made a match between her and Mr. Gertz, who lived three houses the other way. Mrs. Gertz had died a year earlier. Now Grandma kissed Mr. Gertz in our front hall, and married him. Matchmaking prospered on Cottage Avenue; the *shtetl* lived.

We grew up inside a morality play. The lesson taught by the example of the family and the neighborhood was that hard work, prudence, and cooperation were justly rewarded by security—in our house on Cottage Avenue we seemed to have it. You could survive pogroms, we learned; Pop and Grandma had. You could survive the loss of a parent; Honey and Dad had. You could survive a Depression; the family had. And you could survive an illness that went on and on. During the years Honey was sick, Dad worked as many as four jobs at once.

In the larger world, the terms were similar. Hitler, flanked by Tojo and Mussolini, was Evil incarnate. FDR and his trusted friend Churchill were allied in Good. If you worked long and hard enough—helping Honey gather tomatoes from our Victory Garden, collecting scrap metal in Otts' long red wagon with the squeaky wheel, buying a dime or a quarter stamp each week at school to accumulate the $18.75 that would purchase a Liberty Bond—if you lived right and endured, you could triumph in the end.

Or, "If you don't succeed at first, try try again." Achievement was a matter more of will, it seemed, than of opportunity or fortune. *The Little Engine That Could* was the most influential of our children's books; propelled by sheer will, we learned, we could conquer the highest obstacle. After all, FDR himself had been stricken by polio, and look at the heights he had attained, all with a jaunty smile.

Our lives were filled with lessons. Starting at an age I can't remember—perhaps I was as young as three—and continuing for at least a year or two, Otts and I were served our suppers, promptly at five o'clock, at a little table in the little room just off the kitchen, under a chart ruled into columns with headings such as "clean plate" and "elbows off the table." For tasks well fulfilled, we received a silver star; for excellence, a gold. A column for Otts and one for me ran side by side. Dad had learned already at the orphanage about the benefit of rewarding accomplishment rather than punishing error, and competition would provide incentive. Our manila cardboard filled all up and glowed with stars. To this day it is a struggle for us not to clean our plates.

The overt lesson here, of course, was not just "clean your plate" but DO NOT WASTE—in Europe there were starving children who would truly appreciate our food. Do not waste food or water or electricity, do not waste money, and do not waste time. Money was tight, time precious. Life was earnest, and precarious too: BE CAREFUL was another rule. One false step might do us in, wreck the futures we were set for. "It only takes once," Dad would say long afterward in explanation. A tumble from the pear tree on the corner lot might break our necks, a stick carelessly thrust might cost an eye, a quarter-orange taken in one bite might choke us, as had happened long ago, allegedly, to the child of some distant cousin of Grandma's.

Powerful strictures, but none more influential than BE FAIR. Our social consciousness was built upon this rule. "Suppose it was you!" Honey at only twelve had demanded of a realtor who had tried to sell Grandma a leaky house. Otts and I were not only taught this rule in theory; we were raised according to it. But here's the rub: we were taught it with such rigidity that the rule was distorted into a perversion of itself.

To be "fair" came to mean not just that we were treated *equally*, according to our different needs, but that we were treated just the *same*, for fear that one or the other of us might feel cheated. As Honey had, when her sister, Freda, Freda *only*, was given a gold ring. Honey had overheard her parents whisper, "Honey wouldn't take good care of a good ring," and she had never been able to forget.

Yet of course we were *not* just alike. Preeminently, Otts was the older one. Here the Rule of Seniority came into play: OLDER was FIRST. Thus, if both of us were to receive new bedroom chairs, huge overstuffed armchairs covered in a kind of plastic at our family-friend Mr. Mitnick's furniture warehouse, still Otts, being *older*, was to get *first choice* of color. If he chose red, then how could I, even if it was my favorite color? So did I live for years with a green armchair I couldn't stand, while even now Otts' red one occupies a place of honor in his study. Wanting not to be Otts, wanting to be me, I falsified myself. A little suicide.

Older, younger: What to do? This was our fundamental issue: An issue difficult by nature, further complicated by the standards, beliefs, and assumptions of the 1940s, Baltimore, and Cottage Avenue, and further yet, beyond our understanding at the time, by the rules and expectations of our particular family. When one lesson crossed against another—be ambitious, *and* be careful; be yourself, *and* be the same; be fair, *and* respect seniority—just how were we to be? In the midst of these guideposts both reliable and not, in this thicket of ambiguity, Otts and I sought to find our way.

2
Otts

by Howard

DID I EVEN have a big brother? It didn't seem so at the time. Maybe there was someone to measure myself against, even to look up to in certain situations, but not someone who took care of me.

When I was only three, Otts would bring me home by the hand from the corner lot, paternally—so the family stories say. Our older cousin Allen, an only child, wouldn't wait for me, Honey used to tell me; but Otts knew that he should, it was his responsibility. But I don't remember Otts this way. Even now he sometimes calls me "David," his son's name, but from our childhood I have no sense of him as a protector.

In fact, he's not in my earliest memories at all. My memories start when I was four, and I see myself alone, standing on the front porch of our house and looking down at our street, three flights of stairs below. My hands are in the pockets of my first pair of long pants, and I'm wondering what I'm going to do that day, now that Herbie Luntz, a year older than I, has gone to kindergarten. Otts also is at school, but it's not him I miss.

23

When I sift through my memories in search of Otts, what comes is his voice, muted, from another room: "No, Honey, I didn't do it. I don't know anything about it." My first memory of him. "No, Honey, I didn't do it." He sounds a little scared, but firm.

I'm nearly five, and I've broken Honey's perfume bottle. It's cut glass, so it makes rainbows from the sunlight coming in the bedroom window. It sits in the middle of a cut-glass tray on Honey's vanity. In the drawers on the right are Honey's powders and perfumes; Dad puts his keys and wallet at the other end when he lies down after teaching school. Somehow I've broken Honey's perfume bottle, and Honey is accusing Otts. He's firm. He *knows* he didn't do it. So do I.

It was that voice that got me finally to tell, after two days. Hadn't they asked me, or did they ask and then believe my lie? I can't remember. The cleaning woman was under suspicion too, but she hadn't been directly questioned. She wasn't due back to work for almost a week, and I could live with their suspecting her, so far. But when they questioned Otts that way, when it sounded as if they weren't believing him, I had to tell.

Was I punished? I can't remember. What I do remember is my sense of guilt, and the clarity and firmness of his voice.

In my next memory, I've advanced to kindergarten. I remember eating graham crackers and drinking milk, laying my head down on the table to nap, learning how to pass a scissors with its point held toward myself, singing with Miss Kratz at the piano. And I remember weeping convulsively when I was told in January that there wasn't going to be room for me after all in morning kindergarten; I'd have to go for another semester in the afternoon. There wasn't room for anybody from the letter "S" on to the end of the alphabet, but only I am inconsolable. Mimi Shofer doesn't even seem upset.

Though Otts still isn't present in body, in this memory, he is just outside the frame. I've failed, I'm sure I've failed—because Honey has promised me, promised since I was only four, that in the second half of my first year in school, I'd get to go in the morning just like Otts did.

It is in this same year, when I am five, that I first see him clearly. He is sitting up with pillows stuffed behind him, in the big bed where Honey and Daddy sleep at night. I sleep in that room too, behind a green screen, but now, in the middle of the day, Otts is in the big bed, sitting up on Honey's side. He's working with Honey on an Indian bead belt. I watch from the kitchen, through the doorway that joins the kitchen to the bedroom. Honey stands beside the bed, leaning over him, helping him choose the colored beads that will make the pattern come out right. The belt is going to be red and blue and white, with eagles on it. Honey keeps on showing him. Our cousin Allen makes these belts, and now Otts is making one for him. Otts is making it, not me. And Honey's showing him.

The year I didn't get to go to morning kindergarten, Otts didn't go to school at all. He was sick with rheumatic fever, which Honey herself had contracted as a child. But I don't remember feeling sorry for him. He was to spend the entire school year in bed, being nursed and tutored by Honey. She gave him so much attention that not only did he not fall behind, he was able to skip a grade when he went back—a remarkable, almost a miraculous achievement, since P.S. No. 59 made it a point not to skip anybody. Otts was the first, it was said, in thirty years, and he had done it after being out a year.

This sickness was the chief but not the only mark of his fragility. Though I was three years younger, I don't recall ever feeling physically inferior. I was stocky, he was thin. I was plagued each summer, it's true, by a severe case of poison ivy, which meant that Honey wouldn't let me join Otts' Boy Scout troop, since I'd have been in danger even on a hike; but Otts suffered all year with allergies, so he had to be careful about what he ate. Because rye bread was forbidden, he was reduced to eating Koester's packaged white.

He was always breaking bones. His nose, at two. One arm at the roller-skating rink at Carlin's Amusement Park, three blocks away; the other in a fight with Normy Schuman at the corner lot just up the street, a fight that seemed to my spectator's eyes barely to have gotten underway. (All my bones stayed intact. As Dr. Glick assured us, looking at them on the fluoroscope, mine were "massive.")

Beyond his thin body and his allergies and breaking bones, there was his heart, scarred who knew how badly by rheumatic fever. He had a "bad heart," the kids in the neighborhood would say. At least for a while after his illness, he wasn't even to play rough, whereas I was told more than once by Dad that I should avoid hitting anyone with my right hand, lest I accidentally kill him.

So Otts didn't play ball much, and when he did, you couldn't trust him; he always had a tricky interpretation of the rules. Occasionally, when the other kids weren't around for me to play with, I'd convince Otts to play touch football one-on-one. But instead of straight-out running, or trying to pass the ball to himself—a legal tactic, if you started the pass behind the line of scrimmage—he'd *kick* the ball along, shielding it with his body, until he'd reach the goal line, when he'd gather it up and claim a touchdown. My touches along the way hadn't stopped the play, he'd argue, because after all he'd never had full possession of the ball. This from the guy who was so big on doing what was fair!

Instead of playing ball, Otts read. He read the news and the editorial sections of the *Baltimore Sun*; he read widely in American history and all the science fiction he could find. He spent every Saturday reading at the branch library, from the time it opened until suppertime, when Honey would call the librarian to ask her please to send him home. He read faster than Honey, faster than Dad, faster than anyone we knew.

I read too, but not the news or American history or science fiction. I read boys' humor books by Leo Edwards, (*Jerry Todd, Editor-in-Grief; Poppy Ott and the Prancing Pancake*, and as many others in those series as came my way), and I read adventure books (the Tarzan books, *Bomba the Jungle Boy*, the Don Sturdy books, and the Hardy Boys), and I cried quietly over the misfortunes of Bambi, Perri the squirrel, and Twinkly Eyes the cuddly black bear cub. Otts too read the Leo Edwards books, but I read those and the others seven, eight, nine times apiece. And above all I read sports: the Baseball Joe series and the Gary Grayson series (Gary was a three-sport star) and then books by John R. Tunis, *The Kid from Tomkinsville* and *Iron Duke*, and then *Lucky to be a Yankee*, about Lou Gehrig, and *The Yankee*

Clipper, about my hero Joe DiMaggio, who also appeared each September on the cover of my subscription copy of *Sport Magazine*. I read every baseball history in the library and then moved on to football, tennis, boxing, track, and even golf.

Well read in the world of sports I was, but Otts had knowledge so vast and a vocabulary so impressive that his schoolmates called him "Encyclopedia." He did seem always to *know*. If we disagreed on the spelling or the meaning of a word, I was supposed to look it up. If I protested, he didn't care; he already knew that he was right.

My mental picture of him in these years is of a sneer. His eyes, somewhat obscured by the light glinting off his glasses, protrude in disbelief; his badly reset nose is twisted to one side; his lips are scornfully compressed.

He sneered, and he laughed scornfully at me. When I was only five, I begged Honey for a puff on her cigarette (as, I was told later, Otts had done three years before). "All right," she says evenly, "but if you're going to smoke you have to do it right. You have to inhale."

"Inhale?" I ask, all pink and trusting, "What's inhale?"

"Inhale, Howard," Otts contributes, who's standing by at Honey's side, "inhale," he says in the voice of experience itself, "inhale means to go like this"—and he sucks deeply in, the most exaggerated inhalation.

"Oh," I say, "Okay, Honey, I'll inhale." Then as I cough and cough, my eyes streaming and my lungs afire, he laughs at me.

Several years after he taught me the meaning of *inhale*, he caught me and Little Howard in the cellar bathroom, investigating what I later figured out were Honey's douches, trying to insert them in ourselves just to see how it would *feel*. He threatened he would tell on us, he sneered.

And once he crumpled a picture I had drawn of Baseball Joe. Laboring for hours, working with soft pencil and gum eraser against my lack of natural artistic talent, I'd reproduced the picture on the cover of *Baseball Joe on the School Nine*, and he snatched it away and crumpled it, and sneered.

And once he spit right in my face, I can't remember why. I hated him.

Only a few times do I remember our cooperating. Once was in the early years of World War II—I'd have been six and Otts nine—when we spent an entire weekend collecting scrap metal for the Victory effort; it was worth five cents a pound. I recall especially a marvelous find—an old steam iron, five times as heavy as the electric iron Honey used. We worked in busy harmony, Otts and I—knocking at neighbors' doors up and down the whole long block, weighing each donated piece on Honey's kitchen scale, recording excitedly the mounting sum.

Using Otts' red wagon because it was longer than my green one, we piled it high; we had a good two hundred pounds. We stored the loaded wagon overnight near the front porch, until we could get it weighed officially. But we awoke to find the entire load, wagon included, gone without a trace. We hadn't heard a thing; we couldn't find the smallest clue. Surely no one in the neighborhood had done it! But who else would have known the load was there? Our only successful childhood project, disintegrated into shock and disappointment.

(As I write that last sentence, another memory slides into my consciousness: of a magic show Otts and I presented in our living room for a two-cent admission fee. Reality shifts beneath my pen: *this* project was successful too. With him as the magician and me as his turbaned assistant, we filled our living room with kids, sold lemonade and cookies at intermission, and achieved a financial if not a stunning artistic triumph.)

The next time we cooperated, I was probably no more than seven. Having waited at the boys' entrance past the time when we usually met to walk home from school together, I searched for Otts in the cloakroom, in the gym, finally in the boys' bathroom. There I found him in a toilet stall, trying to clean a pair of pants he'd accidentally shit in. Intestinal flu, no doubt; but I assumed that this disaster was caused by the illness that had kept him home from school so long. He asks me would I walk home from school standing right behind him, so that no one will see the stains. I remember feeling touched by his request. Squeezed into the toilet stall with him as he fumbles with his pants, I want to help. So going home, I hold on to him from the rear, pretending that I'm keeping him from running away.

Locked in this awkward embrace, we stumble our way toward Cottage Avenue.

Our next collaborative enterprise—and the last as children, so far as I remember—came a few years later. At the YMHA pool, where the Y Day Camp spent its afternoons, I swim underwater, beneath a rope, to get close to where Otts is treading water at the deeper end. When I realize that I can't touch the bottom of the pool, I panic and try to climb for safety on his back. My weight of course sinks both of us. Bald, big-bellied Uncle Charlie, our usually genial instructor, disgustedly pulls us out, coughing and spitting, and banishes both of us for a whole week. As we wait for the streetcar that will take us home, we squat on our rolled-up suits and towels and hatch a plan to avoid telling Honey what happened. So each afternoon we play checkers in the game room at the Y until the swimming period is done, then take our usual streetcar home and wet our suits in the basement bathroom before we hang them on the line to dry. Honey never does find out.

Why didn't Otts tell on me? I want to believe that he protected me. But maybe he was merely protecting himself along with me, or even just himself. Maybe he was afraid that Honey would bawl him out for screwing up his job as older brother.

I wanted Otts to be my guardian, to save me, but he wouldn't—or he couldn't. If anything, I realize, it was I who did the saving. Not only did I hide his stain, walking home from P.S. No. 59; I saved him even after he crumpled my drawing of Baseball Joe.

Honey got so angry when he did it that she pushed him out the back door into the winter night and locked the door against him. Even though all he had on was pajamas and a robe! Didn't she understand that he'd be cold? I could hardly believe that she had done it, and began to plead for his return. She did allow him in, but he acted as if he didn't care. The two of them were quite a pair. Not a smidgen of appreciation came my way. Maybe he didn't know that I had talked him in.

Still, as I think more about the swimming incident and the Y Day Camp in general, I see that there *was* something different about the way we were with one another there. If Otts couldn't save me, he could, at the Y, be something of a mentor to me. At the age of eight, I joined the staff of the *Y's Owl*, the mimeo-graphed newspaper he had begun. I remember his first instructions to me as he gave me a reporting task—"If you're going to be a reporter, Howard, you must *always* carry a pencil, because you never know when you might need one. You might be at the scene of a fire and have to get some information down! *Always* carry a pencil!"—and to this day I always do carry a pen or pencil in my left pants pocket, lest I be caught, somewhere, unprepared.

The women counselors of the Y! With surreptitious nods, Otts, now sixteen and himself a counselor, would point them out to me: vivacious Ann, who had a dazzling smile; the darkly beautiful Debby, whose arms were covered with black hair; Harriet, a woman no taller than Honey but with enormous breasts, which we could gape at undiscovered as, standing on her boyfriend's shoulders in the pool, she bent over and revealed herself. And the softly erotic, enigmatic Joby, age eighteen, whom Otts took out once to a movie, but with whom I, a counselor in training at thirteen, got further than he did, when she let me feel her up on the bus rides to the downtown Y, and underwater in the pool.

Joby was the first in a long line of Otts' women I competed for. His fiancée Asnah, his almost-fiancée Elly, his wife Irene, his living-partner Rosalie: for all these women I competed with him mentally, imagining myself as their consort. Asnah most vividly. While I was still in high school, fat envelopes for Otts arrived almost daily from Brandeis, addressed in her green ink; they overflowed the drawer of his night table. Sitting on the edge of Otts' bed while he worked late at Hopkins, feverish with lust and panicky with the fear of getting caught, I frantically devoured each torrid page. Many times I visited that drawer, feeding my fantasies with Asnah's imagery.

I wanted Otts to be a guardian, a mentor, but at the same time, almost reflexively it seems, I took him as a rival. I went to war with Otts instead of Dad.

The world of sports, as usual, was where I felt most confident of winning. On the porch of the Mansion House in Druid Hill Park, where the Y Day Camp based its operations, I played ping-pong for hours in the heavy summer heat, developing my cuts and slams until I was one of the best players in the camp. On the softball fields also I was a star—pitcher and clean-up batter for my team.

The finest moment of my camp career came when I was twelve, in my last game as a camper, the annual all-star game in which a team of campers played against the counselors. I am pitching for the campers; Otts is playing left field for the counselors. We are down by a run as we go up for our last at-bats. With one man on, I'm due at the plate. I select a red bat that a little kid has brought—a bat I've never seen before, but it feels exactly right. On the first pitch I hit the ball harder than I ever have, pulling it high and deep to left. As I finish my swing and start toward first, I have a glimpse of Otts' face as he sees how far the ball will go. It is a face of panic and despair. Rounding first, I see that the ball is over him; it will roll forever on the grass, into the trees that ring left field; there is no stopping it.

Ever since, this image has sustained me. With my mind at rest, I see myself at twelve years old, swinging the perfectly weighted bat: the solid impact travels up my arms, my chest opens, I am at peace. The moment lives in me as a time of strength, solidity, and grace—the moment when I defeated Otts, turning his sneering face to fear.

But even this triumph was merely one episode in a long struggle for supremacy. In the mental world, Otts reigned; in the social and physical, I did. I starred on the playing fields, all through grade school I had the lead in class plays, I was elected homeroom president several times, I had boyfriends and some success with girls—achievements none of which could Otts have claimed—yet with the exception of moments here and there, I persisted in feeling his inferior. All my well-roundedness and popularity seemed not to matter much.

In the family too I had found a way to be, made myself a place. Honey was intense, enthusiastic, fiercely protective, and competent at almost everything; despite her lengthy illness, she never relinquished the reins of household management. Dad was warm, playful, careful, and responsible. Otts was brilliant, skeptical, angry, and unpredictable. I became a kind of diplomat.

But there was a lot I didn't understand. What the kids in the neighborhood said of Otts had something to it: while he was smart, very smart, he had no common sense. Why did he throw his white-bread crusts behind the stove? Didn't he know Honey would get mad at him? Why did he listen to the news every hour on the hour, even though it was exactly the same as it had been the hour before? Why did he suddenly begin to yell, rush upstairs, and slam the door? Why did he upset Grandma by insisting that he was an atheist? Why did he read all day on Saturdays? Why did he waste his time imagining major league teams some day on the West Coast and in Canada, when we didn't even have one yet in Baltimore?

He was foolhardly to the point of craziness. It was one of his life's ambitions to be outside in the middle of a Florida hurricane. *Outside!* And when Uncle Mike, Dad's oldest brother, bought a brand-new Schwinn for each of us, the first bikes we had ever owned and by far the most expensive gifts we had ever gotten, Otts didn't wait to find out how to ride but simply mounted it and started off! He steered erratically, wobbling off a cinder path at the entrance to Druid Hill Park and heading toward a deep forested ravine. "Jump!" I yelled, but stubbornly he stayed aboard—and at the very edge of the precipice, he figured out the brakes, barely in time.

Everything he thought and did seemed to go off, like his nose, at a peculiar angle. No wonder he had no friends.

If we never knew when Otts might erupt in anger (like her father, Honey would mutter), the family could depend on me. I was the one who laughed, who helped. Unlike Otts, I was close to Dad, holding the flashlight for him while he fixed a socket, talking sports with him, and practicing my softball pitching; and because I was likable, I was easier than Otts for Honey too, although their tastes were more alike. But even all that, my solid placement in the family, was somehow irrelevant, for what really mattered was the immensity of what Otts knew: the tricky quickness of his mind, the relentless flow of words, one of which at any moment I might fail to understand. All that mattered finally was his look of triumphant contempt when he had clinched his argument.

I wanted to destroy that face. We seldom fought with fists, Otts and I; we fought with words. But there were two fistfights that stand out in my memory.

The first must have been when I was twelve or thirteen, not

long after the first Joe Louis–Jersey Joe Walcott fight. Suddenly, after having been a Yankee fan, a winner, ever since I could remember, I was rooting for an underdog. Bent toward the radio, I felt for Jersey Joe, who was poor and had seven or nine or eleven kids and had fought the fight of his life against the Brown Bomber, only to have the title stolen from him on a bad decision. For weeks afterward I'd lock myself into the upstairs bathroom, right next to Otts' room, and dance and jab in my jockey shorts before the mirror, being Jersey Joe for fifteen sweaty rounds. As I pivoted and grabbed and uppercut, I would call the fight as well, in my best radio announcer's voice. By the end it was Jersey Joe, not Louis, who was Heavyweight Champion of the World. Meanwhile Otts would lie reading in his bed, oblivious to my strenuous attempt to right a grievous wrong.

The next time we got into a quarrel, I decided on the spur of the moment to try out being Jersey Joe for real, even though we were outside in the street. I danced, I jabbed, I borrowed all the grizzled veteran's tricks—but the fight ended inconclusively. I got Otts on the lip, enough to make it swell, but he got me on the nose, enough to make it bleed a little, and before we could determine a victor, Mr. Gertz from up the block came down and stopped us. Jewish brothers fighting in the street! For shame!

The Walcott fight, it turned out, was only a preliminary to the fiercest struggle of our youth, when Otts was eighteen and I was fifteen. Both of us are pretty much full grown, almost identical in size, now that Otts has gained some weight.

It's dinnertime. Honey, who has recently been sick again, has finished ladling out the soup and set it at our places. She's back in her usual spot at one end of the formica table. On the long side of the table, Otts and I are in our regular seats, Otts between Honey and me. Since Dad is at one of his early-evening teaching jobs, his chair at the other end is empty.

The soup is served, but something's wrong—Honey isn't eating. Hunched, drawn, she sits with her jaw clenched, looking hard at Otts. Otts, I see, is *reading at the table*. Otts *knows* that he's not supposed to be reading at the table, and he *knows* that Honey is waiting for him to stop, but he keeps reading anyway— lips compressed, he refuses to look up.

"Otts," I say mildly, "Would you please stop reading, so that Honey can start to eat?" No answer. Honey's jaw gets tighter yet. I wait. Still no answer, and still Honey doesn't eat. Carefully I reach around Otts to his left, not touching him, and pull away his magazine. Eyes bulging with contempt, he slaps my face—and suddenly I am enraged.

I've never been so furious. Years of repressed anger erupt. I lose control and go at Otts. Sprung from her frozen posture, Honey's suddenly between us. Eyes burning, she hangs onto my arms. "Howard, stop!" she orders, but I brush her aside like a mosquito. Meanwhile Otts stands arms folded, sneering at me. Honey grabs my T-shirt; I rip it from her hands and pull it off. As I move again toward Otts, she clutches at my belt. I undo my buckle and thrust my pants away; my jockey shorts go with them.

Now there's nothing left that she will grab. Free at last! I'm Tarzan of the Jungle in the middle of our kitchen. Thick-necked, hairy, with barrel chest and sloping shoulders I'm ready for the kill. I turn again toward Otts.

Honey retreats to the hall telephone, her last resort in an emergency. "Howard, I'll call the police if you don't stop! I swear I will!" Otts and I ignore her.

So now it's just the two of us, facing each other in the narrow corridor between the kitchen table and the work counter. He's removed only his glasses. With a cry of joy I lunge at him. I'll hit him with my right, I'll beat him to a pulp!

But he's as big as I am. He just looks steadily at me, his naked eyes strangely vulnerable, and without a word ties me up in a bear hug. Silently we struggle, locked in combat. Our heads are so close I can smell his sour breath, can hardly tell his panting from my own. Sweat makes my arms and shoulders slippery, but he keeps his hold. I try to push him off, but he's as strong as I am. With my arms entrapped, I can't get any power in my punches; they fall, blunted, on his back. I heave, I strain, I try to batter him. Finally I tire. My rage is all for nought.

Even combat, yet I felt defeated. To feel equal, I would have to win.

3
Older

by Arthur

I DON'T remember anything about myself, I don't remember having a self, until I was three years old and eighteen days. Then Howard came into the world and forced me into the world as well.

It started right away, when we went to visit Howard and Honey in the hospital. This was my first car trip, and I was riding in the taxicab that one of the neighbors owned. (Nobody on our block could afford to own a car to use for pleasure, and nobody on our block could afford to call a cab just for a whim.) So I was enjoying my first ride in a car, staring out the window as the city zipped past. "What street is this?" "It's Howard Street." (Now that's too much. Did they have to name a street for him? Well, if that's the way it is, I can at least find out—) "Where's Arthur Street?"

Silence. Then laughter. "There isn't any."

There isn't any? How come? Why not? And laughing about it? Unfair!

I hated the day Howard was born. And the trouble didn't stop there. It just got worse.

About the broken perfume bottle. Howard says it was two days before he told. I'm sure it was two weeks. I remember endless pain, when Honey was certain I had broken it. Howard was too young to lie, she thought. But I was already mysterious to them; they thought I might know anything, do anything. I had already become the outsider. Howard's silence only made the chasm deeper.

The chasm kept on widening, deepening. I remember when Marty Zeskind, from across the street, got a notion in his head one afternoon that required lining up a bunch of kids and marching us up and down the Cottage Avenue sidewalk. Every once in a while he'd swing a rope across our backs—a lash or two. I think the notion was that we were Alaskan huskies, pulling a sled across the ice, and he was the driver. Anyway, the game gave him license to march us around and occasionally swing that rope.

But suddenly—from off our porch, way across the street and twenty-one steps up—practically another country, there was Honey among us, a Fury scattering the enemy. Suddenly she snatched the rope from Marty's hand. Indeed a Fury—she was furious at everybody: at Marty for hitting us, at us for letting him, and most of all at me.

"Why did you let him do it?" she demanded. "You're old enough to take up for the little kids! Especially for Howard! You're the older brother. You take care of him!"

"But Honey, it was just a game. He wasn't really beating on us hard."

Her glare turned my eyes so hot they couldn't keep from tearing: "Not ever! Not at all! You understand?"

"Yes, Honey."

The intensity of that anger! Defend the underdog!—Yes, Honey. But the underdog is me, Honey.—No, you're the older one, the bigger one; it's someone else who is the underdog.—But Honey, I'm the one who gets left out. When Howard was born, it was me who got left out.

All these years, there hasn't been any place to put that anger. Howard was the reason I got into trouble, but I couldn't turn it against him, because he was the underdog. I couldn't turn it against Honey, because she was Honey and also she was right: I *do* have to defend the underdog. So how can I be angry?

Of course, I can be angry at Marty, at all the Martys who beat up on the underdogs. I don't regret the learning of that outrage. And I can imitate Honey's flaming glare, get it so perfect that it takes me only a momentary glance to wither the oppressor. But I overlearned that glare. The other thing I could do was to keep a hot but secret anger at Howard and Honey. I could glare the blazing glare at them and all the other close and loving people in my life. Howard didn't need to learn that glare: Howard didn't need to defend all those underdogs.

Howard and Honey—that's who I was angry at. They conspired to bring Howard into the world and then to make me responsible for him. Dad somehow wasn't part of the conspiracy; at that point he didn't count. It was Howard tugging at Honey to be with him and Honey pushing me to watch over Howard.

Somehow I got the idea that watching over Howard meant teaching him. I needed him to learn from me. In fact, I was desperate to teach him. I can still see and heft and smell the thick green volume, Cheyney's *History of England,* that stroked and tickled me from every little chart of royal genealogy at the bottom of its pages. When I was eleven or twelve and Howard was eight or nine, I burned and steamed with urgency to teach that book to him.

It was not just any book; it was one of my father's textbooks, one that he taught from. There was even an Arthur in those genealogies: Arthur, the Black Prince, the bravest of the brave who was slain before he could come into his kingship. Here was a tradition to pass on!

And there were patterns—not just facts—to learn, the recurring spirals of those royal families. Patterns: that was why, when I read the baseball standings in the *Sunday Sun,* I invented a real "International League" that included not only Montreal but also Havana and Mexico City; why I invented a real "National League" that included Los Angeles and San Francisco. Without them, the pattern was a fake—unfair. I wanted to teach Howard these patterned waves and curls of royal history—the fair kings, the unfair kings.

I can still taste the sour frustration, the bitter anger, when Howard rebelled, refusing to sit still while I explained the *History of England*. When I failed as a teacher. And when—most bitter of all—Honey said it was okay for Howard to rebel.

To me that made no sense. It ran against the natural flow of life. Honey and Dad watched over me by teaching me; who was I supposed to teach? Honey wanted me to watch over Howard; what better way to do that than to teach him? To me, that was far more to the point than stopping Marty Zeskind from whopping us on the back with a rope.

For me, it was ecstasy to learn from books. Honey thought so; Dad thought so; why didn't Howard think so, and why didn't Honey think it was all right for me to show him that it was?

By being teachers with their lives, Honey and Dad had made me want to be a teacher; but who would be my student? Wasn't Howard assigned by life to be my student? If he rebelled, who else would learn from me? How could I be a teacher if I had no one to teach?

I know that in some sense Howard learned from me, so deeply that he followed in my footsteps. But that felt remote, unsatisfying, and maybe even frightening. Behind me on my path I could hear him slogging along and maybe even catching up. But when I tried to teach him face to face, he wouldn't listen.

The only way I could respond to such a wall of blankness was to turn away. To find responses somewhere else. For years when we were older, there was politeness as a transparent wall between us. But when we were kids, all I can remember is frustration and anger. I was a born teacher, and even though everybody said I was so smart, nobody wanted to learn from me.

But from Howard—this was ridiculous!—they were willing to learn. Especially about the one thing they thought he knew: sports.

There was a myth that Howard was athletic and I wasn't, but it did not come from the facts. The facts were that I learned to swim instantly, while Howard took ages. I learned to ride a bike instantly; Howard took ages. Dad had to hand-letter him a certificate for "intestinal fortitude," he took so long to learn to ride that bike.

What certificates did I get from Dad? Just one about genius being "99% perspiration, only 1% inspiration." Thanks a lot. That was a warning, not an affirmation. Dad gave it to me because I loved to learn the big patterns in a great swoop, not little facts and details step by step. So even for what I was good at, I got "taught," not celebrated. And what Howard got celebrated for—his perseverance—is what I got rebuked for lacking.

But sometimes, even in sports, perseverance was really not the point. Sometimes my way—just jump on the bike and pedal, it doesn't take perspiration—worked just fine. It worked the summer before my senior year at Hopkins when I was a real estate title searcher. All of the title searchers played touch football in a little park near City Hall, and I was the star. (Howard—did you know that, wise guy? Most touchdowns scored, most touchdown passes thrown. Ha!)

And I read *Baseball Joe* and all those other sports books. They were, after all, books. *I* know John McGraw used to tell the old, old Orioles—back around 1900, when the games had only one umpire—to wait until the umpire's back was turned and cut across the diamond from first base straight to third. Next to that, what's a little creative juggling of the rules, like shouting "Fumble!" while I jiggled the football upfield?

But I remember the moment that sealed my identity; nobody in the family ever forgot. One day I noticed a headline in the *Baltimore Sun*: "What Did Senators Do with Johnson?" "Strange question," I said. "They acquitted him from the House impeachment charges. Everybody knows that!"

Howard and Dad guffawed and screamed and shook. "Not Andrew Johnson, *Walter* Johnson! Not the president, the pitcher! Not the U.S. senators, the Washington Senators. Baseball!"

Oh. I was stuck forever, in a stereotype.

I've got to admit, the stereotype was partly true. I *knew* about sports, but I didn't *care* about sports. Howard *knew* about books, but he didn't *care* about books. He cared about sports, so he played ball with other people; I cared about books, so I went off to the library and disconnected from other people. And what happened with Howard happened all over again with the kids at school. The only way I knew of using books to connect with other people was to teach them what I had learned—what I knew and they didn't, what I was better at. But what I learned—the stories I kept finding and the patterns I kept imagining—did not connect with their lives, their experience, so what I tried to teach felt odd and irrelevant to other people. The harder I tried to teach them, the more they resisted; the more frustrated I got and the angrier I grew, the stranger—more estranged—I seemed, and even bossy. And the more comfortable Howard seemed.

Howard came to embody comfort. I was angular; he was roly-poly. I was sharp elbows—keep away; he was round tummy—hold close. I was quicksilver, jumping thought; he was listening, "thoughtful." It was easy to embody strangeness in me and comfort in him, easy to split us into two stereotypes. Easy to like him and not like me. It made me angry then, and it makes me angry now. Because I cared about books more than sports, why should people end up liking him instead of me? Not fair.

Were we really so different anyway?

A memory floats back into my mind, about a time when Howard and I came back to Baltimore as grown-ups for a family celebration—Thanksgiving, maybe. As always, Honey sent us to the neighborhood bakery, and the woman at the counter took one look at us and gasped, "Oh, how you resemble!" All the way home with the rye bread and the bagels, we joked and laughed about how wrong she was—her perception, and her grammar.

What did we resemble? Maybe the lamp post . . . or the rye bread . . . or the oven? But not each other, for surely we resembled not each other. What—we resemble? We who were so different: me thin, Howard "big boned"; me who read the paper for its politics, Howard for the sports; me shy with girls, Howard easy; me given to bursts of anger, Howard placid. Above all, me the older and Howard the younger brother. Even when our tallness had come, even when we both lived somewhere else, when we both had wives and children, I was still the older brother. The source of buried fury for us both.

And yet the bakery lady saw it. We do resemble. Now, when I look at my mind's unreeling movie of us that day—staggering home together, laughing at *"resemble what"*—now I can see us resembling each other. When the neighborhood looked at us, it saw how alike we were.

4

In the Neighborhood

by Howard and Arthur

HOWARD. Not only the bakery lady saw us as "resembling." Even before we had begun to look alike, when I was stocky and Otts was thin, the neighborhood saw us as joined beyond our basic brotherly connection. We had an identity, a meaning, in the neighborhood.

Reminiscing with me at Cottage Avenue after Honey's funeral, Little Howard, whom I had not seen in almost thirty years, exclaimed, "You and Ottie were so smart!" I had thought only Otts was seen that way. The Smart Brothers: evidently that was us.

Not all the brothers on Cottage Avenue had a public meaning. The Zeskinds, Marty and his older brother Leonard, were dark and moved like panthers; they were clearly brothers, but as a duo they had no special role. And the Schumans, Normy and Macky, both had a clean, well-scrubbed quality, but they seemed intellectually so different—Otts recalls Normy as knowing more about politics even than he—that they were difficult for us even to recognize as brothers. What did it mean, anyway, this being brothers?

Girls were scarce on Cottage Avenue, therefore mysterious; boys were plentiful and real. There was Little Howard, short and chubby and with dancing eyes and good ideas; there was Herbie, who had round cheeks and a hurt, puzzled look that he tried to cover with bravado; there were bright, retiring boys; scrawny boys; fat boys who could barely move and very fat boys who were astonishingly agile. The Schumans, with no readily recognizable brotherliness, could have been any two of them.

In contrast, the Fincis, who lived only a block away, had a most distinct identity. Word had it that they and their friends had formed into an outlaw gang. Whether they or our own imaginations formed that gang, I cannot truly say, but at the time I had no doubt. They had tied a girl to the Western Maryland Railroad track, we said shuddering, or perhaps it was only to the pear tree on the corner lot. Dark, high-cheekboned and hooded-eyed, smoldering with what seemed a dangerous energy, the Fincis were outsiders to the neighborhood. They were to be avoided at all costs—no Jewish brothers they!

Marty Tulkoff and his brother also had a neighborhood identity, but a confusing one. Their father was a tough-talking, hard-driving, blue-collar businessman, who was beginning to make it as a producer of horseradish. In a neighborhood that celebrated horseradish as the necessary ingredient at the Passover Seder, this was a mark of some distinction. Equally arresting was the fact that of all the neighborhood, only the Tulkoffs went for their schooling to the Talmudical Academy, just beyond the corner lot, a Hebrew day-school that also housed students overnight. Mr. Tulkoff's brusque manner—Grandma scornfully dismissed him as a "grubbe Yid," a coarse Jew—did not seem to fit with his evident desire to make *Yeshiva buchers*, Jewish scholars, of his children.

TULKOFF'S HOT HORSERADISH blazed in orange flames against the light-green field of the Tulkoffs' battered truck, but Marty himself—of his brother I recall only that he existed—was pale and skinny, waxy-looking, anything but hot, a melancholy fact that reinforced my picture of the squat, forbidding Talmudical Academy as a prison in disguise. Boys with earlocks called down at me from the upper floors—something about my not really being Jewish. Who would want to go to school there? To me at least, the Tulkoffs made no sense.

So what did it mean, to be a brother? The Schumans were miscellaneous, the Zeskinds were alike, the Fincis were Evil, the Tulkoffs were the Sons of Horseradish and Yeshiva Boys. To ourselves, Otts and I were Waskows, part of a family tradition, but to the neighborhood we were the Smart Brothers, linked at the head.

What the neighborhood saw about us was true enough, as far as it went. Although our cousin Allen created fighter-planes and intricately appointed railroad cars from model kits, and fitted sailboats into bottles with remarkable dexterity, his talents were not fully honored, for in our house on Cottage Avenue the intellect was king. Dad tested Otts and me on mental arithmetic and trained us at every opportunity in problem solving: "On an island there is a tribe that always tells the truth and one that always lies . . ." At dinner, disputation was ordinary fare. Honey championed logic as valiantly as Dad; careless thought was shocking and all but unforgivable. Otts and I learned our lessons well, at the kitchen table and at school.

But even as the neighborhood linked us, we were viewing the neighborhood from radically different perspectives. Otts' memory is that the Fincis lived many blocks from us, on the other side of the tracks they were alleged to have put to such deadly purpose; and his sense of the Talmudical Academy is that it was simply there—he didn't think of it as ominous.

And we were using the neighborhood so differently that it was almost as if we lived in two different habitats. I used the streets and the corner lot, for playing ball; Otts used the library. P.S. No. 59 was powerful for both of us, but differently so. The stores seemed not to matter very much to Otts, but to me they were places for adventure, complete with sensuous pleasure and risk.

I played ball—block-ball, step-ball, or step-baseball—at every opportunity. In touch football, Little Howard and I were a perfect passing combination. Button-hooking precisely on the count of three, as Don Hutson had explained in my comic book of football tips, I would look and there it was, softly worn, totally familiar to my touch: the ball. And there was basketball. After the

Talmudical Academy fenced the corner lot and put up hoops, heavy-assed I'd risk the spiky fence, and T.A. wrath, in order to imitate Buddy Jeanette's underhanded foul shot or Fat Freddy Scolari's peculiar one-hand set, delivered from his hip. Although I didn't believe that someday I too might be a Baltimore Bullet, I remembered the little engine that could and worked for perfection nonetheless.

Not until twenty years later did it occur to me to wonder why Otts wasn't shooting baskets with me—or why Little Howard, not Otts, went with me on Saturday afternoons to see the Purple Monster at the Avalon. The simple answer is, Otts was at the library.

I too liked the library. Constructed of warm red brick, it was sturdy and welcoming, and cool inside. All the furniture was solid oak; large, hanging schoolhouse globes provided light; ceiling fans turned noiselessly. At the front desk, the librarian watched with pursed lips and folded arms as I signed my name to prove that I was ready for a card; the pencil moved slowly, making sure to come back to the line. And once a week I sat entranced in a darkened basement room, listening to story hour. But as we grew older the library became more Otts' place than mine. And he didn't just like it. It seemed that if he could have *lived* at the library, he would have.

ARTHUR: I would lie on the slate counters that covered the radiators at Branch 16, head hanging over, book on the floor. I can still taste how slate smells when it's hot. I read all the Rafael Sabatini books, and all of Sinclair Lewis, and all of Upton Sinclair's socialist muckraking novels, and all of Dr. Doolittle that the library had, and all the Arthur Ransome stories about those British kids with a fleet of sailing boats. Now how could that be, I used to wonder. It wasn't possible, was it, for little kids to own their sailboats and live by themselves and go adventuring in the English Channel? *Without their parents?*

Books saved my sanity once. Honey and Dad sent us away to camp for a couple of weeks when I was twelve and Howard nine. Honey was sick and trying to recuperate in the Western Maryland mountains. They tried to get us into a nice middle-class

Jewish boys' camp, but all the places were filled, so they sent us to the Police Boys Camp.

They didn't seem to know the difference, or to care.

All those working-class kids—Polish, Italian, Appalachian! Tough by our standards, cussing, barely held in line by the cops who ran the camp. Not "cops." Po-lees. Officers. Re-spect. From dawn to night, sports and only sports. Nobody *ever* read a book.

But I discovered a cache of books, even Dr. Doolittle books the library didn't have. I hid for three days, AWOL from basketball, baseball, football, and soccer ball, from climbing ropes and leaping "hoises." And AWOL from making friends with kids I was always scared of.

Howard survived. He could talk to those people. It wasn't that he was athletically better than I was. Just that he didn't mind drowning in sports.

HOWARD. The library and P.S. No. 59 were Otts' special places, islands of excitement and delight. They were only two blocks from one another, separated by Park Heights Avenue, the main street of our neighborhood, a four-lane thoroughfare with streetcars running down the middle. Otts would dare fate by walking between the tracks in search of matchbooks for his collection.

No. 59 was only one of eight or nine grade schools Honey had attended before Grandma finally settled in at Cottage Avenue, but Otts and I spent our whole elementary school careers there.

ARTHUR. One of the piercing, transformative moments of my life came in the fourth grade at P.S. 59, just after I came back from my year in bed with rheumatic fever. Miss Rivkin, who was young, pretty, intelligent, and short, and whose intensity poured out of her eyes—who, come to think of it, was like Honey—announced with great excitement that we were about to start learning a whole new subject. Letter by letter she wrote it on the blackboard: H-I-S-T-O-R-Y.

"Look at the word," she said. "It's a *story*. Whose story? *His* story." She smiled at us. "Whose story do you think?" She waited. I sat there, thinking frantically. Being the first with an answer for Miss Rivkin was always a moment of hot joy. "His" with a capital

H like that: could it be God's story? or even Christ's? They kept giving us those hymns to sing in the morning and at Christmastime. It drove us crazy—what was a Jew supposed to do?—but surely they wouldn't make it into a whole regular subject. I was stymied. No swift hot answer this time.

Miss Rivkin was too excited to care that I couldn't answer. "*Man's* story," she said. "And it starts here—" and she pointed to a map of Egypt—"on this river, the Nile. And I know this is a little confusing, the Upper Nile is lower on the map because that's where the river starts and it's in the south . . ."

History. What my father taught at school. And Miss Rivkin thought it was terrific. Now I could learn it. A whole new subject. I was practically grown up!

HOWARD: By the time I got to the fourth grade, Miss Rivkin was no longer there, so I had Mrs. Glassman instead, a niece of the Glassmans who lived next door. Mrs. Glassman the teacher was tall, with prominent cheekbones, stylish glasses, bright red lipstick, and inky black hair, which she piled into a roll that made her even taller.

Otts' attraction to Miss Rivkin had rushed him on into the subject matter of fourth grade; I fell madly for the teacher herself. Mrs. Glassman beamed at me when I knew the answers. She loved it when I played a king in the class play. When she set me straight, challenging my remark that Negroes smelled bad—"How do you think *you'd* smell if you scrubbed floors every day?"—I loved her all the more.

And then!—peeking through the window of the classroom where the teachers gathered to eat lunch, I saw to my amazement that Mrs. Glassman took bites so large from her sandwich that her cheeks were stuffed. Watching, I felt a strange stirring I'd first experienced when Linda, standing in line at the front of our first-grade classroom, suddenly thrust her hips out at the class. As I stood transfixed, watching Mrs. Glassman eat, Barry Klein told me the first dirty joke I'd ever heard.

Honey wanted No. 59 to be a familiar place to us, a home away from home, and so it was sometimes. But also it could be very odd. Although 95 percent of the students were Jewish, at

Chanukah we were gifted with a decorated Christmas tree in the central hall, carols in music class, and a candy cane for each of us, presented by skinny Mr. Hayes, the janitor, who with the aid of pillows was playing Santa Claus. I sucked my candy cane with glee, but like Otts, at Christmastime I was faced with an agonizing question: Should I, in music class, speak the name of Jesus Christ? A word was no small thing.

The corner lot, the library, No. 59: all were places full of drama and discovery for me. It was the excitement of mind that transported Otts at Branch 16 and made him hot and trembly in Miss Rivkin's room; what captured me were the curiosities of daily life.

In the other direction from our house, away from the library and No. 59, there were curiosities aplenty, for in that direction were the stores—a row of shops that extended for two blocks south on Park Heights Avenue. The stores offered us the luxury of choice, for there was one of almost everything, and in some cases not just one: three kosher butcher shops, three groceries, two barbers, two shoemakers, two bakeries, two delicatessens, and even two dry cleaners, along with Larry the Hair-Dresser, Sussman's Drugstore, and stores that sold hardware, newspapers, and nuts.

Money was tight on Cottage Avenue, but life was full and various—at least to my perception. Not that it was unlimited. There were forbidden places: the alleys on the way to school; the poolroom near the Avalon, where we might be contaminated by boys whose lives had gone awry; the swimming pool at Carlin's Amusement Park, on the southern border of the neighborhood, where we might catch polio, the scourge and terror of our childhood; the woods that ran behind the corner lot, where we might hike or even picnic, but also where I might stumble into poison ivy; and a non-Jewish region called Woodbury, to which the woods extended. The other route to Woodbury was down an enormous flight of stairs that began at the rear of Shaarei Zion, the synagogue. Never were we to descend those stairs, lest we disappear forever, lost or stolen in an alien land. Otts did once anyway, to deliver a suit for Snyder's Cleaners, but lived to tell the tale.

We did not have everything, but we had much, and near to

hand. We knew the institutions that sustained our lives—knew them intimately and knew the people who operated them, and so they had profound effect on us.

I say "us" by force of habit, but it seems this was more true for me than Otts. Perhaps it's not just that we saw and used the neighborhood differently but that it made its mark on me more deeply. Or perhaps it's that I touched it in a way that etched its images into my heart and mind. At school Otts could answer quickly and question sharply; he could leap ahead. At the library, he could be alone with thought and fancy, and with information from the world outside the neighborhood. I went for fantasy to adventure stories and to daydreams about the girls and Mrs. Glassman, but otherwise I immersed myself in the life around me. The stores, even more than No. 59, were where I met the world in its variety, ambiguity, and complication.

Kessler's, which began the blocks of stores, was a take-out deli and a tiny restaurant too, run by two brothers, Sam and Barney. On my way there from our house, I'd cross an alley with a steep incline. One balmy afternoon when I was ten, I was headed toward Kessler's for a Hebrew National salami when the neighborhood chicken killer's model-T drifted driverless down the alley and smashed into Kessler's garage doors, missing me by inches. With a curious calm I watched it pass, an observer almost to my end.

As brothers, Sam and Barney were more different even than the Schumans—unalike in looks and temperament as one could imagine brothers being. Sam was hefty, dark, and balding; Barney, of medium build and with a full head of sandy hair. Sam was comic and Barney surly. Yet they seemed to work well enough together, Sam behind the deli counter, Barney at the register with the candy and cigars.

An education awaited me at almost every store. At Kessler's, where I could study a pair of brothers grown adult. At Sussman's Drugstore, where for a year during junior high I yielded to an addiction to pinball. (Otts never played, and was shocked when he learned of my habit years later.) At Brenner's Creamery, where Mr. Brenner sliced our Sunday morning lox, wielding his long knife with a breath-stopping intensity that I now associate with ritual. At Ben's Grocery, where the neighborhood women shoved me aside, taking my "next" away, and where narrow-faced Ben quailed in the presence of his bitter wife. At Hartman's, where the bakery ladies laughed at me because I couldn't say my r's. The stores were one curriculum I did not share with Otts.

Images abounded. Farther down the long block—past the shoemaker, where the machines whirred and the little man with the thick glasses and the green coat pulled tacks from between his lips to nail the soles; past the fruit and vegetable store, where the Italian with the droopy eye, a newcomer to the block, would promise that the meticulously piled grapefruit were "sweeta like sugar," and where Grandma taught me how to pick the juicy ones; past the nut shop, its window strewn with cashews, peanuts, hazelnuts, butternuts, pistachios; past the liquor store—was Roland's.

Roland was our barber, a jolly fat man in white coat and shoes, who had picked up some Yiddish from his customers. Little Howard and his father went to Greenberg's for their haircuts, but Roland was so much our barber that he even came to our house to give Otts haircuts the year Otts had rheumatic fever.

In his shop, Roland cracked jokes and squirted water at us from his sprinkler bottle while we waited, and the incredible tits stared back at me from the calendars. Oh for a touch of them! Oh to bury my head in the dark valley between, while the blonde head smiled down at me who dared. You couldn't look for long; the old men would catch you doing it and laugh. But you could look and then, with your mouth dry from the memory, buy a penny's worth of pistachio nuts from the machine, and suck the salty shells until your lips turned red.

(Why did Otts seem not even to notice the calendars?)

Roland's also was a study in psychology. One Saturday, when I had gone there for my biweekly haircut, waiting in line before me, sprawled in one of the maroon chairs with metal arms, was a large, dark, flushed-faced boy named Joe, who didn't live in the immediate neighborhood but was in Otts' class at Garrison Junior High. No sooner had I sat down, directly across the shop from him, than he started teasing me—about Otts. About how weird Otts was. So weird, he said, that he even ate his boogies.

I knew Otts was a "brain" and was therefore thought by his classmates to be peculiar, and there was much about him that seemed odd to me, but I also knew Joe's specific charge to be an outright lie. So I protested—weakly, probably, because Joe was big and had a buddy with him. But soon I fell silent altogether—because I saw that even as he made his accusations, elbowing his buddy as he sneered at Otts and me, Joe himself was pulling snot from his nose, rolling it into boogies, and popping them into his mouth. I was amazed. How strange some people were.

Altogether, looking back at myself making my way among the shops on Park Heights Avenue, I feel expanded by what happened to me there. But beyond the stores, at the end of the block, its broad stairs and four concrete columns announcing its dominion, was Shaarei Zion, the synagogue—and by it I felt diminished.

Otts and I attended Sunday school there, winning awards for attendance and scholarship, and we were bar mitzvahed there. I boomed my memorized *maftir* in a voice more than loud enough to reach the last row of that enormous hall, singing so strong that afterward the rabbi, with a smile, invited me in front of the whole congregation to join the boys' choir, which was led by the cantor who had married Honey and Dad. But that invitation is the one pleasant memory I have of the synagogue. I never joined the choir, because I feared and hated Shaarei Zion.

It was an Orthodox *shul*. In its services not a word of English was uttered, except for the sermon, and even the sermon sometimes was in Yiddish. The Hebrew prayer books contained no facing-page translation. (That's how I remember it; Otts says otherwise.) We weren't synagogue members because we weren't religious, and we didn't buy seats for the High Holidays because they cost too much.

Without language, I had no understanding, I felt a fool. Without a seat to call my own, I felt humiliated.

On Yom Kippur Dad retired to the bedroom to fast for the prescribed twenty-four hours, drawing the navy-blue blinds that at night protected us against the air raids that never came. Honey did not observe Yom Kippur, and Dad practiced this unusual solitary ritual, yet they expected Otts and me to go to *shul*.

If we were able to spot two seats unoccupied, we would squeeze our way in, to be received by old men babbling payers, who with trembling and accusatory fingers would point to us what page we should be on. All of them could pronounce the Hebrew syllables at sickening speed. We could pronounce them too, but slowly, and since we'd been taught only how to make the sounds, we had no understanding of the words. We were foreigners in a place where we were supposed to feel at home. Row upon row they stretched before us, a sea of old men with wet lips and shaking hands, clutching their prayer shawls or adjusting their yarmulkes as they bobbed, each in his own rhythm, to their prayers. The women were confined to a balcony along the side.

We would stay as long as we could bear it—pretending that we were keeping up, expecting any moment to be ousted from our seats by their true occupants—and then we would bolt for open air. On the wide stone stairs below the great gray pillars that once, absent-minded, I'd thrown snowballs at, the men and boys would lounge, chatting softly in the autumn sun and watching the girls stroll by in their finery, heading for a holy walk in Druid Hill Park.

ARTHUR. I agree but don't agree with Howard's memories about the synagogue way of being Jewish. When I focus on the facts, I think he's right. When I focus on the feelings, I don't agree. Did I feel different back then, or am I feeling defensive now, because my life and work has taken such a Jewish turn?

I think there were some differences between us. Grandmom taught me the Hebrew letters and the sounds—*bah, baw, beh; gah, gaw, geh*—And the peculiar fact that you didn't pronounce God's name. All that was pretty nice, including that close up she had this funny, sweetish grandmom smell. I learned the chanting from Mr. Shavrick, who at regular school taught sheet-metal shops. He had actually chosen to become a public school teachers so as not to work on Saturday—Shabbos, the Sabbath.

I spent a year in the junior congregation when I was twelve years old, preparing to become bar mitzvah. There were some chanted prayers of such sweet yearning that when I hear them today . . .

After that, the big *shul* never seemed quite so strange.

I don't remember minding that in preparing to become bar mitzvah, I learned only the sounds of Hebrew, not the meaning. The week of my ceremony was the one that in the regular rhythm of the Bible readings was the week of reading the Creation: "In the beginning." Now when I think how excited I am to dance and wrestle with those stories—how I love the ironies of the Garden story, how my kids and I wrote playful/serious tales of the Seven Days of Creation that got published—I feel sad about the limits on my learning. And joyful about how much richer in heart and mind is the Judaism I have been able to transmit.

In those days, it was just another task, like learning algebra. I wasn't ravenous; I wasn't rebellious.

The part of being Jewish that I absolutely didn't like was our neighbor Mr. Shapiro's yelling at me, "Goy!" when I broke the Shabbos rules, carrying books to the public library. All he seemed to know was "Don't!" He never explained about the profound Shabbos rest; he never suggested reading Torah together; he never taught the richness of the ritual. Just "Don't."

He did try to save Honey's life when she was sickest by giving her a different name in *shul*, to fool the Angel of Death. Honey was angry—he didn't ask permission—but I never could see why. It worked, after all. At least something did, against the odds.

HOWARD. What to make of these differences between Otts and me?

When I think of Shaarei Zion, I remember accusing fingers and humiliation; when Otts does, he remembers sweetly chanted prayers.

When Otts was twelve at the Y Day Camp, the summer after Hiroshima, he was writing editorials for the *Y's Owl* that said we had to find a way to end all war. When I was twelve there, I was concentrating on hitting a softball over Otts' head.

When I remember Carlin's Park, I think of the forbidden swimming pool, and of a huge wooden rollercoaster called the Mountain Speedway, on which Dad would take both Otts and me at once, his arms around our shoulders as the car crept with terrifying certainty up the first, and highest, hill. What Otts remembers about Carlin's is a giant billboard hanging high above it, painted "No Third Term"—his first political memory. And he remembers Dad explaining that Willkie believed two terms were enough for FDR—and what's more, that Dad agreed!

Otts writes that we were frozen into stereotypes: "Were we really so different, anyway?" he asks. The question, I think, is not *whether* we were different, but *how*. If we weren't actually the rigid roles we played, then who *really* were we?

· · ·

From our experiences in the mile-long stretch that was our neighborhood, Otts and I drew rather different lessons.

That life was a kind of marathon, a test of conditioning and will, an endurance contest that could be won by paying close attention to the rules—that was true for both of us. If you persisted in the Good, life would finally come out right. But Otts had a sense of this "truth" that was both more intense and more skeptical than mine.

I had heard Churchill's rousing sentences come crackling all the way from London to us gathered in a circle in the central hall of P.S. No. 59. But when he was eight and I was only five, Otts had heard the radio announcement that signaled the beginning of the war itself. On that Sunday in December 1941, he had been out in the neighborhood with his blue-and-white round cardboard box, collecting nickels and dimes for the Jewish National Fund, toward the establishment of a Jewish State in Palestine, and just as he returned, there it was, on the Zenith in the living room. With his own ears Otts had heard it: Pearl Harbor had been bombed!

The morning after, talking with Dad in the bathroom as he shaved, Otts had gotten a casual, matter-of-fact heretical analysis of the event: "What did Roosevelt expect? He cut off the oil, they were bound to fight," Dad had said. Nothing I heard all during the long ensuing years of war raised such a question in my mind. Otts had reason for radical political doubt. Not me.

Still, it was true that the family and the neighborhood taught both of us that Right and Wrong could be determined with relative simplicity, given some investigation, and that we should work untiringly for Right. But we learned another lesson too, which lay uneasily beside the first: that life is strange, peculiar, chancy. This lesson, the truth of oddity, seemed to strike me more than Otts.

Otts can recall the characters from Cottage Avenue when I remind him. But they are far more than that for me; they live. Images from the neighborhood wait in the wings of my mind for the least stimulus to bring them center stage. Whenever I see a heavy man laboring on a cane, Mr. Gimpelman from down the street looms instantly behind him. It takes little effort for me to move house by house along our block; forty years vanish in a trice.

Directly across the street lived a man called simply Coonan, who walked bent forward in an urgent, shambling gait, and snuffled, and who sometimes would rush awkwardly at us, insisting in a muffled voice, "I don't know you from Adam! I don't know you from Adam!" He had been gassed in World War I, Honey explained. He was trying to joke with us, she said; we couldn't quite believe her.

On one side of Coonan lived angry Mr. Jacobs, who would burst at a run through his front door, shouting furiously that our punts were endangering his highly waxed red Ford, which we called, scornfully, "the golden car." On the other side lived Goldie, a woman with startlingly blonde hair who often complained of our noisy play and once, shrieking, hurled a pot of boiling water at us. She missed, but Honey warned her of dire consequences should she ever try again.

The Millers and the Tulkoffs, on our side of the street, engaged in a feud of many years duration; summer and winter they kept their side awnings drawn, as if to erase one another from existence. But on our side, the peculiarities were more bodily than psychological.

Mr. Miller wore a black eye patch. Mrs. Shapiro had bunions so large and painful that she could wear only soft bedroom slippers, deeply slit. Mr. Glassman next door had a remarkable head: completely bald, darkly tanned, covered with freckles. He died suddenly, leaving his nervous, wispy, superstitious wife behind. Mr. Gimpelman looked in face and build something like a walrus. He had a stroke early in our childhood that paralyzed one side but did not prevent him from hauling himself daily to the street, down and up the three daunting flights of stairs.

The Greenbergs lived next door in the other direction from the Gimpelmans and Glassmans. Mrs. Greenberg was a tiny hunchback, little more than four feet high. Mr. Greenberg had lost an eye and kept the empty socket bare. I horrified myself by sneaking looks at it. Yet the two of them carried on their lives as if there were nothing out of order.

Even the street vendors were remarkable. Mr. Kaplan the milkman had such a heavy beard that the stubble showed blue-gray just an hour after he had shaved. Mrs. Riggler the egg lady had scarlet wattles, which made her look disconcertingly like the chickens she sometimes brought. Richie the fishmonger was short and squat with a somewhat Oriental face, and he talked only in grunts and nods. Somehow the women understood. As Richie stood on his truck's running board and made his deals, his assistant would snatch the chosen fish from its bed of flakey ice, weigh it on a hanging scale, cut off its head and tail and gut it, then wrap it all in old newspaper—this with the use of but one arm, the other being absent from the bicep down.

Reality, I learned on Cottage Avenue, was a morality play, but also a display of oddity, curious and unpredictable. On the one hand, we could do what was right, study hard, and persevere—and thereby steadily ascend a ladder that led inevitably toward justice and success. On the other, who could tell what affliction, or what marvel, might suddenly appear?

I observed; Otts questioned. About Blacks, for instance. I *noticed* that the only Blacks who came to Cottage Avenue were maids, but Otts, more alive than I to matters of morality, *worried* about it. I was suspicious about Honey's explanation that our maid, Sarah, ate at a separate table for lunch because she'd have been uncomfortable eating with us. Was that really the whole story? But Otts had doubts larger than mine.

ARTHUR: I had a Black nursemaid named Nettie. One day, the way I heard the tale, Nettie took me visiting in her Black neighborhood. When we came back, she laughingly described how I had looked at her neighbors and chortled, delighted and astounded: "One Nettie! Two Netties! A whole lot of Netties!"

The family enjoyed the tale. They thought it showed how

bright and cute I was. But ever since I can remember, I've felt uncomfortable about it. What did it mean that I knew so few Blacks that I saw them all as reflections of one person? And that Honey and Dad and Howard never saw this meaning in the story? (Maybe the very fact that I had a Black nursemaid and Howard didn't made this difference between us?)

Honey and Dad saw themselves as liberals, committed to equality. Honey told another tale—of Grandmom waiting her turn in line at the bakery, overhearing one lady speaking of "the niggers" and interrupting, hot: "In Europe just so they spoke of us, of Jews. We must not do it so!"

But in those days it was equality at quite some distance. The neighborhood and our schools were all white. Not until high school did it even occur to me to question that. But now I keep on wondering how deep inside me those hidden issues got. Somehow those questions of Black and white were not just politics.

Whatever we learned about opposing racism, it sure wasn't from knowing Black people close up. (Except for Nettie.) Even at college, there was only one Black in every entering freshman class—each year an engineer. I remember the rumors that this one was admitted only in deference to the state money that paid for some scholarships. Not that the state of Maryland minded segregation!

On Monday, May 17, 1954, my last spring at home and my last spring at Hopkins, the spring I was already so politically minded that for a date I took my steady girlfriend to see the Army-McCarthy hearings, I happened to be home at 1 P.M. While I was eating lunch and idly listening to the radio on its perch above the kitchen table, I heard the news that the Supreme Court had outlawed racial segregation in the schools. To my astonishment, I started crying. At last the underdog is going to win!

Yet if all that feeling was real, how come I still didn't know any Blacks? How come the clarity of my political views—which I carried on when I did my master's thesis on Blacks and labor unions in the 1880s and my doctorate on the race riots of 1919—didn't carry over into my daily, personal life?

It felt as if I were the only one in the family to worry about these questions. Honey and Dad were liberals, they said, but they didn't ask themselves these questions—not in my hearing, anyway.

HOWARD. It's true. Not until I got to Hopkins myself was *I* asking them. It's also true that while Otts was worrying about such issues, I was observing the peculiarity of the neighborhood; my eye was on detail.

"Much of this is touching and funny," Otts wrote to me, after reading a first draft of my pages about Cottage Avenue, a version considerably longer than this one. "But there are too many details. I know, I know, God is in the details, but who will care about Mrs. Shapiro's bunions? Or about the stores? Almost everything about them (except for the things that differentiated us, like your turn-on to the calendars in Roland's barber shop) ought to be drastically cut or eliminated altogether. You're a detail freak. This needs to be more focused around the brother theme."

"I care, *I* care," I answer. "If this is a book about, among other things, two different consciousnesses, we can't just cut mine out. (Any ideas as to what you *really* want to cut?) Okay, I'll focus it. But under protest: I like the sense of overspilling life; things emerging, being born. *Us* being born out of the original stuff that was the neighborhood. LIFE is in the details, that's how *I'd* say it. Okay, I'll focus it, and cut it here and there, but we have to find a way to include what matters to the *two* of us. Dialogue, dear brother, *dialogue.* To me, Mrs. Shapiro's bunions *matter.*"

It's hard to name these differences between us. They have something to do with the different regions we engaged in: Otts in his reading and his mind, I in the physical context of the neighborhood. And something to do with Otts' orientation toward the future, mine toward the past. Also something to do with his courage, or was it willfulness, or sense of purpose, as against my relative timidity, or inclination to accommodate, or reluctance to close out any options. And something to do with Otts' bent toward speculation and invention, versus mine toward observation and relationship; of his toward the political and theoretical, and mine toward the psychological and the particular.

From here, at fifty-plus, we can start to discern the beginnings of who we have become.

Both of us are teachers—Otts in his books and lectures and in groups, I in classrooms and the office where I do therapy. Both of us are close readers of literary texts. But Otts, more comfortable than I in Shaarei Zion and more focused generally on ethics and morality, pores over the Torah in search of moral lessons, then writes and speaks of politics and theology. I pursue the special-ness of voice, the peculiarity of style and tone that distinguishes one voice from another, in the books and also the lives that open to my scrutiny.

The Smart Brothers—not a description that captured our com-plexity. Nor are my own attempts just now completely satisfying. The reality's still knottier.

As I think and write about these matters of perspective, *Gulliver's Travels* insinuates itself into my thoughts. *Gulliver*, which I always loved to teach, because it was all about different ways of seeing. About the various views of the tiny Lilliputians and the gigantic Brobdingnagians, of the oh-so-rational Houyhnhnms and the brutish Yahoos. And about the peculiar, off-to-one-side views of all the crazies in Book III—which, I am just now remembering, Otts introduced me to. He had an illus-trated edition of *Gulliver*, which had a drawing of Gulliver piss-ing on the Lilliputian queen's palace, to put out a fire. Science-fiction nut that Otts was, he loved Book III of *Gulliver*, which most readers find least satisfying. And he told me about it, when I was in fourth grade, I think it was.

He told me specifically about the Struldbruggs, those poor devils marked like Cain upon their foreheads, miserable because they could not die. Then I went to P.S. No. 59 and passed the knowledge on—"My big brother told me that . . ." (So I *did* learn *something* gladly from him, even if he's so hung up on my getting bored with Cheyney and those lists of English kings!)

Thus did my class create a play about Latin American history with a narrating Struldbrugg, who had seen it all, to hold it all to-gether. That was my invention: the Struldbrugg as narrator. Of course, I played him, complete with a burnt-cork mark upon my forehead. I told the history, held it all together.

Poor Gulliver, tugged so many ways. His own view becomes in-creasingly muddled as he encounters all those other views, until by the end he can't stand the smell of his own wife. In my mind's eye, I see the picture of him on the cover of Otts' edition. He's cast up, shipwrecked, on the shores of Lilliput, his shoulder-length hair, wet from the ocean, streaming out behind him. Tied down by dozens of Lilliputian ropes, swarmed over by the little people, he seems too dazed even to struggle to free himself.

And now I think of Honey giving us baths, first Otts then me, in the long bathtub in the cellar bathroom on Cottage Avenue. I loved to lie back in the water and imagine my hair streaming long behind me, just like Gulliver's on the cover of Otts' book.

Otts, me, Honey, Gulliver—all of it is mixed together. *That's* more like it: how we were different, how joined.

5
Behind the Door

by Howard and Arthur

HOWARD. I think of Otts and me and the question of perspective, and then I think of *Gulliver*. And I think of Otts and me writing this book, hunting together through our history, and instantly, like Mr. Gimpelman appearing to me in Oregon forty years after his stroke, Shreve and Quentin arrive, straight from the pages of Faulkner's *Absalom*.

Quentin Compson and his Canadian room-mate Shreve— brotherly detectives, comrades in speculative research. Sitting together at a table in their ice-cold room at Harvard, they sift through the fading Compson documents, sorting out the dates. They are trying to understand what really happened to the South, and to Quentin's family. They are trying to find a story, or to make one up, that will make some sense of life to Quentin, who is doomed to drown himself.

But then I realize—no, we're not Shreve and Quentin. In the first place, Otts and I don't work at the same table; we're 3,000 miles apart, dependent on the dilatory U.S. Postal Service and the telephone, a dubious connection made even more chancy by a gap of three time zones.

Also, where Shreve and Quentin were thinking right along with one another, from Otts I don't always get the cooperation that I seek. For instance, I ask him if he'll write something more on Cottage Avenue—something more, from his perspective, to balance off against my view.

Well, no, he'd rather not, he answers. Cottage Avenue is my thing more than his, he says; he'd have to work to dredge up memories, which would take him time he'd rather spend on dealing with what's happening now. Isn't it enough, what he's written on the library, the school, the synagogue?

No, I think, it's *not* enough—the *balance* isn't right. So I try another tack. Maybe he'll do a socio-political analysis of the neighborhood? He groans—"I have a crazy schedule this next month"—but after some back and forth he says there is another memory he doesn't have to dredge for. A week later, in the mail comes this:

ARTHUR. Sometimes I used to lie awake at night in my room on the second floor, watching ghostly lights wheel across the ceiling as an occasional car would come around the bend in Cottage Avenue and up the steep hill, playing its headlights into the house. And listening to the freight trains of the Western Maryland Railroad, carrying milk for next morning to the city, rumbling over the tracks four blocks away.

Those railroad tracks were another boundary to the neighborhood. For blocks and blocks there were no streets that crossed them, and nobody lived there. No people; it was awesome. We rarely even went to have an adventure there, I think because it felt so eerie to have no people nearby.

But I loved the sound of the trains at night.

When Phyllis and I went looking for a house in Philadelphia, I found myself drawn to a place that had a tiny strip of woods along the back of the back yard, and then an embankment where a commuter train ran past each hour or so, just a couple of cars rattling and tooting a tiny whistle. The Toonerville Trolley, Dad calls it, after an ancient comic strip.

We had been living in the house eight months before I realized that the woods and the train were echoes of Cottage Avenue.

Once, years and years ago, when I went back to visit Honey and Dad, I was sitting on the front porch, all alone, when I realized that this was exactly the way the universe was meant to be: a large tree looming over there, the shadow of the awnings on my left, the smell of a rain shower on exactly these sidewalks. No question: every other place was slightly foreign; this was home. It looked right, it smelled right, it was where I belonged. But of course I didn't belong there; it wasn't home any more; I didn't feel attracted to come back to Baltimore again. Just an imprint on my brain and blood.

When I found myself at the age of thirty-five enlivened by the emergence of a network of Jews who were praying together, studying the Bible together, dancing and singing and dating and doing politics and teaching our kids together, I think that too was an echo of Cottage Avenue.

There weren't Jewish neighborhoods in space any more, at least in the places I wanted to live; so let's make us Jewish neighborhoods in time. Let's gather from all around the city for an evening, a Saturday morning, a weekend retreat.

If our families are scattered all across the continent, let's make new families here. Let's have the parents share the teaching of the kids so that in the absence of the crazy socialist uncle, or the crazy Orthodox uncle, or the crazy liquor store uncle, one of these friends can be an echo of each uncle. The kids need to learn from all the crazy uncles.

Forty years later, it takes hard work to remake Cottage Avenue—a Cottage Avenue that takes its shape not from its space but from time.

The front porch, somewhen else.

HOWARD. Ah, I think, so there *is* something more of Cottage Avenue in him after all. But even as he claims it, he gives it up— "Of course I didn't belong there. . . . Just an imprint on my brain and blood," he writes.

I too have sought to recreate our childhood setting in my later life: the community I helped begin was twelve houses grouped in a Portland neighborhood, whose doors were open to us who lived as part of it. But there is no "of course" or "just" in my feelings for Cottage Avenue. Only now—since No. 59 was closed and the stores were razed and Grandma and Honey died and Dad has moved to an apartment far out Park Heights Avenue—don't I belong there. And even now, after I have lived in Portland for a quarter-century, have come to love its soft green beauty and its gentle pace, its spaciousness and its relative simplicity, a piece of my heart remains on Cottage Avenue, in the narrow house.

Life was sweet.

When I think of the front porch, I think of the four of us together on a humid summer night. Dad is in the big porch chair with the sling made of canvas the same pattern as the awnings; Honey is at one end of the glider, across from Dad; Otts or I on the glider at the other end; the other in the padded chair. One of us has run up the winding hill from the soda fountain at Sussman's Drugstore, carrying chocolate snowballs with vanilla ice cream in them, and now the four of us are sitting in the dark, slowly stirring the ice cream into the flavored ice. Through the open living room window comes the play-by-play of an Orioles game before they made the major leagues. We eat our snowballs, listen to the exploits of our Triple-A heroes, and watch the fireflies winking off and on.

I think of Sundays. They begin with the four of us sharing the *Sunday Sun* in the big bed, Otts and I sprawled across its foot, Honey and Dad touching toes beneath the covers. Breakfast was bagels and kaiser rolls from Hartman's Bakery, with lox and cream cheese from Mr. Brenner's creamery. We mashed the lox down with our forks so it would cover every spot yet be enough for all of us; it was expensive, fifty cents a quarter-pound. Supper often was waffles made on a round waffle iron that could flip over and make two at once, which we covered with butter and Karo syrup and consumed with cubed salami and Velveeta. We would stay at the table to hear Drew Pearson at six o'clock, predicting things to come, and return at nine to listen to Walter Winchell's urgent voice: "Good evening Mr. and Mrs. North America and all the ships at sea, let's go to press!" In later years, after we had gotten the mahogany console television, we watched "Omnibus" early in the evening, and instead of Walter Winchell, Red Skelton doing a prat-fall and disappearing legs first behind the curtain.

I think of the Seventh of July, Honey and Dad's wedding anniversary, when we celebrated family itself. On 7/7/29—we had the date engraved in memory—Honey and Dad had stood under the chandelier in our living room to be married by Cantor Greenberg of Shaarei Zion.

The Seventh of July meant that Dad brought home a huge bouquet of gladioli for the mantelpiece. When we were little, before Honey got sick, it also meant going out to a restaurant for dinner, the one time of the year we did. It was always Jimmy Wu's, a Chinese restaurant in downtown Baltimore, where Honey and Dad would order egg rolls and chicken chow mein all around, and Otts and I would dare one another to taste the pale, fiery mustard that went straight up our noses to our brains.

After 1952, when the family first got a car, a steel-blue Plymouth bought with savings, the Seventh of July meant hard-shell crabs. Otts and I would drive to Gordon's, a converted garage deep in East Baltimore, where we would order a dozen and a half extra-large steamed crabs, which, Gordon's boasted on a garish sign, had "slept last night in the Chesapeake Bay." We'd race home with the bulging brown bag, our heads reeling with the pungent odor of the peppered crabs, and dump them out in a splendid orange heap on the newspapers Honey had spread on the kitchen table.

There the four of us would sit, each in our accustomed place, with a nutcracker and a pick to probe the shells. On a sweltering Baltimore evening, we would close the kitchen door lest Grandma, upstairs, be offended by the smell. She didn't keep a kosher kitchen, but crab was something else again!

Murmuring, sniffing, grunting, we dug for body meat and sucked the claws. We tried to wipe our noses without infecting ourselves with yet more pepper; with paper towels Honey would pat our pouring brows. She ate two or three crabs at the most, with ginger ale; the rest of us had four or five apiece, with beer.

It was a family orgy, celebrated not in the living room—where at Thanksgiving and Passover long tables spread with crystal, Lenox china, and Stieff's sterling silver were erected to accommodate the entire family—but in the kitchen, the very heart and center of our home, for just the four of us.

It's true, there was a "four of us." Honey and Dad stood at the center, his arm around her shoulder. Otts and I were on each side—secondary in Honey's eyes to Dad, she sometimes reminded us ("I love you both," she'd say, "but Dad is Number One"), but nevertheless connected to the center. It's also true, however, that Otts stood off to one side, by himself. At the edge: part of the family core and also not.

Often Otts was literally away—in his room or at the library, reading. But sometimes even when he occupied the same physical space as the rest of us, he wasn't *with* us, he was off somewhere. On the family drive to Florida in 1954, just after Honey's brother, Dave, had killed himself, Otts curled into the opposite corner of the back seat of our Plymouth and spent all his waking hours reading Charles and Mary Beard, in preparation for graduate school. Once we had arrived at Uncle Herb's, instead of mixing with the uncles and aunts who came to visit us, he holed up in the bedroom that we shared, even though he was leaving for Wisconsin in the fall.

When I read Otts's fond remembrance of the front porch at Cottage Avenue, it strikes me that his picture is of himself alone. When I think of myself alone on the front porch, I remember my distress—I'm waiting for Herbie Luntz to return from kindergarten. When I see myself happy there, it's as part of the picture of the four of us eating snowballs and listening to the Orioles.

As I write this, it is January 1988. My wife, Grey, and I and Grey's two daughters have come back to Portland from a week on the East Coast. (For Grey too, whom I've known since she was seventeen, the trip was a return to origins; she grew up a mile from Cottage Avenue.) The family congregates again, but in Philadelphia, not Baltimore, for the New Year and an early celebration of Dad's eightieth birthday.

It's a packed, lively time. Grey's girls and my sons Dan and Saul, four of the six children we now share, banter at Sunday brunch. Over several days, Otts and I engage in a series of long conversations, taped in case we want to use them for a later chapter, in which we talk about how it has been, so far, to do this book together. We have been at it a year. The final evening is full of jokes and family tales, and after much commotion it produces a group photograph—Dad sitting in the center, children and grandchildren positioned all around: the family as it has become since Honey's death and Otts' and my new marriages.

One incident especially keeps coming back to me. Otts and I have been talking, as the tape recorder runs, about his anger. It's one of the things about him that he hopes working on this book will somehow change.

I'm surprised. I hadn't guessed that he saw our writing together as therapeutic for him in some way.

Soon after, when we join Phyllis and Grey for dinner on New Year's Eve, Otts turns to Phyllis to say something more about his anger. "You think I'm angry when you feel me as remote. But I'm not," he says, leaning toward her, his voice straining to bridge the gap between them. "I don't feel cut off from you, I'm just withdrawn. I do need alone time. I *need* alone time. I know that from my gut!"

Listening, I realize with a kind of shock, more than I ever have, how different about this we are. I simply don't have that sense of myself. I can be alone; sometimes I like to be alone; but I seldom need to be alone. In distress, my reflexive movement is to reach toward someone; Otts goes inside.

The simple reason that Otts wasn't shooting baskets with me is that he preferred books to basketballs, the library to the court. He also needed, evidently, to be alone. Only now, since New Year's Eve in Philadelphia, as we move toward the second portion of this book, do I really understand.

· · ·

How did Otts learn to be alone? It took me many years of struggling with him even to begin to frame this question.

Our fight in the kitchen at Cottage Avenue had ended inconclusively. I had thought I could destroy him. Instead, we were physically so even that we wore each other down. I was physically equal, but I felt inferior. All I knew to do, for twenty years afterward, was to compete.

Not with overt rage. My rage went underground again, until that moment on the Oregon coast when I told Otts that I might

have to kill him some day after all. In the meantime I went head
to head with him in other ways. But not always; instinctively I
picked my spots. As a high school senior, he had placed second in
the national Hearst American history contest, winning $1,500.
Another miraculous achievement: he'd won enough for two years'
tuition at Johns Hopkins. Sensing that it was folly to compete on
that ground, when I got to high school I declined even to enter
the local contest. I became expert instead in sports statistics and
won a calendar watch on a radio quiz program.

Mostly, however, I imitated Otts, then worked hard to surpass
him. Since he had skipped a year at P.S. No. 59, I did three years'
work in two at an accelerated junior high school. At our high
school, curiously named the Baltimore City College, like Otts I
joined the Current Events Club, though I had little interest in
the topic; eventually I went beyond him, being elected president.
Building on the tradition of the *Y's Owl*, like Otts I worked on
The Collegian, my newspaperman's pencil ever at the ready. I dif-
fered from him only in that I became sports instead of features
editor and rose only as high as managing editor (he had been editor-in-chief), because the faculty adviser saw me as usurping the
authority of my own editor-in-chief.

When I followed Otts to Hopkins, I corrected for that setback
by becoming co-editor of the Hopkins *News-Letter*; Otts had
never been more than its managing editor. We were both
Masters of the Hopkins Chapter of AE Pi, which I had joined
because of Otts; and we both made Phi Beta Kappa, he in history, I in literature, which I had taken up in college only partly
because I had discovered that I was good at reading texts—also
because I wanted to avoid history and political science, Otts'
bailiwicks.

I had been graduated from high school with a higher grade
point average than Otts, winning an award that he had not. And I
finished Hopkins in only three and a half years (to his full four)—
not only to save a semester's tuition, I see now, but also to best
Otts academically as well as physically and socially.

As I lay this record out, I recognize that in fact I won at school,
despite Otts' spectacular start at P.S. No. 59. Yet for all my striving and accomplishment, still I didn't feel like his superior, or

even his equal. Still I didn't have whatever I was working toward. Still I wasn't satisfied.

During the period before I started graduate school, I squeezed in six months of active duty in the Army Reserve, part of an eight-year commitment I made to avoid being held back by the post-Korean War draft. For a protected son of Cottage Avenue, basic training was a fall from innocence: a gritty everyday experience, sometimes funny but also frightening—experience that Otts escaped, because of his history of rheumatic fever. Basic training was only eight weeks long, a trivial sample of military life, but full of occasions for deep learning. I lived with people whose thoughts and habits were completely strange to me, tangled with abusive sergeants, experienced the disorientation of being repeatedly awakened, for no reason, in the middle of the night. I found myself barely adequate to the Army's physical demands, and discovered that I would numb my mind in an effort to survive.

I use this knowledge almost daily now, working with clients who've been physically abused or otherwise humiliated; but at the time, neither Otts nor I knew enough to value it. After all, the intellect was king.

Yet my intellectual success at school had not served to make me feel like Otts' equal, nor did it even when it continued at a higher level. I earned my Ph.D. in literature before Otts completed his in history, I published a book on Walt Whitman from which he learned much about how to approach a text, and I was granted tenure at Reed, a prestigious college; but in my ongoing struggle with Otts, none of it was enough to bring me peace.

I was competing with him, but was he with me? Perhaps this was a one-man race. Not much satisfaction there. Besides, even if I had won, what I had won at wasn't sufficiently important. For what Otts knew and did was truly meaningful.

Leaving Wisconsin graduate school, he worked in Washington, D.C., for a congressman and then at the Peace Research Institute and the Institute for Policy Studies, think tanks for the Left. He was at the cutting edge as usual and at the center of power too. His books were on subjects that really mattered: disarmament, civil rights, and peace.

Starting in 1962, these books came to me in the mail, every year or two, in a flow unending as his stream of words when we were kids: *The Limits of Defense, America in Hiding, The Worried Man's Guide to World Peace, From Race Riot to Sit-In, The Freedom Seder, Running Riot*; then Jewish subjects exclusively—*The Bush Is Burning, Godwrestling, These Holy Sparks, Seasons of Our Joy.* Although I reserved a special shelf for them, after the first one I could never bring myself to read through another—until *Godwrestling*, which began with a chapter about the two of us. That one I asked he dedicate to me.

His books were an undeniable indication of our general situation. If I worked locally, in Philadelphia for civil rights or in Portland against the war in Vietnam, Otts had helped to formulate the guiding national policies. I directed a summer Upward Bound program, for "disadvantaged" high school students, as a utopian experiment, where emotion and political awareness counted as well as intellect; and I began the Learning Community as a socialist-humanist alternative to Reed—we'd all live in the same neighborhood, study economics and writing and politics in one another's homes, and share our wealth with one another. I shifted my emphasis from literature to education and psychology—rather than just interpret Whitman's poetry, I thought, I'd do Whitman's democratic work—but still it was all in the service of Otts' theory. In a series of guest lectures at Reed on "The Future as History," he had inspired us. "Imagine what you want," he had taught. "Then make it true."

Otts led the way. Proud of him and wanting his approval, I followed, doing what he said was right. I was good at it, but were my actions truly mine? And was my voice—the voice that defended radical students to the faculty, gave rousing speeches at demonstrations against the war, derided LBJ's policies even at Office of Economic Opportunity conferences—my own voice or Otts' speaking through me? What I'd been doing felt consistent with who I was; my work in alternative education, especially, felt natural to me. But sometimes it was hard to know for sure.

Nothing was important enough, in my struggle to feel as large as Otts, and nothing was clearly enough my own, until I got divorced. Here was some knowledge that was mine: that there was no keeping the marriage together "for the children"; that I felt so trapped I had to leave. This I knew not only in my mind.

After all I'd fought for in the Sixties, compromise I was no longer able to abide. Years of struggling for reform at Reed had gone for naught. Reed was intractable—no room for me there. The leader of the conservative half of the faculty, my opposite number, was a philosopher as intelligent, energetic, and persevering as Otts himself. I would spend my whole professional life fighting this man, I realized, and even if I won, the victories would be small. In a dream I heard a powerful voice instructing me—"You must leave Reed."

A month later, having resigned my tenured job, I knew that reform in my marriage was impossible too. Marriage counseling wasn't working; my body was screaming out that I must leave. Although all three children had been born in Oregon, I knew that Betty might take them back East whence we had come. I knew, in those days of no joint custody, I was powerless to stop her, and I knew I'd miss them terribly. It went fundamentally against my grain to be separated from them. Honey cautioned me: "But Howard, you loved to be with little children even when you were still a child."

But I could not see a way around it. I loved my kids, but I felt hopelessly distant from Betty. In fact, though we'd moved to Oregon for a new start and had welcomed all our children, it seemed we'd really left each other years before. I'd have to leave the marriage first, then work it out about the kids.

In being divorced and separated from my children, I finally learned something that Otts would need to know from me, for his own marriage was in trouble. This was the way I finally "won" in my relationship with Otts.

My divorce shook Otts and me out of the holding pattern we had been in since he had left Cottage Avenue for graduate school in Wisconsin, in the fall of 1954. I called Honey and Dad, in August 1971, to tell them that Betty and I were separating. Just afterward, Otts called, home from a lecture tour. He was concerned, he said, and hurt that I hadn't made a special call to him. "Howard, is there anything that I can do? Do you want me to come out?"

"No, Otts," I said, "it's okay. There's nothing for you to do." Meanwhile I was thinking, "Fuck you! What do you know about my life? Now, for the first time in our lives, you want to be a brother to me! Now! Too late, buddy, too late. No, there's not a fucking thing that you can do."

A few months later, adding a day or two to another lecture tour, he did come to visit anyway—and for the first time told me something about myself I didn't know. "You sound angry," he said, sitting with me in my Nova station wagon, in front of the house I now shared with my new lover, Millie. "You sound angry at Betty." Me angry? Angry rather than regretful, sad, and understanding? I didn't see myself that way. Anger belonged to Otts, not me.

An opening between us, which I pursued. That January, on my first trip East since the separation, I pressed Otts to go away with me. Somewhat reluctantly, he carved three days out of his schedule, and found a cabin for us along the old Chesapeake-Ohio Canal. Once there, however, he was really there. Although he had one leg in a walking cast, we walked for hours in the snow, talking for the first time ever about family, relationships—our inner lives.

Hikers we met looked at us a little strangely: at these two dark, bearded men, lurching shoulder to shoulder along the narrow path, engrossed in talk—our eyebrows lifted or lips pursed in commentary, our hands describing the same patterns in the frosty air, our voices almost indistinguishable. At night, on his suggestion, we even slept together, so we could both be near the woodstove as it lost its glow—Otts snuggling up, his big belly warm against my back, his left hand resting lightly on my hip. I found myself a little shy.

We had made a beginning in Otts' visit to Portland the previous fall; now, in January 1972, we'd gone deeper. The following summer we went deeper yet, in the visit Otts and Irene paid to me and Millie in the cabin on the Oregon coast. He sneers and hurls "Bullshit!" at me, as he always had; I coldly threaten him. Finally I show my rage, for the first time since our fight in the kitchen at Cottage Avenue. The mask is off; something real is touched. When I explain that I feel his "Bullshit!" as a knife—

that I've always felt he wants to do me in—I see something new in his eyes: he understands.

After the canal and then the coast, it was different between Otts and me. Not altogether changed; certainly not healed. But we could talk, finally; we could begin to understand.

We followed up. Each time I traveled East to have time with my kids, who were brought from their new home in Philadelphia with Betty to meet me at Cottage Avenue, I also spent long evenings in Washington, D.C., talking with Otts and Irene about the trouble in their marriage (my first training for the couples counseling I do now). I listened hard, I translated, I tried to help them talk to one another. When they did split up, I saw them separately—more listening, and much telling too, about my own experience.

Since the early 1950s, Otts had been the political leader of the family, always out in front on the important social issues. My divorce, ironically, had made me its psychological leader. No one else in the family knew what it was like.

Only I had lost my children, lost the daily contact with them. At Thanksgiving and Passover I went East; in the summer they came West for nine precious weeks. Still, as I'd known I would, I missed them terribly—felt torn in two between my love for Millie and the boys.

Moving East was no solution; Millie was a Westerner, and Betty was saying she just might move again, maybe even to Vancouver, B.C. I couldn't chase her around, I thought, just to be on the periphery of my children's lives. To have a life at all worth living, I would have to affirm my own, in Oregon with Millie, yet also stay connected to my boys. We would make another home for them in Oregon, a way of life alternative to the one they had back East. They would have two possibilities, I told myself, instead of only one.

My boys. I set myself to know them deeply and to help them to know me, else I might lose them altogether. But this required that my heart and mind be two places simultaneously. After all this, a compromise of sorts—but not one that felt dishonest.

To assuage my constant ache, and hold them daily in my life, I began to keep a journal, and then to write a book in journal form, about what it was like to be a father from across the continent. Gradually I came to believe that to understand us fully, to write in depth about myself and my boys and our relationship, I had to find out more about my father and his father, and indeed about my mother and her mother and her father whom I had never known. And of course I had to learn about Otts too.

At the same time, seeing how little Honey, Dad, and Otts had known about what was happening in my marriage, I realized how far we in the original family had drifted from one another. Here I was out in Oregon, precariously far away. Suddenly I found myself at the edge of the family, as Otts had always been. Wanting not to be alone, outside, I began the long work of finding my children, my parents, and my brother.

Thus I went in pursuit of family history, the better to grasp what was happening to all of us—and the better not to be lonely and adrift. In this way I took on the role of family narrator and interpreter, the one who worked at making sense of all of it—the family Struldbrugg, I suppose.

My major source was Honey. On my visits to Baltimore to see my kids, Honey and I would sit for hours at the kitchen table, long after I'd put the kids to bed. Dad would stay at the table for a while, listening to our stories of our past and present lives, and then nod off, his chin dropping into the V-neck of the forest-green pullover sweater that Honey had knitted for him, and then go off to bed. Honey and I would talk on and on, until 2:00 or 3:00 A.M.

On one of these nights, I told Honey of my vague sense that Otts was felt by her and Dad and Grandma as a kind of stranger. "It's as if you don't quite know how to be with him," I said. "Any of you. As if you're afraid of what he might do. So you sort of stay away. Do you have any idea how that began?" What I wasn't quite allowing into my awareness was that I too didn't know how to be with Otts. I too—maybe I especially—was afraid of him.

Honey looked agitated and then blurted out an answer, in a voice unlike her usual measured one: "Maybe it's about the store, when he used to have to stay in the apartment, behind the door, while Momma and I were out in front."

After Honey's father, Avraham, had died, and after her brother, Dave, had disappeared, having hopped a freight to look for work in the Depression, Grandma had to give up her dream of having everyone together at Cottage Avenue. In order to support herself, she had bought a notions store in East Baltimore. To help her out, Honey and Dad, along with baby Otts, had moved across the city to live with Grandma in the tiny apartment behind the store, leaving Tante Freda and her husband Sam and Allen holding the fort at Cottage Avenue. Dr. Glick, afraid that Otts would catch something from the customers, insisted that he not be allowed into the store; he had to stay in the apartment, behind the door.

The trouble, Honey said, was that Otts hated it. He would crawl to the closed door and pound on it, yelling to be let in. But he was not let in. Until, as Honey told it, her voice now more reflective, "Dr. Glick decided that maybe he'd been wrong, because Arthur developed a nervous stomach. First he accused us of feeding him sweets from the store, but then he thought, maybe it was Arthur's being kept apart from us."

I told this story the next evening to Otts. He had approached me after my divorce, we'd gone deeper with each other in the cabins East and West, and now we took another step. As we sat parked on Cottage Avenue, he and Irene and I crowded into the front seat of their car, I wept long and hard, choking, gagging on the tale, almost unable to say it all. He took it stoically: "Yes, that sounds familiar. That sounds like the way I've always felt." He wondered if I was so moved by it because of my separation from my own children.

That's not why. I was so moved by it because for the first time in my life, I had fully felt what it was like to be Otts. I wept for the baby locked behind the door, I wept for Otts who had suffered all his life from something he wasn't even conscious of, I wept for whatever part I had played in his being kept outside. And I wept because in the long moment of my telling him that tale, I was not competing with him to prove myself, I was not trying to be as large as he, I was not seeking his approval. I was simply meeting him, knowing him, opening my heart to him, wanting with my gathered knowledge to take him in.

6
Call Me Ishmael

by Arthur

WHEN HOWARD told the story of me as a baby howling on one side of the door, cut off from my whole world on the other side, I smiled a little grimly: a smile of recognition. Here was the story I had never heard but always known. The story of why I had always felt an outcast.

Hearing it, I couldn't cry, as Howard did; no doubt the tears had been used up when I was two. But the story began to open up the dry canals that could make possible a flow of tears. It took years more—about ten years—before tears came naturally to me in times of pain.

But the story was a start. It had shattered a wall. Not the wall that kept me out but my own wall, the one that had kept out my knowledge of my own separateness.

Honey and Grandmom had put me right outside the door. I have no conscious memory of this door, but whenever I imagine the scene, it appears to me as a screen door. The message is: Look. Listen. Yell. Look harder, listen harder, yell louder. Don't touch. For your own good, stay outside.

For my own good, they ignored me. It tore at their own hearts, of course. I'm sure they had to clench their jaws and hold their faces tight. But—doctor's orders.

That story brought back another one. This one I had been told but long since tucked away. When I was very tiny, the story went, I cried and cried, night after night, for hours and hours. Honey wanted desperately to pick me up, but the conventional wisdom, and our baby doctor, said she shouldn't. Better to train me to go to sleep when it was time. So they sat and listened, their hearts aching, and I cried and cried.

Yes, I said to Howard, "That's the way I've always felt. Outcast."

And yet, all through our childhood, there was one way to escape my isolation: Howard and I wrestled with each other.

Howard's body grew faster and stronger than mine, so we were well and truly matched in this arena. Rolling on a bed, groaning and laughing, hugging and holding, grabbing and slipping, warring and loving. Too much like loving. When I was fifteen, Honey stopped us. "She won't even let us fight," we yelled, embracing. But after that, no touching, and we soon became as strangers to each other.

We were on the same path—school, career, marriage, the movements of the Sixties—but we were strangers nonetheless. Then even our paths diverged. I discovered Judaism, a new kind of Judaism that was alive and fluid and built on intimate communities. It didn't nag and wag its finger at me for not doing what I "should" do but gave me lively choices and joyful possibilities. This kind of Judaism knew that "Torah" was not just the "Law," not even just the centuries of tales and teachings from the Bible and the rabbis, Hassidim, and philosophers, but also what we ourselves argued and lived. This Judaism knew that the very word *Torah* meant not the truth itself but an arrow's aiming toward the truth.

Howard didn't follow this Jewish path. He walked another path, one with no name, which he stubbornly cut from unpromising woods: a college—experimental; a newspaper—underground; a gourmet restaurant—but with moderate prices; a kind of bootleg psychotherapy; a wonderful book about being a new kind of father—unpublished. And it's true, as Howard writes, that he took one step that made a path I followed: he got divorced. His divorce was the first I knew of all my friends and all my generation. (It seems strange now to recall how strange it was.)

The divorce shook Honey and Dad—especially Dad, who out of his own childhood insecurity had made it a primary rule of his life never to do anything that made his children insecure: never quit a job, never quit a marriage.

But Howard quit the job and then the marriage—and survived it. His wife and his children survived it. My mother and father survived it. And I learned that it could be done, and that I could survive.

In the year all that was happening, we wrestled again. Wrestling—in our bodies and in metaphors—is what I most remember from our fierce and loving sojourn in that tiny cabin above a dry canal in Western Maryland—the cabin where falling snow and my broken ankle all but sealed us in.

My head tells me that with a huge cast on one leg, I couldn't possibly have wrestled with my body, but a memory in my muscles tells me that is what it felt like. We slept in one bed for the first time ever—is that why it felt like wrestling? We talked in depth for the first time ever—is that why it felt like wrestling? We remembered how we felt when we really did wrestle, as kids. We discovered that we might be able to love each other.

The wrestling enriched my new experiments in being Jewish, for I discovered that wrestling—wrestling with a brother!—had given Israel its very name. *Israel* means "Godwrestler." It is the name that Jacob won by wrestling God the night before he was to meet again his enemy, his brother: the barely older brother he had fought with in the womb, from whom he'd robbed his mother's love and father's blessing; the brother he had cheated of his birthright. The brother he met again, twenty years later—and whose face he found God wearing in a night of dread and hope.

On that night of terror, Jacob was wrestling, Godwrestling. He was learning to wrestle with the God who was necessity, inevitability, the God of conflict, the God whose universe had pitted him against his brother. He was learning to wrestle with his brother not to win, as he had done so many times when they were young, but to make love. He was learning to wrestle not for victory but for the sake of the embrace, the loving contact.

That was the wrestling of Jacob with God: a wrestle that taught him how to embrace his brother Esau, to kiss him, to feel his love.

Through this image of Godwrestling, the Torah came alive for me, for the story of Jacob and Esau helped me to understand what was going on between Howard and me. If Torah had meaning for me in my own life, the Torah itself was alive and was worth my effort.

I came to understand that wrestling was a fusion of war and love. I could wrestle with this ancient tradition, fighting it and loving it at the same time, instead of either bowing down or turning away. I saw how the ancient words could wrestle, too, and wake me up. And I saw that if I kept doing this, the ancient tradition became my own—and changed, and grew in new directions in the moments that I wrestled with it.

I could see how all the brothers of Genesis had come to make war upon each other—and sometimes to love each other, too.

Cain and Abel, who came not just to blows, like Howard and me, but to murder.

Ishmael and Isaac, Abraham's two sons, where the older, Ishmael, was turned into an outcast and learned to survive as a loner, and who only after many years found his younger brother coming to seek him out and make a reconciliation.

Esau and Jacob, where again the struggle leads to reconciliation only after years of pain.

Joseph and his brothers, who throw him into a deadly pit and sell him into slavery and long years later find him a royal figure who can forgive them and remake the family.

All these brothers began to sweat and grunt and laugh their way into my life. As they came alive, they gave me new life. I learned from my brother how to learn from them, and I learned from them how to learn from my brother.

This learning came not by my lonesome but in the context of a community, all of whom were wrestling with each other. In the years from 1967 to 1972, a dozen or so groups emerged, scattered across North America, that were making a Jewish renewal. Together we were wrestling with each other and with the most ancient tales and texts of Jewish tradition, to cast light on our own lives. What did resting on the Sabbath have to do with preventing a nuclear war? How did the women who were chanting and dancing and miming their way into Torah change the meaning of the Song of Songs? What did wailing over the burning of the Temple in Jerusalem two thousand years ago have to do with the burning sense of failure when a love relationship collapsed?

Each time we talked about Torah in a living way, we wrestled with each other, and we turned each other into brothers and sisters. It was not easy, for learning how to be brothers and sisters, how to live by sharing and learning from each other, is not something learned overnight. Howard and I were not unique in our estrangement; many of us had never learned to be anything but strangers. If we were married, nothing could be stranger than the Bible's notion, "my sister, my bride." If we worked together, nothing could be harder to create than the love of Jonathan and David, who were comrades despite the fears and jealousies of King Saul's court.

Yet slowly, we who read these ancient tales together and chanted ancient prayers together were remaking ourselves. Our different sparks of being occasionally could be gathered into a glowing wholeness that was larger than ourselves and made us larger, too. We were learning to become a kind of family.

Then I walked even deeper into one of these brother stories in the Torah—deep enough for it to light up one of the dark places in my life: a place of Howard and Honey, of brothers and mothers and being cast out.

In 1973, just after Howard and I had wrestled in that winter cabin, while we were beginning to feel our way toward one another, I gave a sermon on a Rosh Hashanah night about the Biblical story of Isaac and Ishmael. The older brother, Ishmael, and his mother, Hagar, had been cast out of their family by Father Abraham and Mother Sarah. Ishmael was cast out, I said, not because he was too different from the family—but because he too much resembled his brother Isaac.

Isaac's name meant "laughing boy," an echo of the ironic, skeptical laughter the aged Abraham and Sarah had uttered when they were told he would be born, and of their delighted, joyful laughter when he came. Ishmael too was full of laughter, but somehow it mocked and threatened his brother's identity. Was it because he meant to mock, or only because his laughter echoed Isaac's? Either way, Sarah felt her own son's image clouded. So Sarah, who had become Ishmael's "wicked stepmother," said, "Out!" And out he went, his mother Hagar with him—out to a wilderness, a thirsty place where at the very point of death they saw God's well revealed to give them life.

My sermon focused on the tradition that Hagar and Ishmael were the ancestors of the Arab peoples, as Sarah and Isaac were of the Jewish people. That meant Abraham was the forebear of both; it was not so surprising, then, for them to bear a family resemblance. The Palestinians and Israelis, I said, lived in fear and exile from each other not because they were so different but because they were so similar. Each loved the same land, and each denied the other's connection to it, lest that cast doubt upon its own. Each people was a clouded mirror to the other, in which they saw distortions of themselves. When could they see each other clearly, face to face?

For Ishmael and Isaac, it took three steps to bring that moment. First Isaac (or his mother) had to challenge the natural order in which he was the younger, weaker, less entitled brother. Then, instead of fighting back, Ishmael had to surrender his claim to preeminence. He had to let Isaac become the "firstborn" in the esteem and estimation of the family. Finally, upon the death of Abraham, Isaac had to welcome Ishmael back into the family, even leaving his own homestead to move and live near Ishmael's well. Only upon the death of their father could the brothers be reconciled and learn to live face to face with each other. Then when, I asked, could we do this? What would it take, what death, what trauma, for Jews and Arabs, Israelis and Palestinians, to look at each other face to face?

I sent the sermon to Howard, hoping for some comment on the wisdom of its Torah politics. Instead, I got a spare and simple note: "Of course you realize you are Ishmael."

I had realized nothing of the sort and felt bewildered. But his statement hardly needed proof. To be told by my own younger brother that I was Ishmael was proof enough.

His message arrived just as the modern descendants of Ishmael and Isaac exploded in war. I had given the sermon on Rosh Hashanah, in hope that the two peoples, like these brothers, would make peace. But ten days later, on Yom Kippur, in the midst of our deepest prayers, we heard the news that instead the two brother peoples had gone back to war. Ishmael had . . .

And I was Ishmael. So my brother said.

I needed an explanation. So we talked about how Howard had been the "good" son, the one who behaved and who laughed and made sense to the family, while I had been the angry son, the puzzling one who stood at the edge of the family and kept everyone else on edge too, the one who was outcast, mocking, furious. The one, Howard reminded me, who stood an outcast behind the door of the family store in Baltimore.

I began to understand why over and over I had positioned myself on the edges of the groups I had belonged to. Even when I passionately and lovingly plunged into my newly discovered Jewishness, I clung to that taste of being the outsider.

I began to see how much of me is Ishmael. That grim smile when I heard the tale of being put out, behind the door, was like Ishmael's mocking laugh. And then I understood his story far more clearly.

What I learned was that my name was incomplete. I had been named Abraham Isaac—Avraham Yitzchak in Hebrew—when I was eight days old, after Honey's father. The third corner of the triangle, the name "Ishmael" that was called out in a cry of silence, was also me, but got left out.

What a blessing that my brother reached out to me. That he taught me, in the moment that he told me I was Ishmael, that I did not need to be outcast from him. Taught me how harsh and clear redemption needs to be, how reconciliation is anything but gentle, occurring only in the shadow of the death of Abraham. Harsh but possible. The old knots of the family bind, but not forever.

With Howard's help I started testing out the boundaries of my exile. I had been Ishmael all of my life; now I spent almost two years learning *how* to be Ishmael. I discovered what each outcast gesture was that I had known and used for decades; learned what the uses of exile were; worked out what it meant to love being Jewish but to stand one step outside the door.

I learned how my concern for Ishmael the Arab made me an outcast in many Jewish eyes, and I learned how deeply Jewish it is to be the outsider, even or especially among Jews. I learned how deeply Jewish Ishmael was. It was as if the more I learned about being the outcast Ishmael, the more I understaood about the holy nebbish Isaac—how being holy made even Isaac an out-sider in the world.

On the second anniversary of my Rosh Hashanah sermon, someone who was leading our morning service asked me to come up to say the blessings over a portion of the Torah. As is the cus-tom, he asked my Hebrew name. I found myself completing the triangle of my name, telling him, "Avraham Yitzchak Yishmael"—Abraham Isaac Ishmael.

He looked at me laughing, his face lit up with the joke. "That's not your name!" he said. I laughed too—what a theatrical ges-ture, changing my name like that! How ridiculous! And then I sat, trembling with uncertainty. Was this a joke, or did I mean it?

I meant it.

I leaned over and told him, seriously this time, "I mean it. Call me up that way. That's my name now." He blinked, shrugged, called me up. As a few others heard my new name, there was one guffaw of laughter, and I turned red with fury. How dare they make a mockery of this?

Then I paused; it was like replaying the story. Like Sarah, I had laughed; changing my name really was funny. And then, when someone else had dared to laugh at me, suddenly I could see nothing funny in the matter. So also Sarah had, when Ishmael dared to laugh.

I said the blessings and then turned to hear the Torah portion. I had been so involved in deciding whether to rename myself that I had no idea where we were in the text. It was a great shock in that moment to hear sentences about Sarah's laughter and the birth of Isaac.

"Yishma El," said the Torah, the Hebrew for Ishmael's name, which also meant "God heard." Torah had spoken straight back to me. I had chosen right; my name had been confirmed.

My choice had opened up the next birth. By making true and audible the Ishmael part of me, perhaps I had begun the process of giving birth to Isaac. Maybe now I could allow the Isaac part of me to come to life—the laughing one whose laughter is not mockery but joy: the mild one, the younger one, the holy one. Was that the Howard part of me?

Abraham Isaac Ishmael. The soundwaves of new life, beginning at the end of my name, were moving back through it toward the source, toward Abraham. Toward the one whose holiness was expressed not through simplicity and love but through terrifying risks. Toward the holy adventurer who at the call of an unknown God had journeyed into unknown lands. Toward Abraham who was holy like his son Isaac and adventurous like Ishmael. Who was both mild and wild. Toward wholeness.

The story doesn't end there. It would be ten years more before the part of me I had just given a name, the "Ishmael" in me, had grown wise enough to know when to surrender. Perhaps more than ten years, before the newborn "Isaac" in me had learned how to laugh in joy instead of mockery. Ten years of learning how to wrestle, before Howard and I could do a still higher wrestle in facing our mother's death, as Isaac and Ishmael did when they faced the death of Father Abraham.

7
Inside the Family

by Howard

WHY WAS OTTS like Ishmael? Talking with Honey out of my need to understand our family, I had found a telling episode, a turning point, at least in Honey's mind: how Otts had been kept behind the door, cast into what must have seemed to him, at something less than two years old, like exile.

Then Otts had remembered the family story of his crying as an infant. He had been allowed to wail, as *I* then recalled the story, for some truly horrifying stretch of time, eight or ten or even twelve hours. Honey had a powerful will when she thought that she was doing right.

There was yet another incident, not just a story but an event alive in memory: the time that Otts had been locked out as punishment after he had crumpled my drawing of Baseball Joe. Pushed out into the winter night, he had set his jaw and waited— until Honey, persuaded by me, had let him in. By then, at only ten or eleven, he wouldn't even protest.

Three early, painful events. I imagine them piled on top of one another, weighting Otts' life in one direction, defining it the way a metaphor's established in a poem, through repetition and elaboration. Otts' life had curved off early in the direction of exclusion.

There was even more, I've since discovered. As I educated myself to become a psychotherapist, I encountered the writings of Bateson, Laing, Whitaker, and other theorists of family dynamics. I began to wonder if there had been a context that supported and reinforced these incidents of exile, locating Otts as outsider, me as insider. Was there something about the family's very way of being that had pushed Otts to the edge, then declared him odd and troublesome, thus pushing him farther away?

That way, Laing says, lies madness: the victim is made out to be the villain. Not that Otts was *mad*—but he *was* capable of an unpredictable and furious anger. He was a less troubled and much more successful version of the people Laing describes, but recognizably related to them. Honey would "walk on eggshells," as she put it, lest he "explode" at Thanksgiving celebrations even long after he was married. Sometimes he exploded anyway.

Why was he that way? The early incidents would have been enough, it seemed to me. But was it only those, or had something more pervasive happened to him, something basic in the way the family worked? (And had something happened to me too?)

Talking late into the night with Honey, questioning Grandma as she lay in bed, deciphering the spidery handwriting of Pop's letters and stories, studying brown and curled photographs, over the years I've patched together a story of our family. Behind, beneath, around the pretty pictures of "the four of us," I found, lay a strange and complex family web—a web in which Otts especially was caught.

The primary fact was that both Honey and Dad had lost a parent at an early age. So bereft did they feel, and so fragile was their healing, that more than sixty years after their losses, neither could mention the absent parent without tears and tightened throat.

Our family structure stood precariously upon that gaping hole of loss. We were haunted by Honey's father, Avraham, and Dad's mother, Eva, and also by others who had died untimely, as surely as if their spectral figures floated about the upstairs rooms at Cottage Avenue.

The most present of our ghosts was Honey's father. We lived in a family that was not just devoted to the memory of Avraham but that breathed inside his memory. All his children named their first sons after him. Not only Otts, but also Freda's Allen and Uncle Dave's son Adrian all in Hebrew are called "Avraham."

Born only ten years after the death of Avraham and named for him, Otts bore a heavy load that I did not. One reason he was "Ishmael" is that from the beginning he'd been "Avraham."

When Dr. Glick warned that Otts must be protected from contagion by being kept behind the door, his words had special weight because Otts' namesake, Avraham, had died of the disease of poverty, tuberculosis. Besides, it soon turned out, Otts was lean and dark like Avraham (and Honey too). He even walked like Avraham, the family said.

On the fair side, more like Dad, and chunky—and named after a grandfather of Honey's whom she had never known—I was free of the heightened expectations, and the intense attention, that came with being not just the elder son but Avraham returned.

Because even the mention of Avraham made Grandma sad, he was not frequently referred to. But when he was, it was in tones of veneration, so much so that I pictured him all through my childhood as being easily over six feet tall, whereas in fact, I later learned, he was of medium height.

He was a mythic figure: a lover, father, intellectual, and craftsman all rolled into one. If Abraham was "the holy adventurer," as Otts writes, the symbol of wholeness for the Jewish people, so was Avraham for our family. By definition it was impossible for Otts to match him.

We grew up believing that Avraham was a legitimate architect and a bricklayer too, an extraordinary combination of intellect and manual skill, in comparison to which his eldest grandchildren—Allen, who was manual, and Otts, who was mental—were merely specialists. In fact, he was a bricklayer who was a designer on the side. He owned a complete Shakespeare that Honey had devoured when she was twelve, and volumes in Hebrew that none of us could identify but that stood imposingly on the shelves of Grandma's glassed-in bookcase. We concluded, with no other evidence, that he must have been learned in Hebrew as well as architecture.

Beyond this, Avraham was a loving father, Honey said. She did, however, allow that he was capable of sudden anger and that once or twice he punished her when she was innocent. At those times, she would refuse to eat. But usually he was loving.

He would spend each of his children's birthdays alone with that one child, taking her or him out for some special treat—so memorable an experience for Honey that she suggested that I spend a day alone with each of my children when I came East to see them. At least once, she recalled, Avraham appeared at her school with a birthday corsage and took her away from class. He was "not an ordinary guy!" she'd say, her eyes aglow.

It was because Avraham had died that Grandma lost her faith. He had been her first and truest love. Her life was focused on his presence and his absence both, as was Honey's, though not entirely, and therefore as was ours, to some extent.

Of a Polish family that had settled in Holland—part of his specialness to us was that he was "Dutch"—Avraham had emigrated to America in 1904. When Grandma came from Poland in 1906, she met his sister in a sweatshop, was courted by Avraham and married him, and within a year gave birth to Freda.

Very late one night, as I talked with Grandma in her bedroom during one of my visits East, more than fifty years after his death, she explained to me why she had rejected God:

"Avr'am and I, we loved each other. We had only fourteen, fifteen years together, *richtig* only ten, because for the last four he was sick, losing weight, in the sanitarium and out and in again, mmmm I worried so, every time I went I would ask the nurse about his weight, I would think, maybe this time it'll go up a little, maybe this time, just a little maybe, but always it went down.

"And then he died. And I thought, if such a thing could happen to a man thirty-seven years old, with a wife and three children, a man who tried only to work hard and provide for his family, who never talked bad about anyone, then there couldn't be a God."

The Holocaust confirmed her in her judgment. Listening across from her, I nodded, for I thought that though Grandma's tone might be unnecessarily dark, I could easily understand what she felt about God. It had seemed to me since high school that there was no reason to believe in divine benevolence, a hidden plan at work. Dad believed that the Table of Elements was demonstration of divine intelligence, but what about the concentration camps, I thought, the piles of human hair and ripped-out teeth, the stacks of rotting corpses that the newsreels showed? What did *they* demonstrate? And what about the arbitrariness of nature? I saw myself as an agnostic; the unknowable was exactly that. And if that were so, I figured, it made sense to work with what we could know. Clearly life was capable of beauty and horror both; it was up to human beings to make the best of it.

I had always loved Chanukah (one of my favorite books was Howard Fast's *My Glorious Brothers*), and I had always loved Passover: loved them for their food and their ritual and for their message, which I took to be about human courage and the determination to be free. As to the miracle stories—the division of the Red Sea, the oil that lasted eight days—I was a skeptic. Like most other religious stories that I knew, they seemed to me merely made-up—constructions that pretended to be explanations, fantasies that didn't match with life.

Otts as an adolescent had been more overtly skeptical than I, even announcing himself to be an atheist. But by now he had a different view. When Grandma reiterated her theological position, as she, Otts, and I sat in a corner of the living room at Cottage Avenue one Thanksgiving, a few years after she had explained it to me in the middle of the night, Otts flushed and spat out, "Bullshit! That's no argument against a God!" Grandma blinked and pulled her upper body back an inch or two, and immediately my mind began: "Really? The Holocaust's no argument? Maybe not a proof, but surely it's an argument! The problem of evil, it's always been an argument!" Like a machine independent of my will, my mind raced to make out my case, my argument with Otts. But this time I kept silent, because my heart was in my mouth. How could he talk to her that way? How *could* he?—it was *Grandma*!

In mourning for Avraham, Grandma had forbidden her children to go to the movies for two years, and because he had last been home at Passover, she could not bring herself to make a Seder, the ritual Passover meal. This changed only after twenty years, and then only because Honey insisted that it was time for us, the grandchildren, to have a Seder.

"Veh is mir, veh is mir, veh is mir, veh is mir . . ." During the year that I slept in the small back room adjoining Grandma's kitchen, when Otts was still at home and Pop had come to live with us, I would wake to hear Grandma padding about, straightening cupboards, preparing breakfast, muttering. *Veh is mir, veh is mir.* Woe is me.

Her husband had died in the very prime of life, leaving her to raise three children. Her son-in-law, Sam, had shot himself at a race track, abandoning Tante Freda and Allen. She had seen Honey *too* fall desperately ill of tuberculosis, and almost die at thirty-five. Her son, Uncle Dave, had connected a hose to his exhaust pipe and gassed himself at forty-one, leaving behind Aunt Rose and two young boys, Adrian and Stanley. *Veh is mir.* Grandma *was* woe.

At her tallest she was only five-foot-two, but Grandma, like Avraham, had a mythic quality. She was so quick that she could catch a fly one-handed; she was so competent that she could cut noodles fast and fine as a machine; she was so tough that she could hold hot pots in her bare hands. "Asbestos hands," we murmured. But our imaginations were yet more influenced by her darkness. Only five-foot-two, but Grandma cast a giant shadow.

Honey had arranged that we observe Passover, but in deference to Grandma's grimness we did not really celebrate it. At Cottage Avenue, when we were kids, Passover was a solemn, not a joyous, holiday. And whenever I listened to the sports news on the radio, I knew to lower the volume when the racing results came on, because Honey had told me that it would upset Grandma to hear them. I didn't know precisely why—only later did I learn of Sam's gambling-related suicide—but the sense of a dark secret was enough. In the presence of Grandma's woe, we crept about.

But Grandma stood for not only Woe. She stood for Strength and Endurance too. At twenty, in her wedding picture, she has a queenly bearing; her broad Slavic face looks almost haughty, unassailable. At sixty, when we were kids, she wore her hair in an iron-gray bun that seemed to symbolize her fortitude.

Devastated by Avraham's death, she had tried to go back to factory sewing, at which she had been so fast before her marriage that she had made a decent living doing piecework. But, she told me, she began imagining little men before her eyes, leaping between the cloth and her machine. A doctor she consulted told her that she should stop sewing, but should find something else to do at which she could work very hard.

For years she took in foster children. Later she ran the notions store, which was open twenty hours a day. Later yet, during the war, she operated a three-story rooming house for defense workers, who used the beds in shifts. Then she moved back to Cottage Avenue and, when Honey got sick, worked at taking care of us.

My first memory of her is at the rooming house, moving rapidly from room to room as she changed the sheets. One of my last is of watching her climb the stairs to her second-floor apartment at Cottage Avenue, when she was ninety-four. With Dad behind her so that she wouldn't fall, she would pull herself upstairs, resting at every step to catch her breath. She climbed a mountain every day—as she had, I suppose, ever since the death of Avraham.

She had a lively mind. Curious why Otts at almost forty had become so interested in Judaism, she asked me my opinion. "I don't understand it either," I replied. "Maybe it's a way never to run out of stuff to read."

Well past eighty she was still working on her English spelling, in a copybook. She loved the Singer brothers' novels, serialized in the Yiddish paper that arrived daily from New York, and she read into her nineties. When she could no longer see book print even with a magnifying glass, I took to reading to her on my visits East.

The younger Singer's autobiography, *In My Father's Court*, about the Poland she had known, seemed suitable. But when I reached the section about the ancient washerwoman who endured despite her tribulations, I could not go on for weeping. "Howard," she asked, staring in my direction. "Why are you crying? Because you see that I have come to this?"

After Uncle Dave killed himself, he became another ghost, like

Avraham and Allen's father. It wasn't just that he was dead; it's that he was hardly talked about, though he had been a large figure in our lives. Tall, broad, swarthy, and with wavy black hair that matched Aunt Rose's, he had been a handsome man, said Honey, until he ballooned to over 250 pounds. "You can be so handsome," Honey pleaded with me, "if you don't let yourself get fat like Uncle Dave."

Uncle Dave sped around in a red Nash Rambler station wagon. He often brought us spicy Greek olives, a favorite of Honey's, from Lombard Street. He taught me how to use the boxing gloves that Dad's brother Uncle Herb had given us. He hinted smilingly of the erotic tales to be found in his complete set of *The Arabian Nights*. He bragged about his days working around top-secret missiles on an Air Force base in California and about his escapades as a photographer.

But despite this appearance of verve and dash, his suicide seemed to come as no great surprise to Honey and Dad. Uncle Dave had had a troubled life, and there was an air of dark unsettledness about him. As a child, he had been desperately ill. At seventeen, seven years after his father's death, he had hopped a train, running away from home to look for work, and had been hit in the head as the train passed beneath an overpass. He had lain in a hospital unidentified for months.

It was fifteen years later, during the war, that Otts and I first met him, when he and Aunt Rose and the baby Adrian arrived from California, in need of a place to stay. Only long after he killed himself did I learn from Honey that he had been discharged from the Air Force on psychological grounds.

Since our house, modest though it was, was thought of as "infinitely expandable," in Honey's phrase, it seemed little trouble to put up Davey's family in the small upstairs bedroom, the only open spot. It was the same room that a few years later became Honey's room when she was in quarantine, and then my room when she got better and came downstairs, and then Pop's room when he came to live with us, and then Poppa Gertz's bedroom after Grandma had married him but couldn't sleep in the same room because he snored, and finally Grandma's bedroom until she could no longer climb the stairs.

Given some time to recover, Uncle Dave was able to begin a photography studio. He took the usual group photographs for our bar mitzvah books—we can flip the pages and revisit the Shapiros, the Schunicks, the Gimpelmans, Mrs. Glassman from next door, the Gertzes, the Luntzes, our tenants the Zilbers, and cousins, second cousins, and cousins once removed—but he was capable of more. His most telling study was of Tante Freda and Allen her son; in one stroke he captured their relationship.

It's a composite portrait. In it Tante Freda's dark profile dominates the background. From her silhouette, which accentuates her determined jaw and her hair gathered in a bun like Grandma's, Allen's shyly smiling face emerges. This photograph Tante Freda displayed under the protective glass surface of her bedroom vanity, in the house she shared with Allen until her death three years after Honey's. With Allen, the one man who, unlike her father and her husband, would never leave.

Uncle Dave's photography studio succeeded for some years, but in the early 1950s there was a strike at Sparrows Point, where many of his customers worked. The business slid, and Uncle Dave was reduced to walking a pony around residential neighborhoods, trying to convince mothers to pose their children on it.

The night he killed himself was the night before Rosie, who had already had surgery for cancer of the breast, was due to have an operation for a growth on her tongue. Perhaps, Honey and I speculated many years afterward, Uncle Dave had wanted to contribute the insurance money, just as when he'd run away, he'd thought that at least he wouldn't be a drain.

When Uncle Dave killed himself, Otts and I were both at home, both of college age, but Honey and Dad did not talk with us about it, nor did we raise the subject. Together they conveyed a powerful sense that we had to push ahead—that if we even spoke of what had happened, we would never free ourselves from it. They had first practiced this approach, I assume, in response to the deaths of Avraham and Eva. The four of us took the long-planned auto trip to Florida only a few weeks after Davey's funeral; Honey determined that we should go.

It was this family strategy, this conspiracy of silence, that afflicted us with ghosts. The dead were merely absent; it was we ourselves who sucked away our air and clamped our jaws. More than I, Otts rebelled against constraint. Perhaps his refusal to engage with us on that trip—this occurs to me only now, as I revise—was an unconscious silent protest, a kind of civil disobedience. Otts rebelled, and in doing so paid the price of becoming the outsider.

Eva was barely an acknowledged presence. Avraham had left us the brickwork at P.S. No. 59, a wooden shoe that sat atop Grandma's refrigerator, a long painting of Dutch children playing, and his mysterious and intimidating Hebrew books. Sam had left behind the bathroom he had constructed in the cellar and his son Allen's rolling walk. The only physical memento we had of Eva was a small photograph of a woman with a pleasant, solid, square-jawed face, who looks like a more determined version of Dad's second-oldest brother Uncle Jack. She is posed head-by-head with a young child, probably Jack, says Uncle Herb, who also reports that Dad wished the portrait had been of her and *him*.

I've accumulated a few clues as to her nature. She had been a "quiet woman," Uncle Jack told me approvingly some years ago. She had worked hard at getting a kindergarten program in Washington, D.C., he said, and she had died, after bearing five sons in nine years, of an illegal abortion. That last, Otts and I had known from Dad, but that was all he had ever said about her. Perhaps he did not remember more; perhaps he had made himself forget.

Eva was almost invisible to our family, yet she had a powerful effect on us, because her loss had laid out a path for Dad. He came to live at Grandma's only a dozen years after she had died and married Honey when he was only twenty-one and she eighteen. At Grandma's funeral he said that she had been a substitute mother for him. After Honey died, he realized that in some ways so had she.

The loss of Eva was as devastating for Dad's family as the loss of Avraham for Honey's. Indeed, Dad's family was dislocated and divided in a way that Honey's wasn't. But what different tones they took! On Honey's side, Grandma was often grim, Davey was suicidal, Freda sometimes bitterly caustic and possessive, Honey occasionally almost crazily intense. On Dad's side, laughter predominated over sadness.

Pop, who lived in Florida near Dad's four brothers and came for a month or two to Baltimore each summer, was a comic figure. He had a bald head and bulbous nose; false teeth that he would dislodge on request; a Russian-Cockney accent (he called us 'oney, 'enry, 'oward, and Harthur); and a nicotine-yellowed forelock that he pulled at and called his "kveshtion mark," because it always snapped back into its curl.

Pop was somewhat self-deprecating, with a softly ironic, teasing style. Eva had died when he was only thirty-seven, and a second marriage, undertaken in an attempt to provide his five sons with a mother, had ended quickly in divorce, following a fire in which one of the woman's children had been burned to death. (A secret—the fire and the divorce—that Honey told me only after I was grown.) But Pop seemed more wistful than embittered. Honey reported that he had been something of a grouch in the second-hand shop he had owned (perhaps, I guessed in his defense, because he broke in shoes for customers by wearing them himself), but though he grumbled occasionally at us, it was in a joking way. He even laughed at Death, calling it "Uncle Nochem."

To me, Pop was gentle, indulgent, and entertaining. He delighted in the vaudeville shows at the Hippodrome, where once a stage magician called me from the audience, then fiercely whispered to me what to do, to make the trick come out. And he loved Disney cartoons—"That's all, folks!" he would chuckle, laying down his cards in victory; and he taught me casino and gin rummy, which he played with Honey after supper every night, while she did the crossword puzzle on the side, waiting for him to discard. The card games were occasions for his smutty English-Yiddish puns, which Honey would ignore.

Pop and I were buddies. When he listened to his favorite record, "The Volga Boatman," on the wind-up Victrola, I'd join him in a caricature of the lugubrious chorus. On Sunday mornings after breakfast, we'd retire to his room in time to catch "Nat Youngelson's Yiddische Shtunde" on his radio—klezmer music the opposite of mournful. Afterward, he'd begin his weekly letter to his niece, and though I'd lean in to inspect his spelling, he'd protest but wouldn't make me leave.

Pop had been a tailor much of his life, including five voyages on the transatlantic liner the *Leviathan*, of which he proudly told us tales. But at heart he thought of himself as a different kind of stitcher. "Occupation?" the woman asked who registered him for an emergency World War II draft when he was almost sixty-five. "Storyteller," he replied, and stuck to his story through several more, increasingly impatient queries.

My own favorites were "The Little Bad Boy," a cautionary tale about a boy who ran away, causing his parents no end of grief, and "The Woman from Boston," an understated but side-splitting account, all the funnier because it was allegedly autobiographical, of an assignation on a train between "Pop" and what turned out to be a pair of twins.

Honey's side of the family was strong on rectitude. Dad's brothers—"the Florida uncles," we called them—seemed bent on adventure and fun. Florida itself was our family's Promised Land—a place of sun, palm trees, and family warmth, to which Honey and Dad were planning to retire when Dad stopped teaching school.

Dad and his four brothers were our most obvious model of brotherhood, more even than the examples in the neighborhood. But the model was confusing. It was clear that the brothers were different from one another, and especially that all of them together were different from Dad, but it wasn't clear what to make of all this difference.

Uncle Jucky had been in the Navy and Uncle Herb in the Coast Guard during the war, while Dad had had a schoolteacher's deferment; they were romantic figures in their uniforms. That much was fine. But all four of the brothers either ran nightclubs or sold liquor, and by the standards of our house on Cottage Avenue, that was slightly questionable. Also, having more money than Honey and Dad, they gambled on the stock market, and Uncle Mike at least spent a lot more freely than we did. Alien practices, these. Moreover, the brothers were relatively conservative in politics, particularly on labor issues; Dad had never met a payroll, they were fond of saying. They argued and they yelled. Dad did too, when he was in their company. His passions aroused in defense of unionism, he would seem at these moments most like them, despite their contrary positions.

Most remarkable of all, the Florida uncles, except only for Uncle Jack, had dared to marry gentiles or even to marry not at all. (When at ten I told Honey that I was going to be a bachelor like Uncle Mike, who didn't marry until he was fifty, she snapped, "Don't be a fool!")

Beneath their political and temperamental differences, however, Dad and all his brothers were joined by a powerful bond of loyalty. They could rely on each other in a pinch. As the eldest, and the one who throughout our childhood had the most money and no wife or kids, Uncle Mike, we trusted, would be our family's financial protector if we needed. He had, after all, given us those brand-new Schwinns.

Yet though we could depend on Uncle Mike, oddly he didn't wear the eldest brother's somber mantle of responsibility; rather, he seemed the wildest of the crew. It was with him that Honey and Dad had driven, squeezed into the rumble seat of his tiny roadster, on the spur of the moment all the way to Florida from Baltimore.

Such frivolity belonged to the halcyon days that Honey and Dad referred to as "B.A."—the years Before Arthur. (Before Arthur—perhaps another piece of the puzzle. As the firstborn, Otts was not only expected to be responsible but was the very emblem, for Honey and Dad, of the weighty responsibility of family. That would have been another heavy load for him.)

Uncle Mike looked in face, build, and manner like a court jester out of uniform. He had a manic laugh, which he delivered with his tongue protruding. From the middle of our living room, he could throw his voice so as to sound remarkably like a dog barking on the second floor, and when he loudly farted, walking down Cottage Avenue with me and Little Howard toward the stores, with a straight face he'd accuse us of the dirty deed.

Uncle Jucky, Dad's next-younger brother, was a comic figure too, with a line of patter like a stand-up comedian. Uncle Jucky was tall and handsome, with a heroic head. He had been an athlete at the Orphans Asylum and the most popular of the three brothers who had lived there.

Uncle Jack, next older to Dad, had a mildly teasing manner; he seemed the most like Dad but quieter. Uncle Herb, the youngest of the five, spoke out of one side of his mouth and cultivated a tough-guy persona, but actually this also was a sort of joke, for he was warm-hearted and more socially liberal than the other uncles.

Dad was on good terms with all the brothers (though Uncle Herb appeared to be still aggrieved about a broken tooth he blamed on Dad), but he seemed fondest of Uncle Jucky. As was I. I liked his humor, his easy-going ways, his wavy black hair, his larger-than-life proportions, his athleticism. We even almost shared a name, for his real name was Julius and my middle one is Jules.

But though the Florida uncles expanded our horizons, providing living examples of risk-taking, they were sometimes hard for us. Sweet-mannered as he was, Uncle Jucky was given to telling racist jokes. And Uncle Mike, driving us at 80 mph to the Everglades, would swerve his black Buick to hit a turtle, or, pointing out the window toward a dotted hill, shout, "There's a nigger cemetery! There's *gold* in cemeteries!" The four of us, silent in our seats, would cringe. By the time Dad retired, in 1971, the civil rights movement had revealed Florida to be something other than a paradise. Nothing more was said about moving there until Honey died.

Grandma had responded to her loss of Avraham with deep skepticism and everlasting grief; Pop to his of Eva with wistful irony. Honey and Dad, in league against their separate losses, created a sort of blend: our own family's way of being.

It included the humor that we associated with Dad's side. He laughed boomingly at his own risque stories and puns, while Honey twinkled. Although Honey was not good at telling jokes, as we all agreed, she was an appreciator. What made us grin most about her was that she wore no underpants; also that, in need on a long trip, she was not above peeing by the roadside.

But even more fundamentally, the family way was high-serious and rigorous. Our economy was planned with utmost care, as a defense against vicissitude. Dad and Honey drew up an annual budget that allotted every dollar, with flexibility built in. It was an item of family pride that the *Sun* had printed Honey's weekly food budget, submitted to it by Dad, as a model of how to manage in tough times. "Mrs. W. deserves a blue ribbon," said the *Sun*'s home economist.

The family had a master plan: there was the budget, and there was education. By the time he retired, Dad had taught school uninterruptedly for over forty-four years. Honey, though she had never been to college, was at least as true a believer in education and a more avid teacher, though restricted to a student body of just Otts and me.

Formal education was the route to knowledge and stability. Even more important to Dad, it was the visible sign of progress through the generations. Pop was formally uneducated, and Dad alone of his sons had gone to college. From the *shtetl* to our Ph.D.s at Wisconsin and Yale in two long bounds! When we said that our educations had been lacking in some ways, Dad could not let himself believe us.

Hand in hand with this faith in progress went the family's politics. "*We* are Democrats," Honey said, explaining the party system to Dan, my eldest son—and by *we* she meant all of us, the clan. Pop had been a LaFollette Progressive and a Norman Thomas "shoshulist," as he said it; Honey and Dad, who saw themselves as more pragmatic, were Roosevelt Democrats, even if Dad had protested against a third term. When FDR died, Honey told me, she and Mrs. Luntz were crying because it was "like losing a father."

Starting in the 1940s, Dad was an originator, executive secretary, and then president of the Baltimore Teachers Union. He also wrote and pasted up the newsletter, which Honey typed and ran off on the mimeo machine that lived in the cellar bathroom. For more than twenty years after we left home, they were the driving spirit of the Baltimore chapter of the Americans for Democratic Action. In the 1960s, led by Otts' example, they demonstrated for civil rights and against the war in Vietnam. And not only did they remain at Cottage Avenue, the only whites in all the area; they continued to go door to door registering voters. As Democrats, of course.

The budget, our educational program, and the family politics were meant to be stays against confusion and emergency. To a point they worked. But at the same time the family history—a long series of sudden, devastating losses—suggested that life was a tragedy unfolding. In some part of our minds, we held ourselves in readiness. This as much as liberal progressivism was a part of our essential family style, and shaped our attitudes and actions.

Tragedy might reveal itself not only as a random set of terrible surprises—pogroms, tuberculosis, cancer, suicide—but as an awful inevitability passed on down the generations. It was from exposure to her father, Honey assumed, that she had developed a tubercle: the TB bacillus enwrapped in a container that holds the bearer safe from infection—unless the container should break down. If Honey had caught tuberculosis from her father, why not we from her?

("Ironies," Otts writes me, "so many ironies! So, it turned out, how I was likeliest to catch TB wasn't from the Black folks who came to Grandma's store but from Honey herself. Ultimately from Avraham whom I was named for. Who *was* me, according to the family myth. So when I was put behind the door, it was my own self I was sent out in exile from.")

Tuberculosis haunted us. Who knew when it might emerge again, whom among us it might claim? If somehow Otts and I avoided the contagion lurking in discarded Kleenex, what was to guarantee that our children would not be infected by Honey's presence? When our infant sons were circumcised, how close to the ceremony did we dare to let her come?

In the absence of a guarantee, there was vigilance. Honey would not kiss us even when she finally tested negative herself, almost twenty years after she was first diagnosed. She reminded us repeatedly to have ourselves tested periodically. She worried about our getting out of shape. Being fat was too much like Uncle Dave, but thin was no good either. Later she cautioned the grandchildren too.

This sense of lurking danger coexisted with the usual family reticence about disaster. Honey several times underwent life-threatening operations, more than once she almost died before our eyes, yet never did we talk about these facts. Grandma shrieked her lamentations in the hospital solarium, but that was Grandma. If our next-door neighbor Mrs. Glassman asked how Honey was, the proper answer was, "She's fine," even if we had just seen her almost die. It was not for nothing that Honey had taught us, literally, how to grit our teeth. DON'T TELL TALES OUT-SIDE THE FAMILY was another urgent rule.

So—the family style that formed us was a curious amalgam of laughter, optimism, stern vigilance against disaster, and silence when disaster inevitably came. Against this complex background, Otts and I played out our roles.

Part of this setting was an intense, ever-present consciousness of the family itself. During one of his summer visits, Pop told his longest story. This one was truly autobiographical, about his life in Rikitna, a Russian *shtetl*, from the age of five until thirteen, and about his family. For weeks he sat with Honey on our Cottage Avenue front porch, as she translated his spoken Yiddish—it still felt more comfortable to talk about those early times in Yiddish—into English for posterity.

This telling of stories about the family was characteristic of Honey's side as well as Dad's. Until her last year at Cottage Avenue, Grandma was the memory of last resort. Names, dates, places—when Honey got stuck, Grandma had them all. Honey too told stories—about her childhood jealousies of Freda (she had wanted Freda's wavy hair as well as her golden ring); about the silent grudge of many years that had separated Grandma from her older sister Zosha; about Grandma's brother, the missing Uncle Hiel, whose steamer trunk had rested in our cellar, awaiting him, for sixty years.

Working with Pop on his autobiography, Honey was a full part-ner in the telling. She drew him out, read her translation back to him for editing, then typed it in quadruplicate, for presentation to his grandchildren, to whom it is dedicated. Though Honey is not mentioned on the title page, the result is really a collabora-tion. In that sense our own writing, what Otts and I are doing here, is part of a family tradition.

· · ·

As I describe our family—its characters, its structure, its history, its style—it becomes more clear to me than ever that I was in closer relation to every living person in it, except perhaps for Honey, than was Otts. I talked into the early morning hours with Honey; played with Dad and did chores at his side; kibbitzed with Pop; sat with Grandma on her bed and read to her; boxed with Davey, walked with Mike, laughed with Jucky; even had milk and cookies late at night with Tante Freda after she and Allen had moved away from Cottage Avenue.

Where was Otts while all this was going on? Off by himself, pursuing his own interests, while the rest of us were spending a significant portion of our time trying to figure out what he was doing, who and why he was.

Why did he spend so much time alone? Why was he angry? These were the big questions—and then, more recently, why in the middle of his life had he turned so dramatically toward Judaism, taking Jewish renewal on as his life's work? In terms of family tradition, it was the most peculiar thing he had ever done. Honey worried that he would lose his universalism; Grandma wondered about it, and so did I.

I still do. My answer to Grandma, that it was a way for Otts never to run out of stuff to read, was more than just a joke; it was the best I could figure at the time. But recently I woke up with a sudden insight dropping into place.

Passover, I thought. It's all about Passover. Otts' turn toward Judaism swung on the pivot of Passover. In 1968, after Martin Luther King was shot and federal troops occupied Washington, D.C., Otts wrote the Freedom Seder for the following Passover. To the familiar passages from prophets and rabbis, Otts added quotations on freedom from King, the rebels of the Warsaw ghetto, Allen Ginsberg, even Eldridge Cleaver. It was a revolutionary Haggadah, teaching that we in our own time could and should rewrite a used-up text, and reminding us of a dark truth told in the story of Passover: that in the cause of freedom, sometimes blood must spill.

This Haggadah launched Otts into Judaism. Of course, it alienated the traditional Jewish community: Eldridge Cleaver indeed! But that wasn't Otts' audience. He was looking to the young Jews on the Left who had been driven into defiance of the Establishment and who had no radical Jewish voice to support them. Over the next few years, the Freedom Seder spread through the counterculture and the radical political community. There were Freedom Seders celebrated at dozens of college campuses; the Berrigan brothers, radical Catholic priests, came out of hiding to join one at Cornell. It was the most successful of all Otts' organizing tools. It worked in public and it also worked in Otts. He went on from there—one book after another, then one organization after another—deeper into Judaism.

This much I had already known, but in pieces loosely hung together, not gathered into meaning, because I lacked one other piece. Why a Seder? Why did Otts choose a Seder as his form? His Haggadah, his beautiful Haggadah: this was the thought that dropped in just the other morning, which provides me my most satisfying understanding yet of Otts' turn toward Judaism.

Otts had a beautiful Haggadah, illustrated in colorful, heroic drawings of the burning bush, the ten plagues, the parting of the sea, which a neighbor or cousin had given him for his bar mitzvah. At Cottage Avenue Dad led the Seders, reading aloud gravely from his simple, small Haggadah bound in green, paper-clipped where he had shortened it. The rest of us followed along in pamphlets distributed by Manischewitz Foods—the rest of us except for Otts, who, moving back the china and the crystal, ceremoniously spread out before him his glorious Haggadah.

It was the one moment in the year when he was clearly at the center of the family; in fact, *first* of all the family. And his vehicle? Of course, of course: a *book*.

So what was there about the way we were that, except for Passover, put Otts on the edge? What was there about the family that pushed him into needing solitude?

And what was there that put me in the middle, craving contact? And that pressed me into trying to figure it all out? Otts seems not very interested in the why of him. Even his "Ishmael" chapter doesn't explain why he turned toward Judaism; just says he did, as if that should be enough. I get such pleasure, such relief, when a detail falls into place, making sense of the whole. A mental construction alone is not enough for me. It needs to match experience, to be confirmed and grounded in reality. When I tried out my thought on Otts and Judaism and his need to read, he was dubious; it didn't click. But when I tell him this speculation, about his original Haggadah, he says, "Hmmmm. That may have a lot of truth in it. I used that Haggadah for translations I needed for the Freedom Seder." Eureka.

Time for a gathering. Not yet a summing up, but a gathering of what we have so far:

Again, what was it in the family that made these differences between us?

To start with, Otts was more identified with Honey, I with Dad. This was a general family understanding, an amused acknowledgment of how we were. It was as if within "the four of us" there were two couples who overlapped with the central one. Honey-and-Dad stood solid at the center, but to one side there was Honey-and-Otts and to the other Dad-and-me.

There was a magical indicator of this phenomenon. Honey's and Otts' birthdays both fell upon the twelfth—of December and October, respectively—while Dad and I celebrated on the first of February and November.

If we needed more evidence to demonstrate our pairings, we could find it in our tastes. Honey and Otts like cooked cauliflower; Dad and I detested it. Dad and I liked Hershey bars with almonds; Otts and Honey liked them plain. Otts and Honey liked Gosman's Pale Dry Ginger Ale; Dad and I liked Gosman's Golden. Dad and I liked raisin buns with sugar frosting; Honey and Otts liked chocolate. Honey and Otts liked chicken schmaltz on rye with salt. And so forth. The list was long.

It now seems clear to me that these alliances were about temperament as well. Being more identified with Honey, Otts also was more like Honey's side of the family—intense, serious, preoccupied with fairness and rectitude, darker not only in complexion. Being more identified with Dad, I was more easy-going, more accommodating, more ready to see the funny, lighter side of things.

More specifically, Otts was Avraham, and I was not. Otts was in a tighter, more demanding spot—not only intense but outright tense. *Tense* is still the word he most often uses to describe himself. Being tense, he would also have been troublesome.

All this fits, it seems to me, with what Otts has written from his perspective. As the older, he was practiced on; the rules for raising him were more rigid than they were for me. Worse, one of the rules didn't apply to me at all—that as the older he should be responsible for me. These were other reasons he was tense, no doubt.

The family rules were rigorous. If you had to learn them without example, through your own mistakes, they would have been especially difficult to live by—thus the incident with Marty Zeskind and the rope. Beyond that, the rules, despite their seeming clarity, were actually not so clear. If Honey and Dad taught Otts, didn't it follow, he thought, that he should be teaching me? But I resisted his instruction, and the rule he learned—it had the bitterest taste, he says—was that I had the right to do so.

Beyond even that, the rules were not always followed by their promulgators, although Honey and Dad seemed so certain of themselves. If all human beings were equal, as Honey and Dad maintained, why didn't we have any Negro friends? Watching carefully to learn the rules, Otts saw the contradictions too. Another reason to be troublesome.

Being troublesome and angry, he was not well received. Being not well received, he took comfort in being by himself. Is that why Otts took so to solitude?

And what effect did all this have on me?

I had my eye on Otts. By watching him, I learned how not to be—within the family, that is. If trouble lay in Otts' path, I would take a different route. Otts moved ahead, doing what he wanted—never mind the context. But I *needed* to mind the context. I needed to penetrate the secrecy, undo the mystery—to figure it all out.

Otts' portion not for me. Who wanted storm and stress? Who wanted loneliness? Not me. I'd rather court the family, even if that meant not having my own voice. More than anything, I wanted in.

8
The Heart of the Matter

by Howard and Arthur

HOWARD. We hunger, Otts and I, for understanding: to understand and to be understood.

He works by way of Biblical analogies—the ancient, mythic figures vibrate in his pages, giving heroic dimension to his particular experience and everyday reality to theirs. I take a psychological and literary approach: weaving a narrative about the family, creating an explanatory tale, a map that I can use to place myself. We figure and we speculate; we read our lives and we revise. Gradually we come to understand each other's way.

But from the start, this book of ours has gone more easily for me than him. Feeling something of an alien in family territory, he proceeded cautiously. About a year after Honey's death, I had invited him to write with me. It took him six months to agree.

Even then he did so with misgivings, putting aside a political autobiography of his own to join me in a world of family, of close-in relationship, where he felt insecure. "I'm afraid they'll think I'm a schmuck!" he exclaimed a year later, in one of our New

Year's Eve conversations, when we were halfway into the book. "They'll think, Why can Howard do this stuff but not me?"

It wasn't only, I realized, that he was "surrendering" to me in allowing me to start the book. Or that he wouldn't write more about Cottage Avenue because he had other work to do. And I knew better why he had asked me how to go about doing Chapter 3, his piece on me. "Just ask yourself," I'd suggested, wondering silently why all of a sudden Otts seemed stuck for words, "Who has Howard been to me? Who is Howard in my life? That's what I did in writing about you."

Nevertheless, despite these troubles, we've gone forward. A bit like Shreve and Quentin after all, we've worked our way through documents and memories, in an attempt to understand, the better to move on. Our explorations have come far. But there's more: the passion at the center of our struggle with each other. Our differences went deeper than our uses of the neighborhood, deeper even than our stances in relation to the extended family. We wrestled for position, but what did position really *mean*?

In Pop's autobiography, the story he dictated to Honey on the front porch at Cottage Avenue, we find a clue. By indirection we come upon the center of our own drama.

Pop meant his autobiography to be a picture of life in Rikitna, the Russian village of his childhood, but really it's a story about his family. It's about the absence of his father, who had gone to New York when Pop was ten, to earn passage for the others. And it's about Pop's conflict with his older brother, who because "he always was a stuck-up guy" wouldn't join his mother in a business sewing coats.

Above all it's about Pop's connection to his mother. He comes to her rescue, helping make the business a success. They make so much money that they can tell Pop's father to stop sending a portion of his earnings. Thereby Pop, as he tells it, becomes his mother's favorite. "So young and already a man," Pop writes— "and not only a man but all of everything."

Pop's themes are not identical to ours, but they are familiar. Our father too was absent, at work, much of the time. More strikingly, Otts and I, like Pop and his brother, were different from the start, and in such ways that we took each other as an enemy, maybe even as the primary enemy.

And—here's the heart of the matter—like the differences between Pop and his brother, ours were exaggerated by our craving for our mother's love. This was the issue that would never rest, the issue that could drive us on to rage. The question "Is there room for me?" for us could be translated thus: Where did we stand with Honey, each of us?

We have allowed ourselves to see this fully only in the process of this writing. In the neighborhood, Otts was odd and I was not. In the closer-in circle, the extended family, there too Otts was out and I was in. In the nucleus of the family, "the four of us," again Otts was at the edge. And with Honey? Where did we stand with her?

At the very center of "the four of us" was Honey, the fire that energized us, the source that fed us all. What was it like—for Otts, for me—to be her sons?

ARTHUR. One night when I was fifty, I had a dream about two mothers. One was my real mother, my good mother, laughing, hugging me, tickling me, tossing me a softball, teaching me how to have a conversation, telling me rueful tales and ribald tales, eating with utter ecstasy a pistachio ice cream cone, shivering with the chill and the joy of it. And one was my wicked stepmother, distant, propped up in a bed I mustn't touch, coughing, correcting my grammar, tightening her jaw, on strike from eating and on strike from talking until I decided to behave.

They had the same face, these two mothers, and that made sense, because they were one person. The same mother: my real one, "Honey."

Not "Mom," or "Mommy," or "Mother." Not "Hannah," the official name that only the doctor called her; not the Hebrew/Yiddish "Chana" that only her own mother called her. Not even "she," if we happened to refer to her in a conversation that she overheard. "Who is 'she,'" Honey would snort, "the cat's mother?"

No, always "Honey"; always this compulsory name of sweet affection.

At the same time, she would snort and sneer if we bumped into kids who called their parents by their first names. For years and years, it never occurred to me that somewhere in her name there slept a contradiction. When I finally raised the question, Honey was astonished. "But it's not my first name!" she said.

She wanted everyone who loved her to call her by the name her loving father had before he died, as if thereby she could will us into loving her the way her father had. Somewhere here was more than a contradiction: a confusion, an evasion.

For me the confusion soaked in deeper than any words I could have named it with. For I carried Honey's father's name and even walked like him, the family said—my head stuck forward, always trying to get somewhere before my legs could take me. Somehow Honey meant for me to be her father, and I was just odd enough, just bright enough, just grown-up enough, to almost make it work.

There was one mother, but it felt like two. Why is it so hard for me to see that there is just one mother, just one me? Phyllis, my love and my wife, tells me that sometimes I am so angry that she loses me, the me she knows, and someone else appears.

Whose face is that?

Inside, it seems to me that I am just going along being me, but that the world finds me so odd that it cannot see this face of mine. I don't resemble anyone, and so I don't appear. The world pays no attention. And then I yell and scream, or clench my jaw. I look a stony gaze at those who will not see me. The angry face appears. Is it my second mother's face? Do I mirror her, the Honey who is my wicked stepmother? Sometimes I think my daughter mirrors me with both faces. Have I taught her to be double? Have I communicated both my oddness—what makes it easy for the others not to see me—and my anger?

And was my mother mirroring her father—the one who got desperately sick when she was only nine and died when she was twelve, the one whose name I carry? Are we doomed to keep on doing this, to the third and fourth generations?

My earliest conscious memory of Honey is also my earliest memory of Howard. I had just turned three, and Howard was just becoming my younger brother. I first remember hearing Honey's voice crying from her bedroom, birthing Howard.

No, that's not true. I'm censoring my memory; it's still too frightening. She wasn't crying; she was *screaming*. That's the word. Did it have to hurt that much? (Honey never screamed. She even made Grandmom stop screaming at the funeral when Uncle Dave had killed himself.)

More honest: did Howard have to hurt her that much? Howard says she told him he came easy. He thinks that I'm remembering more pain than Honey felt. It's possible. It's possible it was my own pain I was feeling—the pain that was reinforced that day on the way to the hospital to meet him for the first time, when I discovered that there was a Howard Street in Baltimore but no Arthur Street. The pain of being the outsider.

That pain was already there before Howard was born and gave me a usurper to accuse. I was already the outsider. No one had come to me when I screamed to be brought in.

My second face—the angry one, the one that can't bear it if people don't pay attention—could have been born right there, first in my crib, and then behind the door at Grandmom's store. First hours and then days of crying. Then my own clenched jaw when I learned that crying didn't help. And then the stony gaze of anger at those who wouldn't see me.

When Howard told me the story of me behind the door, forty years after it happened, he told it to me crying, with love for me. But he was telling me *my* story. *He* had heard it from *my* mother. Still in cahoots, they were, so I just nodded. Not only did it feel true, as if I'd always known it; it still felt true. In the very telling, I was still left out.

When I was fifty-four, writing this book, I experienced again what it means to be as hungry and as full of yearning as I was at three. I was on a religious retreat, and one of the leaders asked us to experience what it meant to be a rebbe's follower, one of the disciples of the great Hassidic masters. What it meant to feel bereft of God's nurturing, able to taste it only through the rebbe and only when the rebbe was ready to feed us. We paired off into sets of "rebbe" and "follower" and let ourselves flow into an acting out that was physical, emotional, and intellectual all at once.

For me the impact was enormous, and astounding. I let myself grow helpless, hungry, pleading. I found myself unable to say even "I want," because there wasn't enough "I" in me to say anything more than "please."

When the time came for my "rebbe" to channel spiritual warmth and nurture to me, I felt myself glowing with joy, laughing with abandon in the sensation of being fed at last. From deep beneath my mind came the impulse to let myself curl and nestle in the posture of a child about to nurse, reaching up to my "rebbe," looking deeply into her eyes with a passionate desire to be nurtured, loved.

The hunger was so humbling that the release of being "fed" came almost as an orgasm. I think that moment was the first in my conscious, accessible life that I understood how deep was the hunger, the yearning, that I felt in the childhood days I don't remember.

There were moments in my childhood when even that deep hunger got fed. Such a moment was my second memory of Honey: a moment when I felt utterly the insider, utterly well fed. It was the day before I started kindergarten. Honey walked me— just me, no Howard, no Daddy—to see the school so that I'd feel it was familiar, like family. And it was. Her father had laid the bricks that said "P.S. No. 59"; she herself had gone there as a child; it was to be my place. I was to feel at home there.

So Honey taught me, and so I learned to make it. But even such moments of feeling fully fed, fully at home, seemed brief. Worse, they taught me a deeper hunger for what seemed always just out of reach. Taught me that a moment of feeling satisfied and well fed would only lead into a spiral staircase where I would soon find myself hungrier than ever. Taught me to feel a still more poignant sense of being the outsider.

I kept discovering that what to me seemed an obviously sensible way of living seemed to everybody else against the rules. For example: in the second grade, I discovered that every arithmetic test began with the easy questions and ended with the hardest ones, so it was simple and quick to test myself by doing just the last few questions. I always got them right, but flunked the test. After all, two or three right answers out of ten was just not passing.

Silly teacher! Didn't she understand that the point was how

much I understood, not how many questions I answered? So I stuffed the test papers—marked with a big red D in a scale of E, VG, G, F, P, D—into my desk, and went on learning. And flunking.

Then came a PTA meeting, and Honey discovered I was flunking arithmetic. Horror! My desk was rifled, my shame and pride discovered. Brilliance was one thing, rebellion another. "Young man, you bring those papers home to me and get them signed before you take them back!"

But there must have been some other words passed, too, for the teacher also tried to find some carrots to give out. The kid is bright; give him bright work to do. I was assigned to check the weather every morning—look at a school-made barometer, take notes on the temperature, and report. It was nice to be the center of attention after the Lord's Prayer every morning, but when I realized that it didn't matter, it was only make-work, I refused to do it. And that was okay. Even rebellion was okay, seeing through the system was okay, as long as it didn't really rock the boat and threaten the future.

Almost a decade later, the story got replayed. In eleventh-grade trigonometry class, a crazy young math genius, whose hair hung over his eyes like a sheepdog, made friends with me. He sneered at the teacher's and the textbook's rote and got me drunk on the binary system—an arithmetic based on 2 instead of 10. For months I played with twoness and flunked every test of sines and cosines. Now that was trouble! "Flunk math, young man, and you can just forget about college!" Fire, fury, the angry face.

It's okay to be eccentric, Arthur, even a radical, but not a revolutionary. Revolutionaries don't go to college and don't get hired. Or fed. A lesson deeply learned: outsider, insider; learn the limits.

Twice more I remember learning that lesson: Rebel, but take care to set limits. In 1949 or so, the neighborhood newpaper, for which I was paperboy, published a scurrilous front-page attack (I remember a cartoon of a giant menacing rat) on all the groups we held dear: the Teachers Union, Americans for Democratic Action, the liberals who opposed McCarthyism even before McCarthy supplied it with a label.

I was furious and wanted to refuse to deliver the papers. Dad, who had helped found and nurture the Teachers Union, agreed, but Honey said I couldn't do that. I would be breaking my word and compromising my future. I could protest, or quit before delivering the next issue; but I couldn't quit without notice. So I delivered the papers. And I'm still unhappy, thinking about it.

And then in 1950, when I was editor of my school newspaper, I wrote an editorial denouncing the fact that in our racially segregated public schools, even the inter–high school federations of Future Teachers of America clubs were kept segregated. There was a federation of white FTAs from the white high schools and a federation of Black FTAs from the Black high schools. I wrote that this was both immoral and silly: the "future" teachers would someday be teaching in desegregated schools, and they should learn to work with each other.

For years, the newspaper's faculty adviser had been too drunk or too preoccupied to read or care about the content of the paper, but this he got wind of, in time to insist that the editorial be struck. Outraged, I protested to the vice-principal, who blandly explained that the high schools would not be desegregated in his lifetime or mine, so there was no point in making trouble. (This was just four years before the Supreme Court ruled in *Brown v Board of Education*, and Baltimore desegregated.)

I came home ready to quit and call a former high school editor who was now a reporter for the grown-up *Baltimore Sun* and who would have made the story a cause celebre. But no. This time Honey and Dad stood together. If I made trouble, my high school and Johns Hopkins University, where I planned to go to college, would combine to ruin me. No scholarships for sure, and probably no admission either. Again I knuckled under, and still today, I feel disgusted that I did.

Maybe the real question is not why I knuckled under—in the 1950s almost everybody did—but why and how I had enough oddness, enough sense of my own self in the first place, to rebel. It occurs to me that there was one year when I lived, despite all problems, as utterly myself, in the Garden of Delight. That year of almost no limits, no exclusions, made it ever after hard to set the limits.

It was a strange year to think of as the Garden of Delight. It was the year I got rheumatic fever and spent the whole third grade at home in bed. I was officially "sick," but as long as I stayed quiet, I felt fine. And for that year I remember myself as wholly welcome in the circle of the family—or, rather, in the circle of Honey's love. Of that year I remember only Honey. She set a standard for total companionship that no one person—not she, not a brother, not a wife—could ever match. With lively talk, batches of books brought home from the library, patient encouragement to do my homework so as not to lose a year of school, reminders to my teacher to solicit cards from all my schoolmates, backrubs with pungent alcohol, and a project of a billion Indian beads to string with baffled care into a patterned belt to give my cousin—with all that she kept me sane and helped my heart repair itself to make me sound.

Was this her chance to do for her father what she couldn't do for him when she was nine? This is a question that occurs to me only now, when I am in my fifties, searching to understand how I became an outsider. Was even that year of Eden a year when I wasn't me?

It's one thing to experience Eden in the womb; it's another to have it when you're eight, and can remember, and be ever after conscious of its absence.

From being the utter insider at home, when I went back to school I moved to being the outsider. The year of reading confirmed that I was "smarter"—that is, more bookish—than anyone else. Worse, I was now someone eerie, set apart by my illness.

For a couple of years, I wasn't allowed to play ball, or fight the normal fights of ten-year-olds, or even hurry home and back at lunchtime, beause the doctors said my heart might weaken. Imagine! "Don't play games; don't make trouble. He might just fall over dead!" Now that's outsiderness. There were never any hassles. This was a lazy, cossetted, comfortable way of being an outsider.

And then, when I was just eleven, I became an outsider again at home, or so it seemed to me. My mother the dodgeball champion, the joyful, curious, active, running explorer-talker-teacher-looker, was imprisoned in one room with tuberculosis. She would not go away. To hospitals, yes; but a sanitarium? That meant to die, like her father. So she would not leave the house. Fiercely, she stayed—and lived apart. At the age of eleven I learned to stand in the doorway of a room I couldn't enter, to blow a kiss past bedsheets that I couldn't touch. She learned to lift a face that each week grew more gaunt—a face we couldn't kiss.

That was the face that came in my dream, the face of the step-mother who wouldn't kiss me. Not that she was never like that before she got sick; not that she was always like that after she got sick. But that's the other face I see: the gaunt, tense, frightening face of my mother who had turned by evil magic into my step-mother.

Again and again, she went away to hospitals. There was one day I came to visit when every breath came as a gasp; when even an oxygen tent could not relieve her from endless gasping. She listened to my groping efforts to make contact, nodded and whis-pered—correcting my grammar. For she willed herself to be alive, to teach, to mother; but now the mothering came in a harder, tenser way.

She willed herself to be well enough to come to synagogue when I, and then Howard, became bar mitzvah.

She put that will into blazing eyes and a tight jaw when she told me, just before we left for the synagogue on my bar mitzvah morning, "As soon as you finish chanting, you walk over to me in the women's section and kiss me. No matter what anyone says. It's bad enough to have the women separated; I will not be ig-nored!"

She willed herself to live on just one lung, when the doctors decided to collapse the other one so as to halt the spread of the infection. She willed herself to survive when the drug she took to stop the TB gave her a bleeding anemia that took months to diag-nose. She willed herself into a remission, a cure, a relapse, a re-mission, a cure. She willed herself to live until my brother and I graduated, got married, had children. She lived and breathed. She got to hate rooms filled with people; they made it harder to breathe. She got to hate an absent-minded "Huh?" or "Could you repeat that?" for each extra sentence made it harder to breathe. And when she got a cold, or the flu, or bronchitis, she trembled.

The rest of us got used to the shortness of breath, the short-ness of temper. To the insistence on efficiency—not a breath should be wasted. We got used to it all, and we forgot it. Indeed, I myself took great care to forget it. For my fears were never to be spoken aloud, lest they depress and frighten Honey still more.

I did not invent this fear: Dad warned me that everything de-pended on our bearing. Honey would live if she kept her will to live; and she would keep the will to live if we made her proud of us, gave her ourselves as a reason to keep living. If we made life a misery to her, then she would die. This was especially true for me, because I was the older. I had to be the most grown-up.

If I breathed a word of how frightened I was, that itself might diminish her will to live.

I myself could kill her.

Our fears were breathed in—and never breathed out. Like carbon monoxide, they entered our blood and caught hold. The fear that Honey would die. The fear that she would bankrupt us with the bills. The fear that other people would find out she had TB. (In those days, it was shameful—or she thought it was.)

The anger we buried—how dare we be angry at her for getting sick?—until we feared it would burst out. But it rarely did. We succeeded in forgetting our fear and anger. She lived, we lived, and we forgot. Or so we thought.

But much later, I learned how deeply I had needed to forget. It came when I was forty, newly exploring what it meant to be Jewish.

It was a Friday night in spring at my communal prayer group in Washington. We were preparing for the Sabbath that came just before Passover. There appeared a "difficult" woman. She could have been thirty-two, or she could have been fifty-seven. She was from Florida and had almost no money. She had heard there were jobs in New York, so she set out to find one, but her money ran out in Washington. Here she was. Could she stay, after ser-vices, in somebody's home until she was able to get on her way again?

I said yes. How could I say no on the eve of the Passover Sabbath? She might be Elijah the Prophet coming to share our meal, coming to announce the coming of Messiah, coming in well-accustomed guise: the tired, the sick, the poor. I said yes, and we began to chant our prayers.

But she didn't chant. She coughed—deep, wrenching, unending coughs.

My voice in the prayers began to falter and fail. I knew that cough. It was my mother's cough. All those nightmares I had not even let myself dream began to boil up from each page of the prayerbook. My Elijah was coughing her lungs out. And I was about to take her home, to stay with my wife, my children, my self? To cough at the Passover table?

Was she really Elijah, come to my door to bring love and redemption if I would meet her desperate need? Or was she the Angel of Death, come not to pass-over, to free us, but to smear blood upon my doorpost? The thoughts I had never thought about my mother boiled up inside me.

Terror. An ethical nightmare. And nightmares deeper than ethics. My solution was a stay overnight and the next day a visit to a doctor. No! said Elijah. "They said in Florida it was just a bad cold." No! said we. A visit to the doctor or a ticket to New York. In New York we could give her the name of a social worker. Very well, said Elijah: New York.

So she went to New York, and she did call our friend, but when the time came to meet, she didn't show up. Elijah had come and gone, bearing no strange new message, no name of Messiah, but only a harsh old warning: balance your ethics; weigh what you owe to your own and what you owe to the stranger; love the stranger as you love yourself, no more.

Or, bearing Elijah's own message: turn the hearts of children to their parents, the hearts of parents to their children. Turn my heart once more to my mother? Strip away the sheath of numbness, the forgotten cover over the buried nightmare?

Our hearts were hard to turn. What my mother knew best was how to tough it out. If her lungs grew weaker, then oxygen could be towed around in a cart. If the range of her life grew narrow while her passion for life burned brighter, the passion could still be poured in the narrowing circle. If the world got slower and the breath still shorter, the temper could burn still brighter.

And if I felt caught in this narrowing circle, burned by Honey's

Our mother, Honey, holds Howard soon after he is born, November 1936; Arthur is three. "I hated the day when he was born," Arthur writes; but here his expression, if not his gesture, is enigmatic.

Honey's side of the family was somber and strong on rectitude. *Top left:* Szydlowec, Poland, probably around 1895. Honey's mother's parents—Hannah Hitzel Fox Honigman, b. 1846, married 1860, d. 1910, and Hersh Yaakov Honigman, b. 1840, d. 1918—with one of their six children, perhaps Grandma's older sister Zosha. Honey was named after Hannah Hitzel; Howard, after Hersh Yaakov. *Top right:* Honey's parents, Baltimore, perhaps 1918: Avraham Osnowitz, who died in 1923 at 37, but who in some ways was the most powerful person in our family, and Rose Honigman Osnowitz (Grandma), who died in 1984 at 97, a power in her own right. *Bottom left:* Baltimore, probably 1913—*l. to r.,* Honey's sister Freda, her brother Davey, and Honey. Honey was envious of Freda's wavy hair.

These posed photographs do not especially display it, but Dad's side of the family—Pop and "the Florida uncles"—seemed bent on adventure and fun. *Top left:* Dad's mother, Eva, with Jack, the second of her five sons. She died of an abortion in 1914, when Dad was six; many years later, he would say wistfully that he wished this photograph had been of her and him. *Top right: l. to r.,* Julius ("Jucky"), an unidentified friend or cousin, Herb, and Dad, in Indian costumes provided by the photographer. This may have been taken not long after their mother's death in 1914; Jucky would have been five, Herb three, Dad six. *Bottom right:* The five Waskow boys—Mike in a suit, holding Herb; Julius and Jack next to Herb; Dad in the rear, looking like a dad. (Uncle Julius recalls Dad as "phlegmatic," "less animated" than the other brothers.) This may have been taken in 1915, on the occasion of Mike's eighth-grade graduation, or the previous year, at his bar mitzvah. Mike looks very mature for age 13 or 14, and Uncle Herb says that he *was.*

Top left: Grandma (right) and her sister Zosha, 7 years older, at Howard's bar mitzvah, 1949. Grandma is 63. Grandma lived till 97; Zosha, till 103. *Top right:* Freda, Grandma, and Honey (kneeling) at twelve or thirteen, in front of the house on Cottage Avenue, soon after moving in. Avraham is either in a TB sanitarium or already dead. *Bottom left:* Uncle Herb, with pipe, Uncle Jucky, and Dad on the front porch steps at Cottage Avenue. This might have been as early as Honey and Dad's wedding in 1929, when Herb was 17, Julius 19, Dad 21. Mike and Jack were also present at the wedding, but, curiously, are not in this photograph; perhaps it was taken as a memento for the brothers who had been in the Hebrew Orphans Asylum together.

At Howard's bar mitzvah, Baltimore, 1949. *Top:* Honey's side—*l. to r.*, Arthur, Tante Freda, Howard, Grandma, Honey, Aunt Rose, Allen with Adrian in front of him, and Uncle Dave. Stanley is not in the picture. *Bottom:* Dad's side—*l. to r.*, Arthur, Uncle Herb, Uncle Jack, Pop, Howard, Dad, and Uncle Mike. Uncle Jucky is absent.

Top: Baltimore, July 7, 1929.
Wedding picture of Honey, 18,
and Dad, 21. *Bottom:* Baltimore,
1984, a year before Honey's
death. Honey is 73, Dad 76.

"The four of us." *Top left:* in 1940 or 1941, before World War II, on the concrete steps at Cottage Avenue, with "B 'n B," our beagle; *top right:* at the beach with Pop the following year; and, *bottom*, in 1947, in a photograph taken by Uncle Dave (*"Portrait by David"*), where the physical connection between Honey and Arthur, Dad and Howard is obvious.

Before the fall. *Above,* Arthur and Howard at ages five and two. *On facing page, top left,* with Uncle Jucky during World War II; *top right,* on a pony, in a traditional neighborhood pose; and, *bottom,* with friends from the neighborhood at Halloween—*l. to r. front,* a boy whose name we don't recall, Howard Schunick (Little Howard), and Big Howard; *l. to r. rear,* Macky Schuman in a duck costume, Arthur as an American Revolutionary, and Herbie Luntz.

Top: We were raised not only to be allies but to be alike; this was the style of dress Honey believed in. Arthur is 13 and Howard 10. *Bottom:* in summer 1958, we are visiting Cottage Avenue between the academic years of graduate school. By now, Arthur is married. A little difference here: Howard still wears his convenient Army haircut. In the background are the eight identical houses leading to the end of the block, and the Talmudical Academy in the distance.

"Indefatigable teachers . . . , all of us": *top left*, Dad at 31, in 1939; top right, Arthur at 55, in 1988; *bottom*, Howard at 29, in 1966.

Young men with families: *top left,* Arthur, Irene with David (not quite two), Grandma, and Honey in the spring of 1966, in the backyard at Cottage Avenue. *Top right,* Howard wih Saul in lap and Dan on the back steps of their first house in Portland. *Bottom,* a typical holiday, 1967, in the entry hall at Cottage Avenue: *l. to r.,* Betty, Howard, Arthur, and Betty's niece Dina (holding new-born Saul), Dad, Irene (holding new-born Shoshana— then Susanna), and Honey in front reaching across David toward Dan, to adjust him for the photograph. Grandma's portrait is visible in the rear at left.

After divorces: *right,* Arthur with David and Shoshana, 1975, reading the manuscript of their story about Creation, *Before There Was a Before; below,* Howard with his eldest son, Dan, in front of his and his partner Millie's restaurant, Indigine, during one of Dan's summer stays in Portland. *(Photograph by Christopher Rauschenberg)*

Top: The family as it became, gathered at Dad's eightieth birthday celebration, 1988. *L. to r., front:* Morissa Sher (Phyllis' daughter), Betty Fellner (Howard's first wife), Dad, David Waskow, and Phyllis Berman; *l. to r., rear:* David Fellner, Ursula Wolfe-Rocca (Grey's younger daughter), Dan Waskow, Ilan Waskow, Shoshana Elkin Waskow, Grey Wolfe, Saul Waskow, Howard, Arthur, Morgan Wolfe (Grey's older daughter), and Joshua Sher (Phyllis' son). Absent are Honey, who had died two years earlier, Irene Elkin (Arthur's first wife), and Ben Wolfe (Grey's son). *Bottom:* Arthur embraces Dad at Howard and Grey's wedding, March 1986. (Howard: "His face is joyful and sweet— undeniably sweet. I studied that face for many minutes, trying to imprint it on my brain.")

Wedded bliss. *Right,* Howard and Grey at their wedding, March 1986, laughing in response to a comment from someone in the circle of friends and family, to whom they've been reading poems and journal entries. *(Photograph by Dan Wolfe) Below,* Arthur and Phyllis in front of their *huppa,* June 1986.

Different *and* close: *left,* Howard and Arthur with Dad at his eightieth birthday celebration, January 1988, and, *below,* at Shoshana's wedding party, June 1992.

hotter temper, I could do what I knew best: restore the sheath around my heart, look blandly at the oxygen cart, accept her temper as a given.

But underneath, my heart could not keep silent. "Don't breathe a word!" said my history, but my heart of hearts still sighed. With a still, small whispering voice.

The second time that my forgotten fears came bursting into life was ten years later. I was fifty, and the years and the fruits of my Jewishness had kept on growing, against all my imaginings, into a path, a career.

I was sitting in a class to teach about Martin Buber. "The words on the tablets," wrote Buber; "what words came forth from Sinai?" I open my heart to the words: "I . . . Lord . . . your God . . . . Who brought you out of the house of slavery . . ."

"Lord?" But that isn't what came from Sinai. That's the euphemism tradition has substituted for those four mysterious letters: YHWH. The tradition said *Adonai*, "Lord." A masculine being, "up there." The newer scholars say *Yahweh*, the tribal name for a tribal god, like Marduk, Zeus, Osiris. But there are no vowel in this "unpronounceable" name, no "aah" and "ehh." Sinai speaks with a voice that reaches beyond tribe, beyond all tribes.

Why unpronounceable? Be a rebel, I thought. Try to pronounce it.

So I tried to pronounce it with no vowels, no euphemisms. "Yyy—hhh—www—hhh." What came out was a breath. God's name is—breathing? The breath of life. "The breath of all that's living praises Your Name!" the prayerbook says. Aha! If God's name is breathing, then all breathing affirms God's name and expresses God's Being.

Trees breathe, I thought. We breathe in what the trees breathe out, and the trees breathe in what we breathe out. Between us and the trees there is a breathing, in and out. We are breathing together the breath of God.

Time is a breathing, an in-and-out that moves forward as it returns to where it had been.

What does it mean, to take God's name in vain? To empty out the name of God? It means, I thought, to breathe without knowing that our breath is the name of God—to breathe without consciousness, without letting our breath flow into the breath of all that lives.

What does it mean, I wondered, to make a Sabbath? The Bible says that in order to create the restful Sabbath, God paused to catch a breath.

Even then, I still kept part of my discovery a secret from myself. I kept myself from knowing that it was my mother's breath I yearned for. Her breath, once more even and deep: that would be God enough for me.

When did I learn this? Not until my mother died. How did I learn it? Through her death.

In the midst of Passover, forty years late by her doctor's reckoning, she became in the same breath Elijah and the Angel of Death: both the herald of our freedom and the carrier of rest.

Once more, she tried to tough it out. One more bronchitis, and her doctors said she belonged in the hospital. But she would not go: the family was regathering for Pesach. But this time—

I pause in that sentence, pause to catch my breath. Sitting here to write, sitting here at rest, I am short of breath. This last story is hard work to tell.

This time . . .

• • •

"Just tell the story as it happened, Arthur."

• • •

That's her voice. That's Honey's voice.

• • •

Her voice came to me less than a year after she died. So I told the story. I wrote what I remembered, I published it, it moved my brother and my father and my children—and now, now I need to tell the story in a different way.

• • •

But Honey, first I need to talk to you directly. I can still hear that single sentence that you spoke to me back then, but now I hear it in a different way. Now I can hear your tones, your pauses, and I know that voice came from a Honey who was almost new to me.

Your sentence—"Just tell the story, Arthur"—spoke to me not from two faces, but from one mother, unified. How is it I can hear your voice at last? How is it I can hear your voice as one?

I hear your voice at calm, at peace. Not painful, not gasping; not annoyed, correcting, or angry. Not laughing either, or girlish. Not even the mothering voice that kept me happy all the year I spent in bed. But a voice of calm good humor, teaching, sharing knowledge simply. Showing me the path.

And yet this voice is just a glimmer, just a sentence. A bare beginning of how to hear you as a whole, as one, a unity.

If I can tell the story as you told me, this voice of yours may become more than a glimmer.

But I can't tell it alone, all by myself. I did that once before, soon after you died; but because I told it alone, it came out slightly wrong though powerful. One-sided.

For me to hear your voice as one, I must be whole. And for me to be whole, I need Howard. Howard's helping, Howard's teaching, his resembling. Without Howard, I'm not whole. I'm missing something that I need to learn, to absorb, from him—almost to be fed by him. Something of his self I need to feed me.

Feed me. I hear another voice now—is it Howard's? —saying, "Eat of me, my brother. You will be more fully you. More fully one."

Is that the point, Honey? I think somehow you failed to feed me. Suddenly, just now, I am remembering: once you told me in a voice ashamed and sad that you could not nurse me; your breasts could not give milk. Did it all go back so early? I'm not blaming you for failing to feed me; it just didn't happen. And now you can't. But Howard can. Did you tell us to be close because you knew that we would need to feed each other?

I don't know yet *what* it is I need him to feed me, but it's something of him, that is his. I think I can find out, and get it from him, only if I work with him. Maybe that will help me to be one.

HOWARD. It's not clear just what Otts wants from me. Until now, writing this book with him, I've coaxed and encouraged him, asked for his time, his attention, his material. Now he's asking me.

Specifically, he wants my help in telling the story of Honey's death: on the verge of telling it himself, he stops, sensing that his version would be somehow incomplete. More generally, it seems he wants, how consciously I can't quite tell, something else as well—not just my perspective or my insight but my presence: my companionship.

He wants me to join with him, I think—but first things first. What rises out at me from Otts' pages about Honey is what he says about being warned by Dad: that he, Otts himself, could cause Honey to die. Never was I warned this way; it's not true that *we* were warned. Otts must have been warned just because he was older and therefore supposed to be responsible. Or maybe because already he was "difficult"—but what a way to make him even more so!

Even with this said, I can't just leap with Otts into the story of Honey's death, because reading his pages, I see I have a sense of Honey different from his. A sense of her that explains much about her final illness and the way she chose to die. To join him truly, I need to say how *I* understand her life.

Otts writes about two mothers, a good one and a bad; it sounds like a fairy tale, a mythic or romantic view. The good mother he identifies as Honey well, the other Honey ill. My understanding of Honey is that she had many sides, including a scary one, and manifested them from well before her illness until almost the very moment of her death. So I have a different sense from Otts of Honey's "wholeness."

I associate my own view with realism rather than romance: the accumulation of everyday detail, material as seen from closer in; a piling up of insights and incidents, out of which a story line emerges. Otts' mind works something like a lightning flash, illuminating starkly and surprisingly; mine, more like a searchlight, pushing back the darkness bit by bit. Perhaps in my probing, accumulating way, I can reveal aspects of Honey that will help Otts understand her better. And perhaps in doing so, I can reveal myself to Otts. For how can he really know me without knowing my relationship to her?

My own view requires that I start not with Honey on her deathbed but back at the beginning.

• • •

I was born in the back seat of our tenant Mr. Zilber's Dodge, Dad and Mr. Zilber in the front. But I didn't learn that until I was twenty-one. I had asked Honey in what hospital I'd been born. She glanced sideways at Dad, laughed self-consciously, and told me—I hadn't been.

I was delighted. What a mark of distinction! Why hadn't she told me earlier? Such a story I could have been telling, all those years!

"Because," she answered, "I was afraid you'd think that I hadn't been careful enough, that I hadn't taken good care of you. I didn't want to call the doctor too soon. With Arthur he'd told me to wait till the pains were five minutes apart, so I was waiting. But with the second contraction I knew that *you* weren't waiting."

Off they had gone in Mr. Zilber's car. Halfway to the hospital, Dad heard a kind of knocking coming from the back, then Honey murmuring, "Poor butsy, poor butsy." First he thought she was hallucinating, but when he looked, he saw that the knocking was my head against the floorboards.

Ashamed to tell me, because she hadn't done it right. But I've always loved the story. How I wouldn't wait, and "poor butsy, poor butsy." Now I love it more than ever, because I see that it's not just about me being born in the back seat of a Dodge, but about me and Honey doing it all by ourselves, getting me out of her into the world.

I watched everything she did—watched her roll her torso, to tighten her stomach muscles and reduce her hips, as she explained when I asked her why. Probably I was four or five. Later, after she got sick, I watched to see if she was feeling bad. (Maybe that's how I learned to see detail?)

She was only five feet tall. Actually, she admitted late in life, she had been at her tallest only 4 feet 11 3/4 inches. But she didn't look that short, partly because her legs were long and even more because she carried herself tall. Eyes alert, chin raised a bit, she strode forth eagerly.

Five feet tall, and she weighed, in the period when she did those exercises, 117 pounds, if I recall correctly. So she must have been almost chunky when I was small; in photographs she looks filled out. But I don't remember her that way, even if I do see myself watching her roll her hips.

I remember her as flat-chested, wiry, and quick. She moved almost at a run. And her body was so supple that still at fifty-odd she could put one foot behind her head, holding her skirt down so as not to "show" (no underpants, remember), a maneuver that did not always work.

I see her supple, quick, and thin. And then I see her sick and *very* thin. She weighed, at one point, only 79 1/2 pounds. I remember because when I was nine, I got into a fight with Anita Gold in Miss Leutner's class—she hit me first, I hit her back, Miss Leutner sent me (me!) to the cloakroom and said she'd have to see my mother. I began to cry.

"She can't come to see you," I managed to get out.

"Oh, I suppose you're going to tell me that you have a baby brother so that's why she can't come," Miss Leutner sneered. "Well, you should have thought of that before."

"No, that's not why," I said. "She's sick in bed. She weighs only 79 1/2 pounds."

Miss Leutner was shocked. Through my tears I could see that much.

I know that's all Honey weighed because I used to watch the stand-up scale, to see where she had left the markers. And I used to sneak glances at the records that she kept, of her temperature and weight, and I used to look to see how she was breathing and whether there was fever in her eyes. I used to listen, too, for whether her voice was dragging or alive.

She lived in quarantine two years, lying in the smallest upstairs bedroom, propped up on a huge overstuffed reading pillow, with pockets on its armrests for the tissues. A frail figure, her legs barely making mounds in the bedclothes, her dark circled eyes large and animated in her narrowed face. Suspended over her was the adjustable table where she kept her books and papers, her thermometer and pencils and Pall Malls, and where she had her meals from an aluminum tray. She called us with a small brass bell to take away the tray when she was done.

Yes, she smoked even though she had tuberculosis. The doctors did try to dissuade her, but she'd do it her way or not at all. She died in this same spirit.

Honey stayed upstairs two years. I remember sitting across

from her bed when I got home from school, answering her questions and looking at her to see how she was feeling. Always *across from*; almost never did she hold me.

Going through the photographs when we were helping Dad to move, after Honey died, I found a picture of her that I had never seen before, holding me when I was a baby. She is warm and fleshy; she cradles me against her breast and looks lovingly at me. So I know that before she got sick she held me, but I can't remember it. Probably she held me also when she told her story about the tiger-lily that shielded a tiger from the hunters, camouflaging it, but though I remember the story, I can't remember her embrace.

I do remember her holding me once. I had played ball on the school playground instead of coming home the way I was supposed to, and I stood too close behind Zeke Siegel's bat. It got me just below my eye. I should go to Dr. Glick's, Honey said on the phone to Mrs. Goetz, the principal; his office was just a block away. Honey couldn't come because she had to stay in bed, so I went to Dr. Glick's alone. Mrs. Schunick came to be with me, and Dad came too, when he got home from teaching school. Though Dad got faint while Dr. Glick was stitching up the cut—the needle caught a bit—I didn't cry. Mrs. Schunick said I was so brave. I didn't cry until I got home and saw Honey sitting there in bed upstairs, and then she reached her arms to me and held me.

Honey stayed upstairs two years, but that wasn't all of it. We visited her by bus and trolley, then by car, in hospitals all over Baltimore: in Jewish hospitals, lay hospitals, and hospitals where Jesus stretched out healing hands in marble as we entered, or hung suffering over the iron bars of Honey's bed. This went on over a period of many years.

For most of this time, Honey was not actually in bed. Though the scar from the first operation on her lungs curved for ten inches alongside and under her left shoulder blade, she powdered it and wore an open-backed gown to my bar mitzvah reception. She went religiously to PTA meetings. She drove with us to Florida, pointing out the sights—"Look, boys! Look!" But as I write about those years I feel I'm in a swirl of hospital rooms and corridors with no beginning and no end; I feel it was a weight upon my chest. It's difficult to breathe; all I know to do is wait. Wait and eat—I eat all morning, writing this.

Life was in suspension. Honey wasn't fully with us, but neither was she gone. Grandma cooked for us, but Honey never did withdraw. When we were helping Dad move away from Cottage Avenue, I found this letter, water-stained, in her bureau drawer. It is dated December 1946 and addressed to Otts and me, from one of those hospitals:

Dear Boys,

I'm delighted to get your letters. They are interesting and well written.

Please forgive me for scolding you Saturday. The doctor had just been in to give me a treatment and I'm afraid I was rather upset. I had been looking forward to seeing you and was very proud of the way you looked. . . .

You boys just be sure and mind Grandmother and Tante Freda. Do your lessons without fussing. The girl won't be in Thursday so be sure and get up in time to clean up. Have you boys thanked Pop for the allowance? His address is *215 SW 3rd Ave, Ft. Lauderdale, Fla.* Howard, study your spelling carefully Thursday night. Ottie, how are your marks coming? Are you answering in English class? Have you gotten your actual marks?

Howard, I'm sorry you had a sore throat but I think you stay out playing for too long at one time. It is much too cold these days to stay out for more than 3/4 of an hour at one time.

I'm sorry you didn't see my bracelet and earrings but they are lovely and you will see them when I get home. I'm wearing the bracelet and it matches my blue quilted jacket. I wrote to the store in Boston to find out if they have a pin to match the bracelet. Since I have earrings already I would like to exchange them for a pin. If you remember Daddy gave me a pair of earrings several years ago that will go with my bracelet perfectly. Do you know that turquoise is my birthstone and the set makes a lovely birthday present.

The nurse is in to tell me it's time for my light to go out. Can you imagine—*I* a grown-up—have to turn my light off at 9:30. I'm going to burn my light all night when I get home and boy—could

I use my electric blanket.

I doubt if I'll get around to writing again but don't ever doubt that I'm thinking of and loving you. I just get tired easily and must ask your forgiveness for a seeming neglect which isn't really that at all.

My very best of love to you. Please be good as I know you can be.

Love,

Honey

As I read this now, more than forty years after Otts and I received it, I'm overcome by how familiar, how typical it is. This letter is absolutely in her voice.

Her attention moved into every corner of our lives. I should feel bothered, I tell myself, too supervised—wherever did she get that figure, 3/4 of an hour? And I do, a bit—I smile ruefully and shake my head in wonderment. But more than that, I feel cared for and respected. My feelings and intelligence respected. I feel loved.

I feel loved also when I remember her protecting me from Marty Zeskind and his rope, swooping down that way from the porch and scolding him so fiercely: "If you ever touch these boys again, I'll—" She'd what? I don't remember, but I do remember what it felt like to have her on my side.

And I feel loved when I remember another time that she protected me, from the boy with the orange shoes. On my way toward the exit of the bus taking me home from junior high, I had stumbled across a Black teenager's brilliant orange shoes. I'm thirteen; he's about sixteen, and bigger than I am. The bus swerves toward the curb, I stumble across those shining shoes, mumble an apology, and get off. I duck into Kessler's to get my daily chocolate-covered halvah bar, and when I come out, I see that he's gotten off at the next stop and is running back toward me. "Oh, shit," I think, but I hold myself to walking fast. Walking very fast, I make it up our steps about thirty seconds ahead of him—long enough to warn Honey that there's big trouble in pursuit of me. As he dares me to come down and fight, she stands in front of me on the porch, though she's six inches and fifty pounds smaller than I am. He's from Harlem, he yells; he's been warned about Southerners like me. I answer not a word, but my mind is going double-time. "Southerners?" I think. "You're wrong; we're Jews. And we believe in *tolerance*. You've picked the wrong family to be angry at." Nothing will get me off that porch to fight with him. Finally Honey makes him go away.

And I feel loved when I open my bar mitzvah album to the photograph in which she's reaching to adjust my tie. There's a look in her eyes that I can describe only as adoration. It was many years before I found that look again. Really not until now, with Grey.

At twenty she had been an executive assistant to the president of Schleisner's, a Baltimore department store. After Otts and I were born, she poured her energies into the family. She oversaw our mowing of the neighbors' lawns down to an errant blade of grass. Eyes in the back of her head, she joked, but it seemed true enough. She knew somehow when Otts and I were wrestling upstairs. (Later I learned it was because the chandelier was shaking.)

When I was in second grade, she knew it would rain on my walk back to school after lunch. I didn't believe it and refused to wear my brown jacket—and it poured harder than I'd ever seen. The fury of the heavens fell on me. Did she, I wondered, have a direct connection?

She saw everything; knew everything; did everything. She scrubbed clothes on a washboard until I was six and we got a wringer washing machine; she never did see a need for a dryer, not with clothes lines available inside and out. She scrubbed floors on a rubber pad to protect a balky knee; she drilled us in spelling, heard my lines for the class plays, played ball with us, showed Dad how to fix things around the house, typed our papers for school and stencils for the Teachers Union newsletter. She had typed Dad's master's thesis, and Pop's autobiography, and now she typed my Ph.D. thesis and Otts' too.

It was not just support; it was a way of being part of what we did. The typewriter was a fixture, as much her instrument as were the stove and telephone. In later years it had a permanent position. It sat—a heavy standard Royal, with a carriage extra-long for charts—on a card table in the bedroom, wedged between the bed and vanity.

She was the family direction giver until the week she died. When as a kid I had to venture downtown for something—new lenses for my glasses, say—she would take me by the hand and, in the kitchen, walk me through the route, calming my anxiety. "Okay, now you're standing in front of Chambers'," she would say. "It's Howard Street. Now you turn left [we turned] and walk to Monument . . ." On the auto trips to Florida, she was the custodian of the map; ever after, and increasingly, Dad called her his navigator. She would alert him also to the turns.

Above all she was a teacher. She taught me how to read before I went to school and taught me at five how to welcome parents to a kindergarten presentation in the gym, even if I couldn't say my *r*'s. "Look over their heads so you won't get distracted," she advised, so I practiced my speech to the red wall clock that hung above the icebox. (In this way I was readied to deliver lectures and to speak for civil rights and peace.)

And when I was eight and Otts eleven, in the summer of 1945, when Dad went away to Cornell for graduate work, she tried to teach us about sex. Otts and I had asked if we could take turns sleeping in the big bed with her, now that Daddy was away. I feel young even now as I think about this, young and innocent.

"No, that wouldn't be proper," Honey says. Wouldn't be *proper*? And then Honey starts drawing diagrams and telling us how babies come. How did we get to this? What's going on? I remember one diagram especially—of a girl's underside. Girls had three holes, Honey explained. I still didn't get what all that had to do with our sleeping in the big bed, but I was excited by the news about making babies. So excited that I broke my promise not to talk to anyone about it—and told Little Howard that babies came from a man's peeing in a woman. When he repeated what I'd said, the big boys laughed.

She was a teacher to the end. When, six months before she died, I remarked that I had never learned to iron, she swung her legs out of bed and hurried to instruct me, on the ironing board that stood on the opposite side of the bed from the typewriter. Every right move I made, imitating her, she met with encouragement and praise. "This is how Pop taught *me* to do a shirt!" she exclaimed, giving credit where it was due. Her eyes shone, her voice had an urgent excitement I had not heard in years—and I saw mirrored back to me the teaching style and methods I had believed were particularly mine. I thought, "I *lived* with this teacher, she taught me with this excitement every day! What did that *do* to me?"

She shaped me like a sculptor working clay.

She supported me in going after what I wanted. When at six I asked for a gun and holster set for Chanukah—a leather belt and holster painted white and studded with shiny rivets and red glass, with wooden bullets in the loops, and a gray six-shooter that broke apart for loading—she caught her breath but said "okay," though it cost five dollars, a princely sum for the Waskow family in 1942. There were limits—that she made clear—but she stretched them. (For Otts, from his account, she set them hard.)

When I gave up a graduate fellowship at Illinois because I wanted to switch to Yale, Honey encouraged me, though it meant spending every dollar of the educational fund I had been accumulating since I was five. Dad was the cautious one; he thought I ought to stay at Illinois, where the education was good enough and the money guaranteed. When I resigned my tenured teaching job at Reed, again turning my back on that guaranteed income, she swallowed hard and wished me well, then was excited about the tiny restaurant I opened with Millie.

She found the life in things. She loved the old Baltimore—buildings and fountains long since gone, some of which not even Tante Freda could remember—but she was proud of the new one too: the oddly shaped downtown structures and the Harbor Development unfolding. At thirty-five in the spirit of the early 1970s, I let my hair grow long, into a ponytail; she bought me brightly colored bands for it. Visiting Oregon, she picked strawberries for the first time at sixty-five, and gasped in delight at her first sight of mussels layered on the rocks.

In politics you knew what she wanted, where she stood. In the discussions around the kitchen table, she always had opinions, though she'd complain sometimes that she "couldn't get a word in edgewise," or talk loud enough to compete with the voices of three argumentative males.

Her basic position was, she sided with the underdog. When

Otts turned himself from a Jewish radical into a radical Jew, she reminded him that everyone needed help, not only Jews. "Suppose it was you!" she had told the realtor who tried to trick Grandma. "Just suppose! Suppose it was you!"

She was devoted to Grandma. When traveling with Dad, after his retirement, meant displacing Grandma to Tante Freda's, it was a wrench for her to go. Grandma, after all, had taken care of us when Honey was sick. But it was more than that. In Avraham's absence, Honey had stood beside her—facing down the realtor, later moving to help her at the store. They were comrades, two doughty women in league against adversity.

And it was more than even that. When Otts and then I delivered the *Home News*, the weekly ad paper that so offended him politically, Honey and Grandma would spend hours every Thursday in the living room, rolling the papers and rubber-banding them, so that all we had to do was toss them on the porches. As their hands flew and the sea of rolled papers rose above their knees, they talked on and on, Grandma in Yiddish with a little English, Honey in English with a little Yiddish. Why would they give up these hours? I used to wonder. To provide us with a chance to make a dollar? To give us experience at a job? To save us the hours to do homework in? Yes, and yes, and yes—but also, I realize now, because it gave them an excuse to spend the time together. They liked each other's company; they were bound powerfully to one another.

(Visiting Dad daily now that he lives in Portland, I take my cue from Honey being with and caring for Grandma—and feel guilty that Dad lives only near us and not actually in our house.)

Honey was devoted to Grandma—indeed, to the family in general. When Dad and his brothers decided that Pop was too old to continue living by himself, there was no question that it was Honey who'd take care of him. She took him in so deeply that for years after his death, she would forget and set the dinner table for five instead of four. Later she nursed Aunt Rose, her brother Davey's widow, as Rosie died agonizingly of cancer. She did not talk about this afterward—just raised her eyebrows and shook her head as if to clear away the images.

She nursed Grandma after Grandma could no longer make it

up the stairs to her own rooms and so slept on a daybed in our living room—until Honey could no longer rise nightly to respond to Grandma's calls, could barely even with Dad's help prop her up in bed to feed her, and so finally gave up, at Passover two years before the one when Honey died, and let Grandma go into the hospital and then the nursing home. ("Sit me up and finish me off," Grandma had pleaded, in anguish from her damaged back, but no one would.) And only a few weeks before Honey herself died, she insisted on visiting Tante Freda every other day after Freda's stomach operation.

When I urged her to let Grandma go into a nursing home a year before she did, she said simply, "I can't." And when I warned her that she was overtaking herself to visit Freda so frequently, she said, "She's an old woman, Howard, and she's one sick pup." And you? I answered, from across the continent, to no avail.

To no avail, because what she said about Grandma was true in general: she could not stop. All that teaching and monitoring, all that intensity and sense of purpose, all that commitment to the underdog and devotion to the family, also had a darker face. During her father's illness, the family had moved and moved and moved; it was a nightmare time. So she had organized her life around control—and did not know how to give it up.

Control was her necessity. It would show itself in the way she was with store clerks and carpenters: tough, wary, on guard against incompetence or fraud. Or it would flash out, transforming her and terrifying me. Even before she was sick, when we were small.

I'm crossing Park Heights Avenue with her, headed for the streetcar that goes downtown, and I'm digging inside the pocket of my woolly knickers—trying to scratch my chafed thighs? trying to rearrange my dick inside my jockey shorts?—and she glares down at me and says, her voice a knife, "Stop that! You're not fooling anyone!"

Again: at dinner I watch Dad scooping out a large portion of cole slaw and plead only half-jokingly, "Daddy, remember to leave some for the rest of us!"—and out of nowhere, Honey slaps my face. Hard. Sudden. The only time I can remember her slapping me. Disrespect for Father, deadly sin.

And again. All of us are upstairs in Grandma's living room, at a party Grandma is giving for her cousins. I am six or seven, probably, and Otts nine or ten. Suddenly Honey commands us to leave the living room, takes us into Grandma's kitchen, where she drops to her knees and starts sniffing at our rears. What's going on? Then comes that glare, and the accusation in that knifelike voice: "Gas, both of you!"

And again—this one keeps escaping from my memory, I had to make a note of it to make sure I won't forget this time.

I vomited a lot—on long streetcar rides, washing out the garbage can, on boats. Certain foods nauseated me: brussels sprouts, cooked cauliflower—just their smell made me want to vomit. Otts and Honey loved that stuff—Dad and I, we hated it. But Honey insisted that I eat some anyway—because, she said, she had been a picky eater and she wasn't going to see us turn out that way. She persuaded Dad to eat some too, so I would see him doing it.

I'm still not saying it, this memory I censor. I hated lumpy Cream of Wheat. ("Cream of Wheat, it's so good to eat, you can have it every day!"—the theme song of "Let's Pretend" plays in my head. *No*, let's *not* pretend!) Lumpy Cream of Wheat made me vomit. One morning, when I was six perhaps, I vomited right into my bowl. And Honey, furious, "fed up," she said, with all my vomiting, made me eat it.

Is that true? Even as I write it down, I can hardly believe it. But I do believe it's true. I see her eyes blazing and her jaw clenched, and I hear the words forced out between her teeth: "You'll have it for lunch and supper, too, if you don't eat it now!" And I see myself swallowing it all, the vomit and the lumpy Cream of Wheat. I can almost taste it now.

My memory has been wrong before. I used to believe that Honey slapped Grandma at Uncle Dave's funeral to get her to stop screaming, but now I believe she didn't—she only yelled at her in that cutting way. So maybe she didn't make me eat my vomit, but I believe she did. All I can make of it is that she went crazy for a little while that morning. From the pressure of raising us? or the pressure of denying herself a different life? And only now does it occur to me—Why didn't I say no? Why didn't I overturn the bowl, throw it on the kitchen floor? What was it with me that I thought I had to *swallow* everything?

When she got sick, she— I start to write, "she was no less controlling." But actually I think she *was* less controlling after she got sick; I don't remember any crazy moments after she got sick. Maybe she'd used them up in *getting* sick. But she was controlling still. She wouldn't rest, Uncle Dave complained in frustration to Aunt Rose; she was trying to run the household from her hospital bed. And true to form, when she came home, she ruled it from the upstairs bedroom.

To make things right was her passion. This was even more true in her final years. The slower Dad became, the more impatient Honey got. The woman we knew as lively, passionate, and energetic, if a little crazy sometimes, became, to her grandchildren's eyes, caring and supportive still, but also edgy, ill tempered, quarrelsome, and controlling.

I defended my children as I hadn't dared defend myself:

"Honey, if Lonny doesn't like tomatoes, he doesn't have to eat them. He doesn't even have to try them!"

"No, Honey, Saul doesn't have to go visit Betty's mother, even if she's going blind. He'll stay home and play ball with me."

Dan, at six, did it on his own. "Honey," he says, "if I wanted someone to correct my grammar, I could buy a book for a dollar and a half! You only want me around so you can correct me!" Honey, shaken, replies, "Do you really believe that?"

Dan: "Well, it sure seems that way sometimes!" Listening, I'm astonished and delighted. Proud.

The more constrained her life became, the shorter her temper and the tighter her grasp. When we were children, she saved dollar bills from her modest household budget, keeping them in little black purses hidden deep in bureau drawers. By her last years she was saving everything: the least leftovers, in the freezer; stacks of coupons, paper-clipped, worth pennies at the supermarket; piles of recipes cut from the *Sun*; ancient blankets, which in fact would come in handy when we visited.

The cellar became almost impassable. There were boxes full of budget books starting in the 1930s and of newspapers Otts and I had edited in high school; wardrobes bursting with clothes not worn for thirty years (someone someday might want Pop's gray overcoat, it's good as new); a toy-box with my first football, my softballs, and my mitt; provisions of flour, laundry detergent, paper towels, and canned goods sufficient to warm the heart of a survivalist. In the kitchen every surface disappeared—beneath boxes of pencils and erasers, large plastic bags stuffed with smaller ones, glass jars and plastic containers of all sizes, twists to put around the plastic bags, plastic spoons and sugar packets retrieved from trays in airplanes and hospitals, and a huge, ever-growing ball of rubber bands, more than an ordinary family could use in three lifetimes.

She saved because she hated waste. She saved in order to give away; someone might need. The hidden dollar bills bought an expensive mahogany desk for Dad, and the schoolteacher's salary and pension, carefully managed, produced savings that year after year bought airplane tickets to fly me and my kids to visit one another, provided Otts a loan for a house and me a loan toward building a new restaurant, and established educational funds for each of the five grandchildren.

Really she saved in order to heal the present and to shape the future. Because her life was running out.

And I wanted to save *her*—to make her well, to put her right, I guess. While Otts was made to live in fear of killing her, I lived in search of saving her. A mighty difference.

When she first was sick, I wanted to win a gift for her at the carnival that came yearly to the corner lot. There was a stand where you bet on a number and the operator spun a wheel. If the wheel stopped at your number, you won a huge basket of fruit, wrapped in glistening yellow cellophane: pears, apples, oranges shone through.

I knew Honey would love that basket. If I put my dime on my lucky number, seven, maybe I would win. But I was the first and only player at the booth, and the operator wouldn't play until there were more bets up than mine alone. I pleaded with him; I had to go home soon for supper, five o'clock. Finally he relented, spun the wheel. It spun, it spun, and finally it slowed, the nails clicking against the leather tongue that would mark the winning slot. It slowed, it slowed, and it stopped, incredibly, at seven.

I had won for Honey! It was a miracle. She would feel so much better! She would get well even, maybe . . . No—but she *would* feel better, that I knew. Then the operator, looking at me over his left shoulder, raised his right arm and spun the wheel again.

Stunned, barely comprehending, I stammered a protest, but he simply denied the wheel had stopped at seven. Again I protested, but I had no witnesses. "Go on home to supper, sonny," he said sneering, and I did. I don't think I ever told her what had happened.

I wanted to save her, but Honey's tuberculosis was a determined strain. *Clear* was an important word for us. We waited for the day when tests would show that she was "clear," free of the infection. Year after year, the tests showed that she was not. As I moved well into adulthood, I read the daily papers front to back—the *New Haven Register-Guard*, the *Philadelphia Bulletin*, the *Oregonian*—with the same obsessive thoroughness I had used to reserve for the sports section. I didn't know what I was looking for.

It must have been in Portland, more than twenty years after she had gotten sick, that I found what I had been seeking—an article in the medical section about a new drug for TB. I called Honey. Had she heard of it? No, but she'd ask her doctor. He'd heard of it, but hadn't tried it on her. Now he did, and at her next test, she was "clear," finally rid of her infection. I had wanted to make her well, and now I had.

And yet, and yet, and yet . . .

Something about it didn't wholly work. Honey was "clear"— her eyes sparkled, her voice was lively, she traveled with Dad several times to Europe and to Israel—but still I felt that life was somehow in suspension. Something in me was stuck back in the waiting rooms I had sat in as a child. Dad had been a master at the art of waiting, for Honey to get well. To be a man, I'd thought, was to know how to wait like Dad. I had learned, too well, to wait; learned too well how to choke my anger back, and wait and wait for satisfaction.

This I discovered in my forties. I'd been talking to a therapist about how it had been, as a child, to visit Honey in the hospital. He suggests that I crouch over a large pillow and call up an image of her. I see her in an oxygen tent, see myself leaning over her, then I'm shaking her, and then I hear the words breaking out of me: "I want you to get well or to die. Get well or die! Or die, or die, or die! Or die, Honey, die Honey die!" By now I'm strangling her.

But I wasn't ashamed, next time I saw her, as I'd feared. I loved her more fully than I ever had. With the forbidden words said out, I stopped denying the side of her that had wounded me—the stubbornness that had kept her smoking, her willfulness, the urgent need to keep control that had scared me, closed me in, stifled me, choked me. And that took her beyond the limits of her energy, until finally she was to go too far, beyond recovery. This *mishigas*, this craziness, was inseparable, I came to see, from her vitality.

To love Honey, I realized, was to take her whole. This is what I have to say to Otts about "unifying" her: that the very qualities that made her so remarkable—her excitement and intensity, the will that kept her going so she could be a part of our unfolding lives—also could carry her into territory dangerous for her and us. There was no dividing off the one face from the other.

Honey was well for fifteen years. Then her history caught up with her. She entered into a slow three-year degeneration.

Extended travel now was out. On the occasion of Lonny's bar mitzvah in Philadelphia, she refused to let me transport the large oxygen tank for her—too much fuss, and if I insisted, she warned, she wouldn't go at all. She'd ration out the four or five hours of oxygen available in a small tank. "I'll make it," she assured me as I sputtered, and she did, but then was hospitalized a week later. In her last year, she seldom moved beyond the compass of the plastic cord that connected her to the tank beside her bed. It stretched into the kitchen, so she still could cook, but her world was confined largely to two rooms—though she did get herself to an occasional political meeting, and to Tante Freda's bedside.

In these final years I distanced myself somewhat from her. I still went East twice a year to see my kids, and so I saw her, but we didn't talk as much. She waited months to talk with me—to tell me of her feelings about Grandma, and of her worries about Dad as he slowed mentally. But I abbreviated, or avoided altogether, our midnight conversations. Only now, as I write this, am I understanding why. She was slowly dying, and I didn't want to see it. If she was going to not be there, I would leave before she did.

But at Sinai Hospital, in Passover week of 1985, I was to get another chance. Now there was no denying her approaching death. I had another chance to see her fully and to save her.

And where did Otts now stand with her? Angry that he had lost his Eden, he too yearned—somehow to connect with her again, after all the years of baffled, awkward separation.

Unexpectedly, Otts and I were to get another opportunity as well. To work in concert with each other. To move another long step toward the closeness Honey had insisted on.

9
Letting Go

by Arthur and Howard

ARTHUR. From all across the continent, the family was gathering for the Passover Seder: Howard from Oregon, I from Philadelphia with my fiancée Phyllis, two sets of kids from their scattered schools and campuses.

When we were kids, the Seder had been a high and solemn moment for us. First there was the story itself—Jews whom we thought of as more or less like us, going forth from slavery in Egypt to wander forty years in wilderness before finding solace in the Promised Land.

There was the high drama of the ritual, woven with strange foods. Bitter raw horseradish to choke down, gasping, in memory of bitter oppression. Four cups of wine—four, even for kids who hardly ever tasted alcohol! Flat, dry, unleavened matzoh bread. Pouring drops of wine like blood onto our plates. The very fact that all our cousins, aunts, grandparents came together around a formal table.

There was the focus on us kids ourselves. Each year, the smallest child who could be taught to do it, first our cousin Allen and then I and then Howard and then Adrian, then Stanley, chanted four questions in a strange and ancient melody to get the ceremony started.

There was the sense that the story was not over—that Hitler was a kind of pharaoh, that as the wine-stained words of the Haggadah said, in every generation the struggle for freedom was right now.

For us there was some special emotional weight, conveyed not by words but by muffled sobs and gritted teeth. Passover was when Honey's father left for the sanitarium to die, the time when for years we had no Seder because Grandmom was punishing God—until, as the two of us grew up, Honey insisted.

So it had been when we were children.

Now the Seder carried even more freight of life and death for us. By now, 1985, it was the time when Grandmom had almost died and had left Cottage Avenue forever. By now, as well, our old Passover and our old Seventh of July celebrations had almost fused. As our families grew, scattered, splintered, and regrew in new directions, Passover became not only the festival of freedom but also the festival of family. As our two marriages broke up, it became still more urgent, for the kids and for ourselves, to gather, so as to affirm that there was still a family that *could* gather.

Tense and awkward Seders, they became. For now, much more than when we were children, each of us had a distinctive way of being in the world—a distinctive way of being in the Seder:

I, newly dedicated to creative Judaism, wanting to play in a serious but not a solemn way with the traditional Haggadah. Play with its language and its meaning, tell the story with new questions joining the old ones. Resentful of being pestered to "stop playing around and get on with it."

Howard, far more skeptical of the tradition altogether and, furthermore, believing that if Passover was really meant to teach the kids, then we should keep the Seder short. Besides, he thought, Honey shouldn't have to go crazy adjusting her dinner while I "went on and on."

Dad, trying to keep a solemn tone and get the work of reading done just as he had always done it, veering back and forth between three approaches: the hifalutin English of our old translation; the omissions he had worked out forty years before, to meet our needs when we were kids; and the Freedom Seder I had written, so close to Dad's own liberalism and his pride in his sons and our accomplishments.

Honey, wanting to cook an extraordinary dinner as she always had and then to join in the talk, but barely able now to hold the cooking together—panting and trembling every year from the exertion and from the tension of keeping peace.

My kids, David and Shoshana, who liked the Seder with its disputations but who also, one night, sent around a freedom petition: "The undersigned Children of Israel demand that we get to the food."

Howard's kids—Dan, Saul, Ilan—more impatient than their cousins with the talk: Why did their father and their uncle have to debate *every year* about how to treat the "wicked son" described in the Haggadah? Every year, the same raised voices, the same boring argument.

As Passover came in 1985, we thought we were gathering, as always, to marvel and worry and shake our heads over Honey's hard work, to tease and wrestle with each other.

There were some differences. For years, both of us had negotiated with our children and our former wives to arrange which kids could be where and when, so that each set could have a Seder with their father and their mother. Since there are traditionally two Seders, one on each of the first two nights of Passover, these negotiations had been a puzzle but not impossible.

This year was different from all the other years; the system went on overload. Each of the parents had Seder plans so complex that they couldn't fit together. The whole project of a gathering in Baltimore looked shaky, and with it, the unspoken certainty that the family still survived. At almost the last moment, Shoshana, visiting Baltimore for a pre-Passover spring vacation, fiercely demanded that it must be done, and made the telephone calls herself.

We finally agreed that we would gather in Baltimore on the

third night of Passover and have the Seder then. Honey broke in on Shosana's call to Howard, pausing every several words for breath, to say: "You know . . . no one's asked *me* . . . how *I* feel . . . about having Seder . . . on the third night. . . . But that's okay . . . I take it . . . as a compliment . . . because it tells me . . . that you know . . . I'll do anything I can . . . to make it possible . . . for us all . . . to be together."

So it's all set: the family Seder will be the third night of Pesach, Sunday evening. But on the Friday before that Sunday, there are unexpected telephone calls. It's Honey, explaining she isn't feeling well; she's having trouble breathing. She'll need more help than usual; the doctors are saying she belongs in the hospital, but she'll "stagger through the weekend" and then go in for tests. One last Seder at Cottage Avenue, she says: "From now on Arthur will have to do it."

What? Honey, ready to abandon ship, not do the cooking, not gather all of us together? Honey announcing this was it? Well, not quite. Next year. Meanwhile, she would tough it out again.

And then, just an hour later, on the telephone to Howard in Portland: the doctors have insisted, and she's agreed to go into the hospital immediately. (Later we learn that she has bronchitis; she can't get enough oxygen through her TB-damaged lungs, and so the various gases in her blood are dangerously in disproportion.) No final Seder at Cottage Avenue after all. But a Seder there will be, she says. She has it planned.

Phyllis and I get to Baltimore mid-day on Saturday and go straight to the hospital. At first it seems just like the last time I came to visit her in the hospital, and the time before that. Honey begins with plans—still plans, still teaching the grammar of how to manage life.

Plans for the Passover Seder. She has already taken control of her world, negotiating with the hospital to allow a dozen people to have the Seder in her room. "All the cooking . . . catch a breath . . . finished . . . catch a breath . . . except the knishes . . . Finish them . . . bring the matzoh ball knaidloch . . . and the gefilte fish . . . And wine . . ."

And then, almost with no transition, plans for her death—papers to sign, where they are filed, what Dad could do, should do, where he should live.

And then—in a kind of testament of clear-eyed love—she turns to Phyllis: "Arthur has a terrible temper. But at the core he's good." Handing over the loving knowledge of me to my lover, to draw on when the stores of our own love might dwindle low.

HOWARD. Saturday evening Saul and I arrive from Portland, where he's been visiting, stop at Cottage Avenue to rest a bit and join up with Dan and Ilan, then drive to the hospital, where we find Honey sitting up in bed. She's getting oxygen, but she seems fine—witty, vivacious, even sparkling. She teases the nurse about how pretty she is and tells family stories to my kids in a strong, excited voice. But suddenly she warns Saul, a senior in high school, "Don't bank on my coming to your graduation. I'll try to get Granddad to go, but I don't know if I can get him to leave me for a day." And knowing that visiting hours are already over, she abruptly turns to me, to make sure I understand some financial details she's already given Otts.

I understand that she's being careful, covering all the bases, thinking that this time she may die. I understand, but I don't believe it. So many times . . . And after all, she looks so good, she sounds so strong. I leave saying that we'll see her at noon on Sunday, bring the Seder food that she has prepared, have the service in her room.

At 7:30 Sunday morning, reading the *Sun* as I stretch out on one of the love-seats in the living room, I hear Dad on the bedroom telephone, insisting on getting through to Honey. She hasn't called when he expected her. After three rebuffs from nurses, he's able to get through. Sure enough, she's in trouble. "You sound bad," I hear him say; a pause; then "Should I come?"; another pause, and he hangs up.

I hurry to accompany him, stopping only to wake up Otts and tell him where Dad and I are going. He insists we wait a minute so he can come along.

We are there in fifteen minutes. Honey can hardly breathe. With a folded newspaper we fan her, to get air into her, as sixty years earlier she had fanned her father in the TB sanitarium. A nurse clears her lungs with a machine, and her breathing eases. She tells us she had little sleep—so many details racing through her mind. Again we revise the plans for Passover. We'll have the service in the waiting room, she says, and visit her one at a time; and we should bring her, please, a glass of wine, a knish.

ARTHUR. I think: For her, just breathing has been decades of pushing tons of air uphill. She is simply exhausted. But the lung muscles come back. She begins to breathe again but has no energy left over to talk.

I gently rub her back, stop for a moment. She thinks I have been troubled by the old scar under her shoulder blade, the scar she hated because it was one more reminder of the TB, the operations, the pain, the defeats. Says ruefully, "Where they put in . . . the lucite balls . . . to hold my lungs down." I say, "You have been a wonderful teacher of never giving up." She says, "I'm ready . . . to give up now."

My breath catches in my throat. Never has she hinted such a thing.

But she rallies and urges us to go home, have lunch, nap, and then come back. When we return, she is barely breathing. The muscles are played out. The doctors ask us to leave the room. A nurse emerges to say calmly—this is not a question, not a request—that they are going to help her breathe with a "procedure." Shoshana peers in and hurries back to us: "She's fighting it!" Fighting what? We rush back in. A respirator.

The doctors say Honey will die within hours if we do not authorize them to insert it. They say it will give her muscles time to recover, give her time to beat the bronchitis. Howard explains the situation to her and asks her what she wants. No answer. She struggles against the drugs to stay alert. Howard asks her, "Did you understand?" She mutters, "No. Repeat." We cannot get through.

We are frightened of the nightmare scene: once the respirator is in, no one will take it out; it will breathe her, she will not really live and breathe. The floor doctor says, "We want four days to try." We ask him, again and again: if it does not work and we say to stop, will they stop? "Yes," he says. Only later do we learn it is a lie.

So we say yes. They overwhelm her, insert the respirator. The

oxygen reaches her lungs, her blood, her brain. Honey reawak-
ens. Realizes the respirator is in. Is furious. Cannot talk—the respirator makes talking impossible. Shakes her head violently, no
no no. Reaches to disconnect the respirator. This is not a body re-
flex to get it out of her throat where it is invading but a mindful
act, reaching down to disconnect the pump. She knows what she
is doing. Firm. Fierce.

HOWARD. Dad stands at the foot of the bed. Otts and I kneel at
either side, trying gently to restrain her. She will not be soothed.
She turns with pleading burning eyes to me.

She looks at me. The respirator tube is down her throat; her
tongue is clamped. She looks at me.

Every ounce of her spirit, the will that has kept her alive for
forty extra years, pours through her eyes. Muted by the tube, she
speaks to me with her eyes. "Save me," she says. "Free me."

I have watched her, read her, all my life. Into this moment all
my learning concentrates. I know exactly what she wants. And
there is nothing I can do.

In rage and shame I flee. With no consciousness of getting
there, I find myself in the waiting room. The rest of the family is
waiting there, but for now they are merely shadowy presences. I
am alone, locked inside my mother's eyes. I pound couch pillows
in frustration while in the bed she fights to free herself.

There was nothing I could do. Or was there? What if I had
helped her pull apart the tubes? Or shielded her the way she
shielded me when I was a kid? Would the orderlies have over-
whelmed me? What if I'd told Dad and Otts that we'd decided
wrong?

ARTHUR. The doctors and nurses overpower her again. They hold
her arms. They give her tranquilizers, three times the normal
dose, to knock her out.

We are in tears, distraught. Have we chosen wrong? Is she
making a rational choice? She has always fiercely insisted on living, and to her this has meant organizing her own life. Have we
conspired to deny her what to her meant living, in the guise of
helping her to live?

We are told to leave. We go home to look at each other. We are frightened, baffled. From the hospital we get a troubling call. By now we have reached our former wives, Irene and Betty. Honey has loved them for decades, cried over our divorces. They are entitled to know she may be dying. They have rushed from Washington and Philadelphia to be with her, and now they call us from the hospital. She has awakened to find them with her. She begins making cutting motions with her fingers. Finally they figure it out: "Honey, are you saying that you want the machine to be cut off?" The answers comes—a nod. They have called to let us know.

The three of us—a father and two sons—wrestle with the story. We disagree. But in this crisis, at last there is no sneer, no snarl anywhere in all the disagreement. We honor one another.

Dad is clear: he wants to follow out the chance that she will recover.—Even if this is not what she herself is saying that she wants?—Yes. She has never instructed him, he says, as to this situation. He must do what he thinks best. Besides, he says, how can we be sure she knows what she is saying?

All right, I think. He has lived with her all these years; it is he who will have to live without her. He is entitled. But how many days must she be bound and tormented, if it is not helping her to live on her own? They said: four days.

So we begin the vigil. Four times a day, for half an hour at a time, we can visit Intensive Care. Each half-hour is like a day itself; each day feels like a week. Monday morning Honey begins by gesturing that her head is held too tight by a chin strap. (Oh, God, how could we not have seen? We know she's claustrophobic! Nurse, get her out of that!) The nurse removes the strap.

Honey is speechless—Honey who so loved speech and words.

(When I was eight years old, I watched her at the ironing board and asked her what it meant to have a conversation. "Let's talk!" she laughed, and then an hour later, went back and showed me how the stream of words had flowed and turned from place to place. "Now, that's a conversation!")

She tries to spell out words, letter by letter, on our arms. We try to decipher them, but fail and fail. She will not stop, will not give up. After an hour, the nurse notices and offers us a pad and pencil. So at last she has a voice again, a voice of sorts. The notes begin.

"WRONG," says the first note. Loud and clear. Absolutely her voice, even on paper ringing with her tones, even though her voice has been taken away, her breath is not her own. "WRONG." It is the right to give up, her decision to give up, that she will not give up.

"Won't forgive," she writes, looking at Dad.

"Silly."

"Stop."

The doctor comes in to explain to us: "Her blood gases are better. Her muscles can recover. We think she can make it."

I put it to her clearly: "If several days of this might get you back to where you were, is it okay? Will you take the chance? Will you try?" A long pause. Slowly, reluctantly, she nods. "How long?" she scribbles. I answer, "They say four days."

She writes, "3 DAYS TOPS."

"That's why Dad decided to try," Howard says. She takes Dad's hand. Forgiven.

But the struggle is only beginning. "Promise," she writes, her eyes blazing. "I promise," Dad replies.

Then, "Untie my arms." Honey, they're afraid you'll pull apart the tubing. "Promise won't. If necessary, loosen some."

Then the notes are rueful, even perky. "Messed up the weekend," she writes, and "Hell of a vacation."

Saul writes—if Honey can't talk, he won't talk either, only write like her—that she shouldn't worry about that, she should think about getting better, we love her. She writes across his note, "Reciprocate." When Howard jokes that she's showing off, she smiles. But her limit is three days.

Later that morning, Dad, Irene, Shoshana, and I stand around the bed together. Honey writes, "Glad friends," and nods in the direction of Irene and me. Shoshana fumbles to interpret, finally says, "You're glad that Mom and Dad are friends?" Honey nods. Shoshana bursts into tears. Honey then writes, "All," and underlines it.

HOWARD. By early Monday afternoon, she's tiring. Her chest, forced by the respirator to expand, has not moved so much in years. If each visiting hour is like a day to us, each hour on the machine must seem like a day to her. Fluid gathers in her mouth and throat. ("Throat," she writes, but first we do not understand; then we can't get anyone to clean it out.)

The nurses probe for a vein from which to draw blood; they jab again, again, again. And she's aware, not asleep to her suffering, as they had promised us. (So sure were we that she'd be asleep that Dan and David have gone back to their colleges.)

Over and over, despite her agreement to try for three days, Honey writes, "What day?" "Torture." "Silly." "Promise."

When she writes, "How much longer?" and we respond "Three days," she makes clear that she has meant three days from yesterday, when she was put on the respirator. Then she asks for more sedation. "A very intelligent woman," the Intensive Care doctor says.

Meanwhile, in the hours when we are not with her, we gather information. Later Monday afternoon, in a meeting with her major doctor, a woman we know Honey respects, we learn that Honey normally takes in with each breath less than one-third the usual amount of air for a person of her size (and in crisis, much less than that). She never breathes "at rest." Every breath she draws is like a breath of ours after running a vigorous race.

We learn also that the blood gas condition that has required Honey to use oxygen at home is a terminal disease. The average patient remains alive with it two years, and Honey has lived, already, three. (Did Honey know this and keep it from us?)

Worst of all, the doctor tells us it isn't true that Honey can be removed from the respirator after three days if she and we want that. We have been misinformed by the resident physician. There would be legal problems: a life support system cannot be removed.

Moreover, she can be kept alive on it indefinitely. "Mrs. Waskow," the doctor says, "is suffering from only a one-system failure." To be sure, she says, the system is an important one, the respiratory system. "But still the heart and the kidneys and the brain are working pretty well."

"I have great respect for Mrs. Waskow," she says, "I want to give her every chance to live."

My voice shakes with fury, understanding, and despair: "I too have great respect for Mrs. Waskow, and the deepest love. She is my mother, and I am ready, if she wants it, to *let her go.*"

ARTHUR. The doctor nods. She does not fool us or herself. She acknowledges that the respirator is painful. That one doctor has spoken not-the-truth. That it distresses her to carry out the ethic she believes she must carry out. Tears in her eyes—the only doctor who has tears in this whole story.

Afterward Howard says that in a different world, a different generation, Honey would have been this doctor. Her clarity, her intelligence, her passion to shape the world could have been poured into this broader cup of living.

We are appalled that the life support system cannot be removed. Our nightmare has come true. We have promised, "3 DAYS TOPS." And now we may not be able to deliver on our promise.

HOWARD. From this meeting on, we work as a team. Before this we've been cooperative enough but as individuals: first one of us and then the other has made sense of a gesture or a note. Now, given the information from the doctor and the changing tone of Honey's notes, we start to plan.

Two gray, burly, bearded men—clear of mind, full of feeling, steeped in political experience, sure of our position—two brothers on either side of fifty, in the full power of our lives we unite to help our mother die.

For the issues have clarified. It is obvious to us that Honey knows exactly what the situation is and what she wants. Dad hopes this is not so, and the doctor says that the blood gas condition could well be distorting her responses. But Otts and I know what we know: that she is *clear.* Finally, with Honey's notes as evidence, they too become convinced.

What Honey wants is not to be kept alive on the respirator. For me, this would be enough right now. For Otts, the three days she has reluctantly agreed to are still a necessary test of her ability to recover—but also an absolute deadline. For both of us, it is clear that it is over.

Enough is enough. Honey has struggled with illness for forty years, has lived a full and joyful life despite it, and finally, at seventy-four, has spoken for the first time in our memories of "giving up." She who began as a dodgeball and kickball champion, who loved to travel, loved to see, has spent much of the past three years tethered to the green oxygen tank looming by her bedside; and now the respirator, invading her body, muting her, choking her, is a last insult.

And there is more. Given the doctor's information about the nature of her disease, it seems to us a kind of sadism to insist that she go on. Why keep her alive, suffering, against her will? Why "save" her from this crisis only to condemn her to suffer another crisis in a month or two?

This is the moment. She hates to be dependent. She would hate to lose her mental acuity. She would hate to languish like Grandma in a nursing home. At this moment she can still barely, barely, influence her fate. And we, deluded by a representative of the hospital, have made a deal with her, we *promised* her: if she cannot wean herself from the respirator in three days, she gets to stop. She gets to rest. We will not betray her. She with our help, we with hers, will find a way.

Our work is with the hospital and with Dad. For Dad, even more than for Otts and me, this is all so sudden. For years he has stood vigil—driving, shopping, doing odd jobs around the house, staying there always, just in case—as first Grandma and then Honey took to their beds. Now he needs time to absorb that this is not an emergency like any other.

Honey's telling remarks—that this Seder is the last one she will do, that she won't make it to Saul's and Shoshana's graduations, that she has felt for the first time like giving up—have been made to Otts and me, not to Dad. Dad hasn't heard.

Met suddenly with the danger of losing the woman he has been married to for fifty-five years, the woman who along with Grandma replaced the mother who died when he was six, Dad blinks in pain, his hazel eyes filmed behind his spectacles. He thinks as clearly as he can, then does what is familiar: depends on the experts for advice. If the doctors want to try, then he'll agree.

From the Hebrew Orphans Asylum on up through a successful career as a teacher and a union leader, his whole life has been built on hope. So he asks the doctor to give Honey a "pep-talk," and reminds us that once before, when she was first sick, Honey recovered when everyone thought she would die. Listening, we catch our breaths—he doesn't see!—and answer him: "But Dad, that was forty years ago!" Beneath his white moustache his mouth turns down; he sets himself and waits.

Out of our meeting with the doctor comes not only increased clarity for us but an understanding with the doctor: she too does not want to keep Honey alive *indefinitely* on the respirator.

The machine is set to produce a certain number of breaths per minute, to aid the patient's breathing. The muscles need a rest, but there's a catch: since the muscles aided will eventually weaken and become unable to work on their own, a patient in Honey's condition must be got off the respirator soon or not at all.

So the doctor, it turns out, has attempted Sunday night to wean Honey from it rapidly. From eight machine breaths per minute at the start, Honey had gotten down to five, but then she'd gone back up. Now the doctor wants to try again, but slowly. How slowly she will not say, yet we leave the meeting with a precious understanding: this is a trial that has an ending.

After this meeting, Dad hugs both of us at once. His voice choked with emotion, he says that we have been "two towers of strength"; that he could never have done this meeting by himself. From his tone even more than from his words we hear he is asking something of us: not to defer to him so much but take the lead.

So Monday night, in one of the upstairs bedrooms, Phyllis, Otts, and I hold a conference as Dad naps below. Otts asks whether we should get a lawyer. If the hospital should try to keep Honey on the machine, we may need to challenge it legally, on the grounds that it obtained our consent to put her on it by promising that we could get her off when we wanted to.

Fear rises in my throat—my old fear of Otts' anger, his inclination to confront. I'm scared that talk of legal action will alienate the doctor, who seems to be an ally, and leave us head to head with the administration, embroiled in a lengthy, messy legal fight, with Honey paying the price. We're on the right track, I say, let's not get off. Eventually we agree simply to find out where we are legally.

Late in the middle of the night, an incident fragmentary, dream-like in my memory. Otts enters the room where I am sleeping in the bed that was first his, before he went off to graduate school, and then was mine, for my three remaining years at Cottage Avenue. He has risen naked from where he's been in bed with Phyllis—both of them squeezed into the single bed in the room next door, where Honey lay in quarantine two years—and he has come to me.

He's worried, fearful—about what, it is not clear to me. He climbs into bed with me and weeps, and tries to say. All I can remember of it is that he's worried, terribly worried. The only words that remain with me are that he's afraid that he lacks faith, and that God won't love him.

I'm half asleep, can't get why he's so upset, but I do know that he's worried and I'm not. So I can hold him, tell him that we're doing fine and that events will take their course. Either Honey will be weaned slowly from the machine, within a few days, or she will not, and the doctor will do something to release her.

Otts relaxes. As Dad sleeps fitfully downstairs, next to Honey's empty spot, and Honey has an agitated night in Intensive Care (so they tell us the next day), Otts and I lie in one another's arms.

ARTHUR. It wasn't that I thought God wouldn't love me; it was the reverse. I was afraid I didn't know how to love God—to "surrender" in the ancient sense of knowing that there is a flow of Truth that we can join in. I was afraid I couldn't do it. My instinct was to fight instead.

Howard's distress at my wanting to open up the legal track had gotten to me. He said we were already on the right track, just follow it, don't fuck it up by fighting. Am I always doomed to wrestle, even when it isn't necessary? Can't I . . . just . . . breathe?

HOWARD. The next morning, the machine is at nine breaths. Standing at the foot of Honey's bed, we watch snow flurries falling. Phyllis says, "Honey, it's Tuesday, April 9th, and it's snowing!" To which Honey in a clear hand responds, "Mother."

My calm of the night before deserts me. I think she thinks that

Grandma is still alive and is asking about her health, as she's asked about other members of the family. But then, noticing my dismay, Honey adds, "Birthday," and I realize that not only isn't she adrift, she's more alert than any of the rest of us. It's Grandma's birthday, April 9. We don't remember that, but Honey does. The reversal is too much for me. I rush weeping to the waiting room.

Honey's notes continue. Whatever has happened during her "agitated" night, it seems to have bolstered her resolve to die. "Silly to keep trying," she writes. "How much longer?" "Three days of torture." Armed with these documents, we request another meeting with the doctors.

One of them begins that he has just visited Honey. She "seems to be doing well," since she gestured to him to adjust her pillow. How remarkably enduring Honey and Grandma before her have been! He's sure she'll be okay, just needs some time.

We're aghast. I'm speechless, but Otts is on the doctor instantly: "I'm sure it's true that she wants to be as comfortable as possible as long as she's alive," he retorts, his eyes flashing, "but that *doesn't* mean she wants to *stay* alive this way."

We show the notes as evidence; we probe to find out how much longer the major doctor will keep trying. We get back nothing firm, and suddenly my chest is breaking open, as it did when Honey looked at me on Sunday afternoon. Each hour is a day to her! Through my tears I speak:

"Since she cannot be in this meeting, I want to say something in my mother's voice. No one is talking here about the torture. These procedures may seem standard to you, but to her, and to us, they are TORTURE. 'Three days of torture,' is what she says. TORTURE. To what end?"

These words are meant not only for the doctors but for Dad.

To Honey we report only that her doctor still is trying to wean her from the machine. We have never been able to bring ourselves to tell her that we don't know whether we can keep our promise of "3 DAYS TOPS" to her.

But perhaps she senses that "something's off," as she would say, for on Tuesday afternoon she asks for a reaffirmation. The hand that wrote "Mother" so clearly in the morning now shakily spells out this note, its letters tipsily crowded close to one another: "Promise you pull"—and she jabs me in the belly when she's done.

The "you" is me, I realize: she wants *me* to promise her that whatever happens, I will pull the plug. I am filled with pride and shame at once.

She trusts me. She has chosen ME. Yet I cannot give her what she wants. I honestly don't know if I can pull the plug. Can I get the opportunity to do it safely? There are monitors, buzzers, whistles to warn attendants. Would I risk a murder charge? And would she want me to?

I honestly don't know if I would do it; it would all depend. I want to believe that there's another way to save her. So I sidestep, I waffle: I promise only I'll do everything I can.

Of course Honey hears the omission, and before the visiting period is over, she is taking the next step. Her fingers now barely able to grasp the pencil, she scrawls a word we can't decipher. Again she tries, again we fail. Finally we understand. It's her doctor's name, misspelled. Honey wants to "talk" with her herself.

Hours later the doctor goes to her. How Honey did it we probably will never know, but when we meet with the doctor for the second time that day, she has been convinced. "Mrs. Waskow," she begins the meeting, "has made a decision to die."

The doctor still wants to continue her attempt to wean Honey slowly from the respirator, but now she is prepared to set a specific limit on the trial. If by tomorrow morning Honey has not made significant progress (which the doctor will not now define), she will agree to stop.

In response to our requests for detail, she explains that she is not able, legally, to remove Honey from a life support system. But she can move her from Intensive Care, where every aspect of her condition is intensely monitored, back to a regular hospital room, and in doing so, switch her from a highly sophisticated respirator to the inefficient model used on the floor. There *is* a way out: a grotesque one, but a way.

Now, reporting to Honey, we need not be mealy-mouthed.

There is a plan. I tell it all to her: tomorrow is the day. Now she is satisfied. She nods that she understands, and rests.

ARTHUR. I'm horrified to realize that when I walk into Honey's section of Intensive Care, I look first at the setting of the machine, not her. Tuesday night it is at ten breaths per minute; the numbers are up, not down.

We go home to talk. It is clear to us all now, even to Dad, and we say it out loud to each other. She is dying. We see it; we see that the doctors see it. For the first time, we feel at peace: she will have the peace that she is ready for. Somehow, despite the rules, she will have peace.

The morning of the fourth day dawns. It has been almost seventy-two hours, three days, since the respirator was inserted. We walk in, glance at the machine. The breath count is at eleven; the machine is having to do still more of her breathing. For Howard, this is enough. He asks for time alone with Honey.

HOWARD. The words and tears burst out of me.

"Honey, thank you for being such a good teacher. [As they rush forth, they sound to me more like Otts' words than mine.] Honey, don't worry about me and Otts. I know we're both a little fat, but we're healthy, we really are. [These are mine; this is my voice.]

"Honey, I'm remembering what you said about Grandma when she died, that she looked so peaceful to you, and I'm thinking that you want that for yourself. [She nods.]

"And Honey, Honey, I love you so much, but if you want to die, I want that for you. [She places her right hand upon her chest and offers it to me, once twice three times she gives me from her heart.] Goodbye, Honey, goodbye."

All my life I have resisted letting go—of almost anything: books, letters, souvenirs; relationships, children, memories; pain itself. To let go has seemed like death to me, my mother's death. Now she is dying and I am saying *yes*.

ARTHUR. Soon after, the doctors come to tell us that Honey has had an unexplained sudden drop in blood pressure. Do we want to use heroic measures? No, we say. They nod. It is clear to us: she said "3 DAYS TOPS," and even at the level deep beneath her mind, the level of the heart and blood, she is making sure that her decision will be carried out. She still rules her life. And death.

The doctors come again. Her blood pressure has picked up, but they accept the truth. There is no reversing the decree, the disease. They could force Honey to stay alive, but they cannot help her become well—even as well as she had been. The respirator is not the temporary crutch they had hoped it would be. Indeed it never was.

So they are willing to move her downstairs, to change to the less efficient respirator. "How long do patients live that way?" we ask. "Up to a week," they say.

A week! Twice as long as Honey has already said was torture?

Dad says, "A week is unacceptable." Silently we cheer for him. Sick at heart, we gather ourselves once more for action. Maybe the legal track will be necessary after all.

But meanwhile, the doctors are preparing to move Honey out of Intensive Care. For me, this is the time to say goodbye.

It doesn't quite work. Honey is conscious but not quite responsive. I can't say the words *die* and *death*, but I tell her the doctors have admitted that she cannot make it. They will move her. She has won the battle with them.

I cannot bear to say there may still be a week of torture. I am determined that there won't be. I ask, "Is it all right?" She nods.

I start to say that when I look at Shoshana, I will be able to see a breath of Honey. She looks back at me, not answering.

I ask myself, "Did I do it wrong? Did I get it wrong, even now?" I tell her that I know she never intended to keep me an outsider, that this past year or so I have felt at last in touch with her.

Her hand under mine shifts ever so lightly, so gently I am not sure whether it is a message or an accident. She slips into something between sleep and coma. I walk out crying.

HOWARD. We turn ourselves to politics. Otts' lawyer tells us that we can insist on taking Honey home to die. For the first time we talk directly to a hospital administrator, and tell him about the resident physician's promise. "Oh," he answers, startled to get this information. We suggest that legal action might be appropriate. He nods. "I'm quite sure that we can work something out."

So we have created two alternatives, but this last flurry turns out to be unnecessary. Two hours after she has been put on the inefficient respirator, Honey dies.

After I have said goodbye, I feel no need to see her. I do only fleetingly before she dies. Her eyes are open wide and luminous—but empty. She has no intelligence; her will is gone. The machine is tossing to and fro a shell. This is a travesty. I turn to leave, motioning for Dad to follow. When I open the door again, on intuition, only minutes later, the machine is still.

ARTHUR. When I realize it is fully over, I remember Grandmom's story of my grandfather's death—Avraham Yitzchak, the one I'm named for. She would not say the ancient blessing, the hardest, the harshest, the curtest of all blessings, the one Jews say when they hear about a death—"Blessed is the true Judge." "How could I say such a thing? What kind of true Judge would kill such a decent man, so young?"

But now I can say it, and I can mean it. It has been a harsh battle, but the One Who Judges has judged truly.

Baruch dayan ha-emet. Blessed is the true Judge.

This is the one blessing in which the "YHWH," "Lord," "Yyy-hhh-www-hhh," the Breath of Life, does not appear. Of course.

HOWARD. Fifty years ago, I tumbled out of her onto the floor of a Dodge sedan rushing to the hospital. Together we gave me life. Together, all of us, Honey in the lead, passed Honey into death. In her dying she gave to us again: courage, clarity, and love. For her funeral I wore what I had brought from Oregon to wear for Passover: the clothes of celebration.

ARTHUR. Thirty-two days later, on the first Mother's Day of my life when I do not have both a grandmother and a mother, I can put on the gorgeous rainbow tallis, a prayer shawl, that Honey sewed for me when I turned fifty. Then I can say:

Blessed is the One Who frees those whose hands are tied down.

Blessed is the One Who sends Elijah, to turn the hearts of children and parents to each other.

Blessed is the One Who mothers the world.

Blessed is the One Who is the Breath of Life.

• • •

And blessed is the one who in the time of her dying brought the two of us together.

10
To Wrestle a Brother

by Arthur

HONEY'S DYING had brought us into the closest relationship we had ever had as brothers; her funeral posed the danger of an intense explosion.

How to shape a funeral that would honor her truth? That she would want it to be Jewish was clear; that she had no institutional connections—not even to a friendly rabbi or a once-a-year synagogue—was equally clear. I alone had focused my life around Judaism. Did that make me the maven, the expert, even the "rabbi," for this moment? What would that do to my father or my brother?

We agreed that I would call a rabbi who was a friend of mine, a man of unusual learning, openness, and wisdom. He agreed to lead the service. But he had a suggestion: perhaps Howard and I should each speak about Honey's life—what she had meant to us and in the world. Better us than someone who barely knew her.

To me that seemed perfect. I went back to Howard to propose it. "No," he said. "To you it's perfect because you know how to take what's intimate and make it public. That's how you write;

that's how you speak. I can't do that. I would break down, just stand there weeping. It's too close, too intimate, for me to do.

"My closeness to her was different from yours," he went on. "Maybe you are more like her than I am. But I could talk with her. You couldn't. And she could talk with me. She *did* talk with me. I can't tell all that, and I can't talk without telling all that. So I can't talk."

For one murderous moment, a flash of hatred ran through me. "He's saying Honey loved him more than me!" I thought.

And then I thought, "So what?" —"But if he says that, I ought to kill him." —"Really?" —"Well, at least I ought to hate him." —"Really?" —"Well, I do hate him!" —"Really?"

So I looked for the murderous flash, to prove I hated him. But it was gone. The days of loving wrestle were still there. With a shiver of regret, almost nostalgia—"Where are you, Murder, now that I really need you?"—I turned back to my brother.

"All right, I understand. If you can't do it, you can't. But I can, and it's what I know to do to give her honor. You said it; it's true that I can take what's intimate and say it in the world. Is that okay?"

After a long pause, he responded, "Well, I'd feel terrible, I'd feel diminished. It would look as if you were speaking for us all— as if your version were the truth. My truth of her would get left out. I know I'm choosing to leave it out, but I don't want yours there and mine not. So I wish you wouldn't speak."

"But that's not fair! That's not legitimate! You decide you won't speak, and then because you won't speak I shouldn't speak. Come on!"

"I know it's not 'legitimate.' But if you talk, I'll feel diminished."

I walked away in total pain. Pain for me, pain for him. A double bind.

To be who I fully am—in the moment out of my whole life when I most want to be my fullest self—means to speak aloud my love, my honor, my truth about my mother. But what honor would it be to my mother to make my brother feel terrible? What fulfillment of my self would it be to make my brother feel diminished? Back and forth, back and forth . . .

Would it be my responsibility if he made himself feel terrible? No! I thought, and for a moment I felt released. I could do what was mine to do; *he* would be responsible for feeling bad.

But it didn't matter. Did I want him to feel diminished? No! Did I want him to feel fully himself? Yes! Then must I take the positive steps to make that possible? Not for his sake but because I wanted it that way?—Yes, yes!—But what about my own fulfillment? Back and forth, back and forth.

I went to Phyllis. She suggested: "Ask Max [our rabbi friend] to meet with all of us, to hear our stories of Honey and retell them—as our stories, not as his. It won't pretend to be a polished eulogy; it won't shimmer and flow. It will be real; it will have in it what you want to say and whatever Howard is able to say and whatever the rest of us say."

I went back to Howard. He listened, nodded. "That's fine, that's what I'd want." Me again: "But not what *I* want!" And for a few minutes we go through the whole thing again.

My heart is hammering and knocking with a silent voice of its own: "You know what you're supposed to do. You're the older brother. You've been first. You wrote about it even—all that stuff about Ishmael and Isaac, and Esau and Jacob. You *know* what you're supposed to do. Give it up, give it up, give it up!" And me, in silence answering back, a voice not from my head or heart or lungs but even deeper: "I can't do it, all right I know but I can't do it. Why should I do it? No, don't tell me why—it doesn't matter; I can't do it. I can't."

And then an outburst, yelling at Howard. "It's not a compromise; it's not halfway, you understand? I don't want it; it's not what fits me. It fits you and not me, you understand? I *don't* want it, you understand?"

He looks at me quietly: "I understand."

And then the barrier between my two silent voices collapses. My vocal voice says aloud: "Okay. Let's do it. Let's ask Max to collect our stories. I'll call him." And I feel solid—not joy, not love, not sadness, not anger, not relief, not resignation. Not anything "peculiar." Solid. There's work to do; let's do it.

I went off to call the rabbi, ask the family to think of the stories they wanted to tell, and jot down some of my own. The rabbi said all right. The work was under way.

An hour later, my brother came to talk. "Would *you* do it? The way we said to have Max do it? Would *you* collect the stories and then tell them—not in your own voice but in all our voices? I'd like for you to do that."

And then I cried. Then I remembered: Surrender, and space opens up. Maybe your brother will surrender back to you. (Maybe not.) Surrender, and the universe might surrender back. Surrender what you wanted: it might use the new open space to open up some new path, some new possibility. It might turn out you want the new path even more.

So that is what we did. I gathered stories, and I told them. I began with a story about Honey's love of pistachio ice cream, and I went on with stories of her passionate, curious love of all of us and all of life, and I ended with the story of her passionate love of Dad. Howard hugged me and said he felt his voice well spoken.

I had been the best that I could be—even better than my own best self, because the wrestle had forced me to hear the other selves as well and speak them.

"Two brothers," I said in my talk. "Two brothers from the same womb; so different. From the same womb, two different intertwining stories."

Up to that moment, Howard and I had wrestled many wrestles. Some were simply for the joy of it; some had been for power and advantage; and some had been a higher, more subtle interplay of love and struggle. But this had been the highest of our wrestles, because we were most conscious of each other's pain, as well as each his own. The highest, but probably not the last, for now we know it goes in spirals. One wrestle may lead to reconciliation, and then the new relationship will somehow spark again that flash of murder. And we will find ourselves in still a different wrestle.

What is growing on these spirals? What makes them go somewhere instead of just around in circles?

It comes to me that the spiral is about the teaching, and the knowing, between us. For years I tried to teach him, and for years he refused to learn from me. I know he imitated what I did, but face to face, from me, he wouldn't learn. And then it changed. I began to learn from him.

When I think about the years of his divorce, when he was asking, probing, digging in the half-forgotten tales of Cottage Avenue in order to uncover his own story, the few years just after our long talk in the snowed-in cabin when I was learning to wrestle with him and with Torah, the years when I was learning to discover my own story in the "family history" of the Bible: when I think of what was changing in those years, it was that I had begun to learn from Howard.

What was I learning? Not just that divorce could be survived. I was learning to look more closely at the people close to me. All my life I had been "far-sighted," looking beyond the family and the neighborhood toward the larger world. After all, if the family locked me out and left me wailing there, what could I do but turn my back and look outward toward all those shimmering distances?

In those years when I began to learn from Howard, I began to look more closely at the close-in people in my life. Not just to look at them, but to see those relationships as part of the work of my life. I didn't give up politics, trying to heal the broken relationships in the "big" world. But I began to see what it might mean to try to heal the broken relationships closer to home.

When I wrote a book, *Godwrestling*, about what was emerging from my wrestle with the Torah and my intimate Jewish community, the family was in it too. Howard was in it, my marriage and divorce were in it, intertwined with the "big world" of Israelis and Palestinians, the powerless and the powerful, men and women.

Howard was in it not only in the content but in the process, for my very willingness to think and write like this I had learned from my new connection with Howard and from Howard's exploration of the close-in world around him. It was in the conversations with him that I had learned how to think this way, and it was partly from a book of his that I had learned to write this way—a book he had written about fathering his kids, a book in which his own childhood and theirs had become intertwined as ways to learn about each other.

But now I see that even then I was looking at the people of my close-in world more in memory than in actuality. I was looking at them in the past, in history, learning the ancient tangled family tales from Howard. I was untangling what had made me Ishmael. But I was not yet ready to stop being Ishmael.

In the present, in my relationships with my wife, my kids, with Honey and Dad, with the "band of brothers" at the Institute for Policy Studies in Washington where I shared a politics in a time of utter intensity in politics, even with the fellowship of Jews with whom I prayed and studied Torah—with all these close-in people I still kept my distance.

In the spiral of relationship with Howard, that was where things stayed for about ten years. I was clear enough about having learned from him that in the dedication of my book *Godwrestling* I could say it—say that it was from Howard that I had learned how to wrestle and how to write in this new way.

It's true that it did not occur to me to do this on my own. Howard asked me, and at once I saw how truthful it would be. But even his willingness to ask—his voice trembled when he took the chance of being refused—even his willingness to ask, and mine to agree, signaled that we were a great deal closer to each other.

The next curve upward on the spiral came with Honey's dying. I spent that week looking at the people closest to me. At Honey, over and over to see whether she was dying, how she was dying. At Howard and Dad, to see what they were thinking and feeling. At my kids, and Phyllis, and Irene, and Betty. Even at the doctors. There was no one else to look at—no bigger world. And there was no wall between me and the family. No one had the strength to put one up.

During our wrestle over the funeral, Howard said, and I agreed, that I knew how to take what was intimate and make it public. But we were mistaken. Until then all I knew how to do was take what *had been* intimate and make it public. I knew how to take a hurtful past, in which I had not even been fully conscious of what hurts I was suffering, and learn what it had meant; and then to make that intimate knowledge public.

But to expose my present suffering? That I really did for the first time at the funeral itself, when I spoke about Honey. For the first time I was not uncovering an ancient past but sharing present consciousness. "This is not the past walking into the future, the walk is painful, into the present," says Muriel Rukeyser in a wonderful poem on the great rabbi Akiba. Painful indeed. Now comes the test of whether I can continue to make the intimate public.

The first round of wrestling with Howard was when we were children. The wrestle was on its lowest level. It was only about power and control and ended with the polite invisible wall.

The second round began in the snow-bound cabin and continued along the Oregon coast; it was about our pasts and about our willingness in the present to explore our pasts together, even when there were overtones of murder in our memories.

The third was in the week of Honey's dying. The wrestle then was wholly in the present, and much more as making love than making war. It was intense and short because it was focused so intensely on Honey's life and death.

And then, a year later, began a fourth round of wrestling, in which the thinking and writing of this book is the arena. It has been a strange kind of wrestle, since each of us was groping toward ending the very split that made for wrestling in the first place. Howard reached beyond it when he asked me to write a book with him about the two of us. I reached beyond it when, in telling the story of Honey's life and death, I realized I needed him to join with me in telling it.

In the midst of this wrestle, I have come to see that it is my job to end the split within me, to end the stereotype I have been frozen in.

The split between us can end only if the split within each of us is ended.

11
Life after Death

by Arthur and Howard

ARTHUR. Honey gone. The crisis of her dying, and her burial, behind us.

What did her disappearance do to us, her sons?

For years, we had got along fair-to-middling well, to use one of her expressions. You might say the weather between us was "cautiously warmer, with patches of fog." But in the week of Honey's dying and her burial, that fog was ended.

Even more than her life, her death was a fireball of energy, hot and bright. It burned away the fog.

And, of course, it burned away Honey herself, who had been the center of energy in the family: the sun around which all the rest revolved. With her gone, communication, storytelling, and new understanding could no longer be channeled through her.

Maybe the timid steps we had been taking toward each other depended on her being there. And maybe what happened between Howard and me in that week in Baltimore, our loving work together, was only what happens in a crisis. Now we had a life to live—month by month and year by year. Maybe, like a system of planets bereft of its sun, we would float out of touch with each other. Or maybe we would strengthen our connections.

If Howard and I were really to be brothers, we would have to make it happen ourselves.

The first test turned out to be dealing with Dad.

Over the past few years, as Grandmom and Honey and Dad had grown more feeble, they had lost their ability to function independently of one another. Dad spent less and less energy on the outside world. More and more he stayed at home, hovering to make sure he would be there if he was needed.

Especially after Grandmom died and Honey's exhaustion got deeper and deeper, Honey and Dad survived by giving each other the energy that neither could generate alone. He was arms and legs; she, intensity and focus. But as long as Honey lived, this was not obvious. Together they *did* seem to make one whole, effective person.

With Honey gone, Dad's frailties became more and more disabling, and more evident. For the first time, in his moment of need, I saw that we had never had an independent father-son relationship. With Honey so strong and so central, it had never seemed possible to create one.

Now I had to make my own relationship with Dad or abandon him altogether.

I began to let him be my father.

This was hardly what I had expected. I had read the social workers' warnings that, as our parents grow more aged nowadays, we can expect to feel ourselves turned inside out; we become their parents, watching over them as they once watched over us. This reversal, they keep saying, is a painful one.

Their predictions were accurate enough. Dad was seventy-seven when Honey died, and it instantly became apparent how much he needed mothering. The kitchen was both a gauge and a symbol of his dependency, for in the kitchen he was helpless, to a degree that left us flabbergasted.

Maybe we should have known. He never had had the need, or the opportunity, to cook for himself. Just think about his history: from babyhood to orphanage to foster homes to Grandmom's boarding house. Then he married the landlady's daughter, and lived in that same house for more than sixty years. No Boy Scouts, no Army service, no college apartment, no hunting or fishing or camping trips, no "batching it" when a wife went home to mother. When Honey was too sick to cook, Grandmom took over. And at seventy-seven, bereft of the wife who had been his one close friend, Dad had not much resilience to learn new ways.

All of that surprised us, but it was not especially upsetting. For Dad to need "mothering" and "wifing" was one thing; he had, after all, never been a mother or a wife, and in his life the distinctions between those roles and the roles of father and husband had been sharply defined. What became a great deal more frightening was that more and more he needed "fathering" and "husbanding." In the very roles for which he had been the house expert, he began to slip and fail. It became harder for him to deal with the details of household planning and money managing that he had once found so easy and pleasant.

The network of possibilities and choices from which decisions grow became cloudy and indistinct for him. Only a straight line of choices here, a single possibility there, remained visible. The interconnections faded. He found every decision hard to make, and some contradicted each other.

One day when I was visiting, I came across some letters from the Internal Revenue Service. They said he had failed to file one necessary form and had made a mistake on another. They were sitting in a pile, along with appeals from a variety of causes and some other business letters. "What's this?" I said, my throat already tight. "Oh, I'm trying to decide about all that," he said. "It takes so long just to clean up the mail that keeps on coming."

"But the IRS! The IRS! Don't fuck around with the IRS!"

"By that verb," he said with a sniff, "do you mean don't delay, don't put it off?"

"Oh God," I said. "Of course!" And I got didactic—the worst way to be a teacher, which, I'm tempted to say, I learned from him when *he* was at his worst. Pained explanation of the obvious. Step by step. What he *must* do, repeated each time in a louder and bossier voice. His response was a mixture of meekness with no willingness to do, and stubbornness with no willingness to hear. So I'd repeat it all again, this time louder, more pointed, and more pained.

Finally, we reach an impasse. I am trembling with frustration, fright, and rage. I am able to get hold of myself just short of an explosion, turn aside, and ask Phyllis what is going on. She points to the heart of it: my fear that Dad will find himself in trouble and the more terrible fear that I will have to take responsibility for sorting all this out.

She is right. Without realizing it, I have decided that "fathering" him means protecting him, and that means managing his business affairs. But it scares me. I have enough trouble keeping track of my own. I go back to Dad and say I am sorry to be yelling at him; it's just that I am scared. "Scared of what?" he says, putting an arm around me. "Are you scared they'll send me to jail?"

I nod—it is part of the truth, anyway—and to my astonishment burst into tears. "Oh come on," he says, "they'll never put an *alter cocker* like me in jail. They owe me money anyway. It's just these forms that I owe them. Don't worry. It'll be all right."

Soothing. Comforting. Holding me. It's only a nightmare, Otts. Fathering me.

At that point I really wanted to bawl. "Daddy fathering me? Where di that come from? It's been a long time since that! So long I can't remember it at all. Did it ever really happen before?"

"I'm pretty mixed up," I thought. "Is he learning for the first time how to father me, or am I learning how to father him? Maybe the problem is that I never knew how to let him be my father, and that's what I'm supposed to be learning."

Finally I said, "Look. I'll make a bargain with you. On your side,"—I could see him tense up—"you feel totally free that if you want help with this stuff, you ask Howard or me, and you'll get whatever help you need. On my side, I promise not to kvetch about it." He relaxed, and so did I. His fathering had worked. And Phyllis' good sense. And my own ability—barely—to step back from the brink and ask for help.

But there is something else. I don't remember being fathered like that, ever. Still, he had been my father, hadn't he? He had done something to father me, hadn't he? What was it? What had it meant to him, all those years, to be fathering me? I am a father myself now—have been for twenty-five years. What had I learned, or mislearned, that it meant to be a father?

Something about that wrestle over the taxes must have spoken to Dad as well as me, churning up in him some painful memories of fathering. No sooner had we worked our way out of that tangle than this new father of mine began telling a story that explained what my old father had thought it was all about.

When I was two and a half and Honey was pregnant again, he reminisced, he was just finishing a probationary year as a senior high school teacher. It brought more pay and more prestige than teaching in junior high school. His principal had to approve his work, or back he would go to junior high. And then, without ever observing a class, his principal said no.

"I didn't know why," my father said. "I never knew why. It was absolutely unfair! So I said to him—I'm revolted whenever I think of it—that I had a wife and a son, and another baby coming. I needed the money. I begged, and he put his hand on my shoulder and said it would be all right. And he gave me the job, since I begged. I'm still ashamed to remember."

So I said to him later, "I'm glad you told me that story. It's important to me to know how it felt, what you did for us."

"I'm not glad," he said. "I hate to remember the past when it rips me up." And he turned around, still ashamed, and beginning to cry.

"But look," I said. "You don't need to be ashamed. It's what the principal did that was shameful. You did what you had to, to protect Honey and Howard and me. I'm *proud* of you for protecting us. And I'm proud of you for going out to organize the teachers' union, so people wouldn't have to beg and principals couldn't get away with being unfair."

"I did do that," he said. "That's true, I did do that."

That was what it had meant to him to be a father: to protect us—by eating shit if he had to—and patiently building the union so he and the other teachers wouldn't have to, and could win decent salaries besides. (That union took a long time to organize. For a lot of the time he was president, it had only forty members. The *Sunpapers* thought it was ten times bigger. He laughed, but he never let on.)

But it never occurred to him that being a father meant telling us that story. To him it meant just the reverse: How could he be a good father if he shared what he was ashamed of?

Although he had never told the story, the event itself had had an impact on us. When I told Howard about it, he said, "No wonder he was so upset when I quit Reed College. I had kids to feed, and I just quit—for a principle and a hope. No wonder he got upset."

But we hadn't known, so we couldn't piece it together: the way Dad fathered, protecting us financially and shielding us emotionally. But that shield kept out some of the light that would have helped us grow.

That's why it feels as if only now, after all these years, he is becoming my father.

But it also becomes clear to me, now that I'm bringing the stories together, that what I was trying to do to him, was more or less what he had done to us: protect him, manage him, save him from the IRS. I certainly wasn't going to tell him I was scared, especially that I was scared of having to manage his affairs. I was ashamed of that. And if I had to be the strong one now, the fatherly one, how could I share what made me feel ashamed?

So now it's perfectly clear, isn't it? I learned all this from him. He thought that "fathering" meant to protect, to manage affairs so it all worked out, and so did I.

No, it's not so perfectly clear. It wasn't just Dad doing it to me, teaching me that fathering was managing. When I told these stories to Howard, he didn't seem surprised. He knew from long ago the father who was "new" to me—the one who comforted me, who explained it was only a nightmare.

"Sweetness," said Howard. "He was always full of sweetness."

Then Howard looked at me. "There's sweetness in you too," he said, "though I never would have expected it. These last few years, there's sweetness. I like it."

So it wasn't only Dad's responsibility. Somehow a wall rose up between us. No, not "somehow." Walls get built by people. I must have been helping to block out that sweetness, hearing only the father who managed the family's affairs and kept an emotional silence.

Walls get built by people. Me a brick, him a brick, him a brick, me a brick . . .

HOWARD. A brick layer yet, like Avraham. Still being Avraham.

Maybe that was the first brick laid, Otts, in the wall that rose up between you and Dad—the very fact that you were Avraham. If you were "Avraham" for Honey, where would that leave Dad? And you-and-Dad?

Whatever caused this separation, I can see now that it's true. I didn't realize it so much when we were growing up. After all, for a couple of years in high school, you spent hours, days, weeks alone with Dad, studying for the Hearst American history contests. But when I read what you write about him, I see it now.

We were different with Honey, you and I, and we write about her differently. Yet she is essentially the same person in our two accounts. But not Dad. When you say he didn't father you, I can barely recognize him as the man who was, and is, my father. It's as if we grew up knowing two different men as "Dad." It must be the largest single difference between us.

To me he seemed solidity itself. Do you remember the snapshot we found in the bureau at Cottage Avenue, tucked beneath the extra sheets, of Dad, Uncle Jucky, and Uncle Herb when they lived at the Orphans Asylum? Jucky is grinning jauntily, little Herb is scowling, and Dad is standing sweetly and responsibly behind them, an older brother looking like—a dad.

That's what I see in the photograph. When I showed it to Dad, he winced; what he saw was their unpressed, ill-fitting clothes and his tangle of a tie. Since then I've had the fancy that he measures the progress of his life by the distance he has put between him and that snapshot. Yet it has never ceased to be, for him, an image of himself.

"Dad needs bolstering," Honey often said to me, over the years. The last time was the evening before she was put on the respirator, when it was no longer just an implied instruction.

Since I've been taking care of him in Portland, I have a better sense of what she meant, but when we lived on Cottage Avenue, he seemed solidly, dependably, steadfastly *there*, even though he worked so much.

Honey could surprise me, sometimes scarily, but not Dad. He was slow to anger, though come to think of it, I do remember his hitting us glancingly across the back of the head when he was pissed. He had short, strong arms and heavy hands. Honey would stop him with a word: "Hen—ry!"

Still, he was slow to anger, at least in my experience, and very slow to tears. Only once can I remember his crying when we were kids, at Pop's funeral, as he passed his mother's gravesite. Then he pulled at his suitcoat and walked on, alone. Honey stood aside, with us.

His range was narrower than Honey's. Her intensity took up more space. He saw himself primarily as the provider, who even before Honey was sick, worked an extra job, at a department store. I just learned this the other day. "Not enough money in teaching—I had to!" he explained.

But in retrospect, he seems to have been not just the provider but the secret of the family, a kind of balance wheel. Although he was away earning the income much of the time, it was not only Honey who did the work of parenting. Dad too is part of the story. Behind Honey's burning clarity and fierce determination, he was the steady one, whose values, behavior, and temperament could be assumed—at least by me.

When at eleven or twelve I challenged the family politics, he was unflappable. A backer of winners, a Yankee lover to the core, I derided the progressive income tax. He merely chuckled and said, "The soul of a contractor!" And even when I snorted about union practices, questioning the forced payment of dues, he didn't storm or turn scornful but simply remarked soberly, "You don't know enough labor history." Soon enough I came around.

I competed for Honey with you, Otts. She, not Joby, was the first of your women that I coveted. But Dad was not an issue. Dad I had.

His bawdy sense of humor; his cleverness in budgeting; his playfulness; the sexual energy I could see when he kissed Honey passionately each New Year's Eve (and which I inferred from the stack of rubbers I discovered in their chest of drawers, when I was looking there for my old elementary school report cards); the roaring laugh that distinguished him even in a crowded, darkened movie theater: all these I took from him, so deeply that they seem essential to my own identity. Also his wariness of the unfamiliar, his dependency on closeness to a woman, his need to be responsible, his tendency to wait and hope; these too are me. Watching him prepare a tangerine for Honey—peeling it and then removing the white threads so carefully, so caringly—I learned something about making love.

All this I know, but even more alive in me are my memories of us.

I remember him carrying me upstairs piggyback, so I wouldn't get my feet dirty, after Honey had given us our baths in the long tub in the cellar bathroom. And diving underwater between our legs at the Co-op's annual excursions to Tolchester. He'd come up spouting like a whale.

I remember him in the bedroom kicking off his jockey shorts and catching them mid-air, and in the bathroom, under the wooden owl that held his comb and brush, sputtering and snorting as he washed his face, making a big production of it for my delight. Or shaving with his gold Gillette while I perched on the cracked toilet lid. We were practicing my r's:

"Say rrrred."

"Wwwwed."

"Say rrrrat."

"Wwwwat."

"Say rrrrose."

"Wwwwrrrose."

"Good, good—very good, Butch, very good."

I remember him dashing through a drizzle to the corner mailbox and somehow returning home without a spot of wet. He'd been "dodging the raindrops," he claimed. It was quite a magic trick.

And I remember him running behind me as I learned to ride my bike, then making me that diploma of accomplishment, its seal a bicycle wheel with a Red Cross crayoned over it, in honor of my scrapes. And catching my softball pitches on the pavement at Cottage Avenue. I was fast and wild, so there were lots of balls to chase, but never once did he complain.

With that same sweet patience he'd wake me up to go to school. "Butch, Butch, it's getting late," he'd say, gentle with me even though I'd turned off my alarm and he'd had to come upstairs a second time. Waking Grey's daughters now—*our* daughters, Morgan and Ursula—I imitate his voice.

He took me to a Forest Park High School football game one night when I was nine or ten. An adventure—Honey seldom let me stay up late. Huddling together in the autumn cold, we rooted loudly for the Green and Gray, and especially for Reinke and Buckholz, a fullback and quarterback of All-Star proportions. That duo was powerful to my imagination.

Like Blanchard and Davis, Mr. Inside and Mr. Outside for Army's undefeated football teams in the 1940s, Reinke and Buckholz were an unbeatable combination. Watching them lead Forest Park to victory, I decided that I'd go for high school there, where Honey had gone (a photograph of Forest Park hung on her sickroom wall) and where Dad taught.

When you, Otts, went to City, I changed my mind about Forest Park. But the dark Reinke's bull-like rushes, the lanky blond Buckholz's crisp passes, the green and gray uniforms glowing in the floodlit night, Dad and I rooting together with a blanket thrown across our laps: these images have never gone away.

Dad and I, we did things side by side. I don't remember it, because I was only two, but a family story told how we had our tonsils out together, going in to surgery holding hands. A dozen years later, in Florida, we got so badly sunburned, lying on our stomachs with our legs outside the shadow of a beach umbrella, that we could barely walk. Suddenly two hobbling old men, we "raced," roaring with laughter, inch by inch across Uncle Herb's long living room.

A few years later yet, toward the end of another Florida vacation, we dogpaddled in the Atlantic, as he counseled me against taking on too much in my upcoming sophomore year at Johns Hopkins. I was deep into the *News-Letter* and the fraternity, I was signed up for five or six courses, and I thought that I could do it all. And I did do it all, ignoring his advice. But I've always felt warmed that he talked to me about it.

We watched boxing together on Wednesday night TV—Willie Pep, Chico Vejar, Chuck Davies, and Kid Gavilan—comparing our scoring round by round. We hung storm windows together, and the front porch awnings when the seasons changed. As I stood on the porch railings, stretching to fit the last awning eye over the farthest hook, he held on to my belt.

One of my most vivid memories of those years is of Dad and me peering into the toilet in the cellar bathroom. We are studying a giant turd that you have laid. I am, perhaps, eleven. You yourself are nowhere to be found. You have simply left your turd behind.

It is medium brown, that turd, and winds out of the water halfway up the porcelain, quiet in its coil like the sleeping boa constrictor in one of my Don Sturdy books. It is not only long but broad, so broad it cannot make it down the hole, and so dense that the action of the flushing water cannot disturb it.

"There's only one thing to do," Dad says. "We have to break it up." And he goes to the tool bench for the big wooden-handled screwdriver.

"How could Otts have produced that turd?" I wonder silently. "He's not that big. Who is this guy?" Bemused, I watch Dad hack away. We cheer when it goes down.

What happened between you and Dad, Otts, that you were so far away from him?

Of course, there was his warning you to behave in such a way that Honey wouldn't die. That must have not only scared you but made you furious. But that doesn't explain enough; your distance from him went back earlier.

As I said starting out, if you were Avraham for Honey, perhaps you were a threat to Dad. But maybe there's more. This is a thought I've never had till now: maybe we saw Dad differently because for Dad I was a version of Uncle Jucky, much easier for him than your version of Avraham.

Jucky the next-younger brother. Jucky the popular—the athlete, the handsome one, the laughing one.

After Honey died, when Dad toyed again with his ancient fantasy of moving to Florida, it was really Uncle Jucky whom he imagined living near, even living with. And when Jucky visited him while Dad still lived in Baltimore, on the telephone I could hear how pleased Dad was to have taken him to see the Orioles, satisfying Jucky's life-long desire to see an Opening Day game. In his voice I could hear the excitement and the sweet fatherliness that I remember from my childhood.

So—as an older brother Dad got his father training at the Orphans Asylum, and I was Jucky come again.

Otts, Otts—this feels like the missing piece. Not only did *I* identify with Jucky; *Dad* identified me with him.

. . . But how come *you* weren't Jucky?

. . . Because you were Avraham.

. . . Okay, but is there more?

. . . Maybe. Maybe you *were* Jucky—but only for a little while.

Once at Cottage Avenue, on one of my visits East to see my kids, I watched Dad holding Ilan on his lap—Lonny the youngest grandchild—and singing ditties from the Home to him.

"Was he like that with us?" I asked Honey.

"Of course," she said.

"With Otts?" I pressed.

"Of course," she said, "until you came along."

Of course. Is *that* what caused your separation? Was it *me*? I don't want that to be true, but as I write it down, I feel as though it is.

Dear Otts, what can I say? You were displaced by me.

I didn't do it, it was done to me *and* you, but for sure I liked it and I built upon it. I liked being the insider, the favorite. I liked being handsome too.

When I see you saying that Honey and I were in cahoots when we talked about your being kept behind the door, I want to protest. But I know there's something true about it, even if I was asking out of love for you. And when I write the story of breaking up your turd with Dad, I want to reduce the importance of our laughing *at* you, of our being not just together but in league against you. But I know that part is true, along with my desire to understand the mystery of you.

Will you forgive me?

I want to go back and do it over, but we can't. But we can go forward and make it different.

That's what we're doing, isn't it? Not only in our thinking together about Dad; in our writing together too.

When I tell people that we've been doing a book together, from across the country yet, they smile knowingly and ask, "And are you still friends?"

"We're closer, far closer," I tell them proudly, with a kind of awe. "We're far closer than we've ever been."

It's happened, hasn't it? We've met each other. I invited you, and you've responded—haltingly, it's true—but you are so courageous (I see you on your Schwinn, teaching yourself to ride even on the brink of that precipice in Druid Hill Park) and maybe underneath you're so ready to be loved, that you've been coming slowly in.

Doing this book with you, I've learned about your courage. I admire you for it. And I'm proud of you for your politics, the work you've done.

Now I want to say more about you and Dad.

Him a brick, you a brick, him a brick, you a brick: the wall was built. How can you take it down?

Think of all the ways you *were* connected.

He introduced you to politics: his heretical position on FDR; his heretical analysis of Pearl Harbor. It's right there in our chapter on the neighborhood. What do you *make* of that? Didn't he not only introduce you to politics but teach you something of your special brand?

He whistled, whistles, all the time, and so do you. It's practically his trademark, and it's yours as well. You even whistle a melody on your answering machine.

You speak often of your "crazy" schedule. I realized some years ago, looking at my own crazy schedule, that somewhere inside me I thought I had to do that—manage the equivalent of all Dad's jobs—in order really to be a man. Can that also be part of what's pushing you?

Do you remember when we were teen-agers and you encouraged me to say the Lord's Prayer with you backward (to see if the Devil would come as advertised)? Dad asked us please not to be blasphemous just for the sake of blasphemy. His stand impressed you—you stopped without an argument—but I've never known quite how. Can you get that feeling back?

He loves the Freedom Seder. I know you think he's stuck on it, and you're annoyed that he doesn't take the next step along with you as you go further in your Jewishness. But he does love the Freedom Seder. What about that?

Now that I think about it, he has taken the next steps; he loves your new community, P'nai Or, too. You've introduced him to a new way of being Jewish—you've given him a way of being Jewish for the first time in his life—and he's responded. He comes to retreats with you, participates, and writes a public letter of appreciation. What do you make of that?

Some of my memories are readily available, but others I've learned to search for. If you work at it, I bet you'll find things that join you and Dad, one way or another. Let go of your solitude. Reach for connection, take down the wall: you a brick, him a brick; you a brick, me a brick, him a brick; me a brick, him a brick, you a brick. . . . I know that you've been doing it already. I just want to encourage you.

One more thing—a story about me and Dad, with implications for you and me. After he began to live in Portland, we got into a talk as I was driving him to a doctor's appointment, about my leaving college teaching eighteen years ago. He'd said again, as he has so many times, "I've always thought you were cut out to be a dean of students."

Oh no, I groan inwardly, this again.

"Well, Dad, I think you're right. That would have been the thing for me to do, had I stayed in the academy. In fact, being a therapist is close to that."

"Yes," he says, with that quiet stubbornness, "but I've always thought you were such a good teacher, and that being a dean would be so right for you—"

"Look, Dad," I interrupt, my guts twisting slowly as I drive. "What would ou say if I told you that what I'm doing right now— the therapy and the writing, and an occasional class in humanities or lit—is perfect for me, exactly what I want to do? I was a very good teacher, and I would have made a good dean, but that's not what I chose to stay with and that's not what I intend to go back to! What would you say if I told you that what I'm doing is perfect for me?"

"Well," he says, pausing here and there, "I'd have to defer to your judgment on that matter."

Okay, I think. But my guts are not quite satisfied. "Dad, I'd like to tell you what I've done in this town since I left Reed, because I don't think you really know. I want to tell you for yourself, so you can be content, okay?" I slide into a parking spot and tell him what I've done.

He reaches over and puts a hand on my knee. "Butch," he says—he has not called me "Butch" in thirty years—"I guess I've been stuck in an old idea. I'm very proud of what you've done. I'm very proud of you."

My heart turns over. So it wasn't just for him that I was saying it, I realize. Who knows if he'll remember tomorrow that we've had this conversation, I think, but I guess I've gotten what I really wanted.

(Who knows if *I'll* remember, in twenty years?)

So, Otts, for all my easy sense of him, for all my confidence that he was steadfastly there for me, I'm not so sure of him that I didn't need to go for more. That makes us brothers, doesn't it, in need? It means—doesn't it, dear Otts?—that you're, that we're, not so alone?

ARTHUR. Dear Howard, loving Howard, beloved Howard—

Your letter made me cry. Actually, I guess it isn't a letter. It's a response to and a comment on what I've written about Dad. But it felt like a love letter, written straight to me.

The first part got me tense. You were saying all those "I remembers" about Dad—all the things *I* don't remember. Reading them felt like watching Tarzan beat his chest, booming, "Me son. Him father." You bragging again about being "in cahoots," this time with Dad, and warning me off again. Reminding me again that I was really the outsider.

But part of me knew that even the first part of your response was loving as well as competitive. And then came the second part, where the loving took over.

Well, not entirely. The second part is teaching, too. You really badly want to be my teacher. This is different from when I asked you to help tell Honey's story. This time I didn't ask. You just started in, teaching away.

I do want to learn from you; I feel the teaching as full of loving. But there's still something in there of your wanting finally to have me understand that you can teach, that you have plenty to teach me. There's still a smidgen of the more earthy wrestle, I think, and wanting to win.

And it's okay. I *do* know it's a love letter. And I can learn from it. But I also think you were reading more into my stories about Dad than I meant. I know that I owe him a great deal as a model for my work as an historian and political activist, even as a writer. All those evenings when he would be concocting letters to the editor of the *Sun* on behalf of the Teachers Union—such a careful craft. What would they print? What would persuade people if they did print it?

I can remember talking with Honey when I was maybe fourteen about what work I wanted to do, and saying how much I enjoyed history. She asked, "What kind of history?" and I said, "Like Cheyney, that book of English history." She mused that that was interesting; Dad liked American history much more. I can still practically feel myself switch over: if that was what Dad liked, then I should like it too. It was a kind of family patriotism.

So Dad was indeed a model for me. Or was I responding to Honey? Was I figuring that if she liked a guy who most liked U.S. history, then that was what I should be doing?

But the point I want to make is that there's no real contradiction between all of this and what I said about only now discovering Dad as a father. All of "this" is about work—about teaching history, doing politics, writing. It's not the same as fathering. At least it doesn't feel the same to me. I could say it is. I could say that one of the things fathering was about, in the generation when we were kids, was teaching a vocation to your children— both the sense of calling and the practical details of how to do it. I could say that—it would be a gift to myself—but it doesn't feel that way.

What is getting in the way for me? Why was it Honey that I was having that conversation about teaching with, and not Dad? And why was it that when he decided to have a serious go at thinking about my future, he took me off to Philadelphia for a battery of aptitude tests? They said the obvious: I was terrific in vocabulary and ideas, terrible in three-dimensional imaging and in manual dexterity. I knew perfectly well that's who I was. Why didn't Dad? Why did he need experts to tell him? It's almost as if he was my vocational counselor and then my tutor—for that U.S. history test the Hearst newspapers ran—more than my father.

What was missing? What was the glass wall between us? That

trip to Philadelphia could have been a bonding emotional experience. Maybe that's what he intended it to be: a couple of days for just the two of us, staying overnight in a strange and interesting city, learning each other, loving each other. But that's not how I recall it. The same with studying for the Hearst history test. It could have been the kind of bonding that you recall from learning to ride the bike. But that's not how I remember it. I remember just learning history.

I'm not saying it was Dad's fault or his failure. It could very well have been mine. By that time I knew my solitude so well.

I was startled that you mentioned that story of chanting the Lord's Prayer backward. I didn't know you experienced it as a powerful moment. I certainly did. With one sentence—asking us not to be blasphemous just for the sake of blasphemy—Dad washed away any trace of a desire I had to do it. He was so firm, so clear that there was such a thing as holiness.

In most ways his ideas of holiness and sacredness were so vague and unclear that when I try to "see" that firm, clear sentence, I imagine beneath it a whole swamp of uncertainties. But still deeper there must have rested one rock of certainty. Otherwise that one firm sentence would have had no grounding. God only knows exactly what is sacred, I imagine Dad thinking, but something is, so poking fun at the very idea of the sacred really is a blasphemy.

It wasn't the idea that convinced me, though; it was the way he said it. He said his one firm sentence with such dignity that the sentence itself became a banner of sacredness. Was there holiness in the world? Of course. Dad had it. Or was it.

There were few moments when I could see Dad's wholeness. I think about your story of his mistake about you—his thinking, even now, that you should have been a dean—with irony and chagrin. He does that to me too, proposing I should follow paths that are exactly what I've tested and rejected, or paths so grandiose that they also miss the mark of who I am.

I think I could feel okay about that, if the story ever ended the way yours does, with his realizing that he is caught in an old idea, and saying so. It would mean he was allowing me to see his wholeness: the special kind of wholeness that could come from his seeing that he was stuck, broken—and letting me see that he sees it.

But whether it's his not opening that up to me, or my not opening my eyes to see it, I rarely feel it happening. In fact, one of my most important revelations of Dad's wholeness came not from him but from a friend of mine, a few months ago. I was taking a lengthy training seminar in psychological and spiritual growth. One of the exercises was to pair off so that each member of the pair could ask the other to be one of his or her parents. The "parent" and "child" were then to have a conversation about some important issue between them.

My partner was a good friend, who knew the story of Honey's life and death. I asked him to be Dad. Then I told him how much it had hurt and frightened me for him to tell me that Honey's life depended on my being a good boy—how frightened I was that I couldn't be a good boy and would be responsible for killing her.

My friend said, "I'm really sorry, Arthur. I was very scared myself. Remember, my mother died when I was six. I was really scared that Honey was dying. There was something about you as a kid whose mother was dying and me as a kid whose mother had died, and now was dying all over again. It really scared me. I'm sorry I scared you."

Whoosh. All my anger and my bravado in challenging him went whoosh. So *he* was scared! It seems obvious, but I never focused on it. He was indeed the dependable, solid, stolid one. Him scared? And especially, him the victim-kid whose mother did the worst possible thing—died—and who was frightened for us too, that our mother might?

I did a lot of forgiving in that moment. More than forgiving, I understood Dad's wholeness. I wish it had come from him, not from someone else playing his part, but I realize it couldn't have: I had never told him about my fear, as I did my friend.

I hear, dear Howard, what you're saying to me: It still is possible. I can do a lot to break through the glass wall. I know it's important to do. Whatever that wall was, I'm worried that it left me with the same glass wall when it comes to my kids. In that same growth seminar exercise, my friend also asked me to play his father. I felt inane. I didn't know how to do it; I didn't know the script. I can't even remember what I did. Whatever it was, I was astonished when he told me that I had been a good father, that he felt well fathered. I couldn't believe him; I asked two or three times, incredulous. But he insisted.

I'm not so sure that David and Shoshana would agree. Sometimes I feel as if the best I can do is be a good vocational counselor for them.

So all right, Howard. Let me go back to your "love letter," and start there. Yes, Dad and I both whistle, and I've noticed something odd about that. Often I whistle out of joy, wanting to give my own special thing to the music when people are singing, especially when the chanting of the prayers gets wonderful. But sometimes I whistle when I'm ill at ease. At a party where I don't know anybody, I might sidle over to the appetizer table, whistling half aloud. I've noticed Dad does that too. When he and I have come to the edge of an argument and there's some uneasy silence, or he's feeling awkward with new people, there he goes, whistling. I've never mentioned it to him, for fear it would make him feel bad. So it's given me a kind of double secret: I know a secret about his secret, and he, without knowing it, knows a secret about my secret.

But you have it wrong about the Freedom Seder. I'm not angry that Dad doesn't take the next steps along with me. I feel trapped whenever he rests it all on me. I wish he'd take the next steps by himself.

But I get the point. I could probably say a lot of this to him, even about the whistling, if I were putting myself at risk too, and if it didn't come out in such a way that I was dumping on him.

Okay, teacher, brother, okay.

I've been wondering why you think it's so important that I reconnect with Dad. I understand the part that is your effort to make a gift to me. But I wonder if there's something else. Do you think that now with Honey dead, it's Dad who makes us brothers?

It isn't so, you know. It's us who make us brothers. We make each other brothers. We can end the split between us if we can end the split within us.

It is time to make myself whole again: time to forgive you for splitting me in two by being born, time to ask you to forgive me for hating the day when you were born. I need to do this for my own sake, and I see now it has been for my own life's sake that I needed to join you in writing this book.

We make each other brothers. This book has made us brothers.

Just to write it together, we are having to forgive each other a lot and ask each other's forgiveness a lot. And say to each other a lot this new thing: "I love you."

Right.

Dear Howard,

I love you.

Otts

HOWARD

Dear Otts,

I know it isn't Dad who makes us brothers.

I do want for you to be connected to him; otherwise it would all be up to me. But it goes beyond that, I guess. It must be that I want you to be not only connected to him now, but retrospectively. I want *you* to have our history too.

In a way I *do* want to go back and make it different, after all. I guess I want to make it up to you.

I want to teach you not so much to win over you as to give you something. And this, even more than my account of Honey, is what I have to give.

And perhaps I want to give you something *back*.

Reading what you write and listening to those tapes of our New Year's Eve conversations, I see you and hear you as determined, probing, stubborn in your search to understand yourself. I read and hear myself that way as well. Both of us asking the next question, going one step farther, one step deeper. Indefatigable teachers and learners, both of us.

Where did we get it? From Avraham and Pop, from Grandma and Eva, from Honey and Dad—all of them independent thinkers.

But where did *I* get it? Not only from them but also from you. You did come before me, after all.

Even as I resisted learning from you, Otts, I was learning from you anyhow, and not just by following in your footsteps. I was learning how to question and explore, learning how to use my mind.

I couldn't teach you without the mind you helped to make. Thank you, brother. Older brother.

And Otts—I do forgive you.

Love,

Howard

12
Face to Face

by Arthur and Howard

HOWARD. I asked Otts to join me in writing one last chapter, in which we'd gather up some threads. Now that Dad has died, we should finish the story of his last few years, I thought. Also we might say what it had been like to do this book together.

At first he wasn't interested. He wanted to get on with his daily work, his latest wrestle with a stubborn world. So, I thought, it's mine alone to do, and maybe that even makes good sense. Maybe what fits for Otts is to move on, leaving loose ends flapping in his trail, while what fits for me is to linger, to gather and stitch.

But then Otts changes his direction. He wants to write something more on being Jewish, about our differences on this. Just as we're about to end, Otts seizes the initiative.

I suppose that I should welcome this. Otts has written more as we've gone along, and now he wants to come assertively into the book. But his idea's not what I had in mind. I'd rather not get into it, I say to him. Is it really relevant? If that's what he's after, I say, maybe we could do a double reading of the Book of Job. That would get to some fundamental philosophic differences.

But Otts persists. There's something missing from this book that he wants in; he needs a chapter *before* the last. Eventually I come around. If he's really interested, I say, I'll go along. I'm willing to explore the possibility at least; maybe something telling will emerge.

So then Otts sends me this:

Dear Howard,

I want to do this despite your doubts because when I ask myself whether there are still any taboos between us, what comes to me is this question of our Jewishness. In a way, it is *because* of your doubts that I want to go ahead, plunge off the cliff, even though it feels dangerous.

It seems to me we acknowledge—politely—our different ways of being Jewish and our different ways of experiencing wholeness, but we have not wrestled with each other about what this means to us. Is it too dangerous to try? Are we afraid of falling into denigration of the other's path—or afraid that the other will think so?

I think of our two second weddings. Yours and Grey's, in the midst of an intimate community, spare and personal, saying aloud words of commitment written in your own diaries, your own poetry. The only Jewish presence was something you asked of me: to say the ancient prayers in memory of the dead, in memory of Honey. My own ironic thought, which I have been afraid to say until now, is that for you the Jewish part is focused on the dead.

It is true that you recognized me by asking me to do the special Jewish part, but you didn't ask me to choose or to create some Jewish element that would delight me and be my Jewish gift to you. You chose for me, and of all the possibilities what you chose was to bring a Jewish way of remembering the dead, as if to signal: This for us is about the past, about the dead. And also as if to signal: Don't bring us some lively piece of this renewed Judaism that gives you so much joy.

The rest of your wedding was full of life. I tried to give some life to what you assigned me, too, but I didn't want to give too much life to death—especially to Honey's death; especially at a wedding; especially with Dad right there, still torn in pain; and you and me, still raw. The sense of your community around you was wonderful and moving. From them, with them, and in the midst of them, there came many of those moments of tears and caught breaths that come only when a time, a community, are spiritually alive and rich.

All of this richness was in a language that was both purely personal and universal, not in the special language of the Jewish family, the stories and poems and metaphors of the Jewish people. The languages you used were mine as well. I shared the tears and the caught breaths. But I felt my own *mamaloshen* missing— not the Yiddish that Grandmom and Honey made sure I didn't learn, but the mother tongue I mothered for myself, in myself, much more than Honey or Grandmom mothered it for me. I felt partly tongue-tied.

I'm not sure I'd have felt this as strongly if Phyllis' and my wedding had not followed so quickly: a weekend long, three hundred strong, gorgeous and gaudy and baroque in its playful use of all the ins and outs of Jewish weddings. Baroque for sure—I don't think it would even occur to me to call your wedding "spare" except in contrast to the way we piled symbols on symbols, intertwined metaphors with metaphors. In patterns new and unexpected, surely; all our own. But all from Jewish tales and ceremonials.

What is it we wrote at the beginning of this book? "Arthur's political, Howard's personal; Arthur's spiritual, Howard's psychological; Arthur's Jewish, Howard's humanist." The first two of these contrasts seem to me dark, rough lines dashed off in a charcoal sketch, begging for softer grays. We may lean in those directions, but in you there's also plenty of political, plenty of spiritual. The last polarity feels real. Does that make a distance between us?

What draws me so powerfully to Torah—Torah reworked and reinterpreted? No, that's not quite right, that passive tense. More like, "What draws me to the reworking of Torah, the reinterpreting of Torah?"

Torah is a family story, just like this book, only many generations longer. Hundreds of generations of the family are telling each other these noble, disgusting, funny, outrageous, puzzling, insightful, opaque stories of their lives. Constantly rewriting and reinterpreting the stories in the light of new information, new

frameworks, new winks and nudges from reality. Learning from
them even while we're noticing what is missing, who is missing.
Many of the women, for example; there's hardly a tale in which
any woman comes through with such intensity and power as
Honey had for us.

And here I sit, convinced that in that Torah story, this tale of
many many many tales, is God. Not in the conventional senses;
more, as some of the Jewish mystics say, that the story *is* God—
God unfinished as the story is unfinished.

I want to join the story, and rewrite it. What you get out of digging up Grandmom's conspiracy with Mrs. Shapiro, I get from
tales of rabbis, shepherds, milkmaids, and revolutionaries who
have tangled themselves so thoroughly in each other's tales that
one of them who was born three thousand years ago might easily
pop up to argue with my next-door neighbor. In fact, I think the
tale of Mrs. Shapiro's Passover conspiracy with Grandmom belongs right there, in the weave of the Jewish family story, in the
unfinished Torah. (There! I proclaim Grandmom and Mrs.
Shapiro part of the ongoing Talmud!)

Not that I think God shows up in just these stories, that our
Jewish tale is the only one in which is God. God forbid! All these
other stories—what you and Grey wrote and read at your wedding, the poems you and your friends brought—these also have
God, are God.

But the stories, symbols, metaphors, the language I find easiest
to talk is the language of my "family," the Jews. And the people I
spend my life's energy trying to persuade to see the other pieces
of the Unity are also my "family," the Jews.

Even when they push me out, treat me like brother Ishmael.
Why?

A shred of thought floats up my mind—it feels like a secret,
even slightly shameful:

I used to think that when my first book had got its catalog card
in the Library of Congress, I had achieved immortality. The card
would be there forever, even if nobody read the book. But that
kind of immortality came to be nowhere near enough. Not only
did I want real readers, I wanted people to learn from something
I had taught.

Somewhere along the way it occurred to me that the nearest to immortality in any human culture was the stories that the Jews tell across the generations—so long ago, so new! So able to outlive the great and deadly powers of the world: Pharaoh, Babylonia, Rome, the Crusade Church, Hitler, Stalin. If just one thought, one tale, of mine could get into that bloodstream, that's Forever!

Why am I a little ashamed of this? Because my highest image of myself is that my teaching "works" because the best of me intertwines with the best in someone else. Both of us get joy out of it. But if I grab off some immortality for myself besides, that's cheating. It's a little bribe, accepted under the table.

Still, there it is. I imagine that the Jews—like me, both outcasts and explorers—will tell their tales forever. What else is there to do, in that campfire outside the boundaries and borders, that campfire in the wilderness where there is only matzoh to eat and only stories to tell? Stories of what it was like to get out of the house that was too tight to live in. (That's what the Hebrew for "Egypt" means—"the tight spot.") And stories of what it was like to be thrown out before we were ready to go.

It wasn't just that huge and colorful Haggadah that I carried from Cottage Avenue into my Freedom Seder. It was some sense of narrowness within that house, within the narrow coils of Cottage Avenue, that sent me out to breathe. And some tug between the littleness of this little and sometimes narrow-minded people and their living on the fringes, in the wilderness, that makes me like their metaphors for telling.

And here's the bite, the taboo, Howard. It drives me a little crazy not to be able to talk that language with you. I feel the way I imagine you feel when I say I'm not interested in telling or hearing stories about the family or Cottage Avenue. I imagine you feel that I'm keeping you at arm's length because that's the language you talk best and also that I'm missing some richness and wonder from my own life because I shut away those stories.

So that's the way I feel: there's a lot I want to say to you that's hard to say because you haven't learned the tongue I'd say it in, and there's a lot of richness you miss by doing that.

I also feel helpless, because I don't know how to invite you in.

One more reason that this keeps us apart, and then I'll stop. I'm baffled, and maybe a little hurt, by the puzzlement you keep expressing about why and how I chose this Jewish path. Does it annoy you that I chose it? Does it feel like a betrayal, as it did to Tante Freda when she got the invitation to my and Phyllis' wedding and called Dad to say, "Where does he get off being so Jewish? We never raised him that way!"

But why are you so puzzled? I've written about it, I've told you about it: how Passover came in 1968 just days after Martin Luther King was killed and the city of Washington exploded and Lyndon Johnson's army occupied my neighborhood, a jeep with a machine gun pointed at our house, armed soldiers standing guard on the Capitol steps. How I found myself walking home past that Army jeep, more shaken than I've been in my life except when Honey died, my city and my country and my hopes burning around me. Walking home and saying over and over to myself, "This is Passover and here is Pharaoh's army all around me!" Going home to do the Passover Seder, the only Jewish thing I was still doing in my grown-up life, to find the old Haggadah shrieking at me, to find the barrier between this ancient solemn document and the raucous bloody streets gone. To find the childish Jewishness of Cottage Avenue—not just my own childishness; the Jewish path there was not, I think, a mature, fulfilling one—suddenly connecting in a great "Klang!" to my grown-up politics.

My life became whole.

And all this at a Seder, built for intensifying emotional experience, the meal where everything you eat is literally food for thought, where you pour out drops of wine like blood and eat the herb so bitter that it takes your breath away, and eat the bread of poverty and haste and freedom—the bread you take with you when you jump off the cliff into new territory, just in case you survive to walk away.

A conversion experience. What's to baffle? The fact that you keep searching for reasons feels like a rejection in itself.

There's one more piece. Maybe I haven't told you about it. I know I haven't written it. That August of '68, you remember, I was an alternate delegate to the Democratic Convention in Chicago, the one that was torn apart by Mayor Daley and his cops and finished by tearing the country apart. I had been elected from my neighborhood to support Bobby Kennedy. Now my candidate was dead, and King was dead. We Washingtonians nominated our own chairman, a remarkable clergyman in the King mold, the first Black person ever nominated for president at a major party convention. That was an act of life in the face of deadened hope.

When we got to Chicago, I didn't just stay inside Convention Hall. I spoke over and over in the antiwar demonstrations in Grant Park, and I wrote inside-dopester stories for the "wall poster" that *Ramparts* magazine was publishing and posting on the streets, and I had a hand in the fourth party that my colleagues at the Institute for Policy Studies were trying to found. I hardly slept.

But on Thursday night of the convention I found every piece of that, every piece of my self, blown away.

First I set out to join the demonstrators at Grant Park. But when a friend of mine said, matter-of-factly, that a dozen or so of us would be killed by the police that night, I fled. Too scared to be a street radical. One identity gone.

I went back to the convention, and almost vomited when Hubert Humphrey actually appeared. And then I left. Too angry to be a liberal Democrat, even in that amazing D.C. delegation. Another identity gone.

I went to find my Institute friends and found them drinking Scotch at the Stockyards Inn, waiting for dissident delegates from the convention to cross the parking lot and join the new party. I knew those delegates weren't coming. And after all the pain of that week, the Scotch and the steaks were too much. Then I hunted up the *Ramparts* people and found them smoking dope. Until the last minute they had been spinning silly fantasies, horror stories at "the highest level" to give themselves a thrill. Maybe Lyndon Johnson would drop into the convention by helicopter and get himself nominated for president after all. Now they were bereft of these fantasies. Real horror on the streets was not high-toned enough.

I couldn't stand it—not the Scotch, not the dope. Not on a night of blood and tears and vomit. Too scruffy, or maybe puritanical, to be an *engagé* intellectual with a coat and tie. Another identity gone.

Then I drove back to Grant Park. By now it was empty and desolate, the crowds and cops all gone. Empty except for clouds of tear gas, so thick it was actually visible, blowing across the trampled, torn-up grass.

Empty. Empty. Empty. Gas. Poison. Tears.

I was all used up. Emptied out. No identities left.

In one corner of Grant Park I found a college kid I knew, tear-gassed and semiconscious. I took him back to my hotel room, gave him my bed, and slept on the floor, dead tired.

I think that night left me all the more open to what had happened in the spring before, my discovery of Jewishness: the bitter herb but also joyful wine; the old seed of new life for me, sprouting spring-like. There is a sardonic/hopeful Jewish saying that before God sends the disease, He (but maybe in this case really She) sends the cure. I felt like that after Chicago: even before my plague of emptiness had come, I found the cure. A tiny sprig of life in my own desolation. An identity that had withstood many many such moments, years and decades and centuries of such moments.

So what is there to be baffled about? Why do you need to keep asking why? Is there something about this path I've chosen that not only feels alien to you but feels as if I've alienated myself from you? And—taboo again—how do I invite you into this language, as you invited me into the language of the inner family and Cottage Avenue?

Love and

(with a wink)

shalom—

Otts

HOWARD

Dear Otts,

You misremember, and misinterpret too, what our wedding was. "The only Jewish presence," you write, was the Hebrew prayer for Honey. You'd thought, "ironically," that the "only" Jewishness for us had to do with death. But we wanted that prayer as a way of honoring you as well as Honey—a prayer meant to give you both a place, to bring you in your Jewishness and Honey in her death into the loving circle we had gathered. It had all to do with present time.

Also we ended the ceremony with the smashing of a glass, an ancient Jewish custom, recalling the destruction of the Temple even in the moment of greatest joy—a custom we specifically wanted to include. It would have felt weird, foreign, empty to be married without it, and without the cries of "Mazel tov!" that follow.

We didn't speak the traditional Hebrew vows because we wanted our wedding to be a place of truth. Our hearts are not in those vows; it would have been hypocrisy. But it *was* a Jewish wedding. Live music after the ceremony was played by a klezmer band. It was interspersed, throughout the evening, with reggae tapes. How's *that* for Jewish and "other" joined? And the food, also by conscious and deliberate choice, was traditionally Jewish deli, much of it prepared by a Black chef who was a long-time friend. A twenty-foot buffet table overspilled with whitefish, corned beef, chopped liver, brisket, helzel, knishes, kishke, herring, rye and pumpernickel and challah—all our favorite Jewish foods from northwest Baltimore reproduced in Portland, Oregon.

And it's true, it was a spiritual as well as a personal event—spiritual precisely in its being fully personal. As spiritual an event as Grey and I have ever been involved in, comparable for her only to the births of her three children. Incomparably more spiritual than the formal "Jewish" ceremonies of our first marriages, where both of us were merely going through the motions. Years later people still were telling Grey and me how special our wedding had been to them—the ceremony and the party, the words and the music and the food. It's a shame that your joy was nibbled around the edges by the worm of irony. What was spare to you, even inadequate in certain ways, was rich for us beyond our fondest dreams.

How come you did not, do not, see it the way we do? How come you see it as not (or barely) a Jewish wedding? Is there insufficient "head" in food and music? Or are you now so deep into the Jewish family tradition that you see Jews who aren't as *out*? It feels as if you're bothered by our not being Jewish *enough*.

Or is this judgment an unconscious retribution for all those years when *you* were out, on the edge of our family and of the neighborhood? There's a lot of that in what you write. At our wedding you wanted us to let you play, that's how it sounds to me. And now you want for me to play with you by joining you in thinking about, talking about, and living in relation to all those ancient stories.

The sense of being judged—the notion that I'm not Jewish enough—obviously makes me bristle. You'll get a lot further with me if you just say you want me to play, to engage with you in a Jewish way.

But even this would be a harder task for me than you seem to realize. Maybe you don't fully understand how hurt I've been by my contact with formal Jewishness. I was humiliated, not once but many times, by the Jewish standard-bearers on Cottage Avenue: by Shaarei Zion, by its rabbi, by the boys who called mockingly down from the Talmudical Academy, by the self-righteous Orthodox elders in the neighborhood. I was laughed at, scorned, and made to feel an alien. Honey and Dad also, and Pop and Grandma for that matter, had no fond feelings for the rabbis. I'd thought you felt that way too. But evidently, from what you write in our chapter on the neighborhood, you had a different experience.

Or maybe you dealt differently with humiliation: bided your time; then, with the Freedom Seder, entered more deeply into Jewishness but at the same time confronted the Jewish establishment just as you confronted what we used to call Amerika. When I was laughed at, made to feel outside, I backed away, and eventually tried a peculiarly personal accommodation.

Betty and her family, as you know, were observant Conserva-tive Jews. They followed the rules of *kashrut*, attended synagogue on Shabbat, gave deep credence to the High Holy Days; Betty finished Hebrew College alongside her Goucher studies. "What are you going to do with such a religious girl?" Tante Freda asked me in her kitchen late one night, when I had stopped by to visit after an evening at Betty's. Not yet twenty, I answered blithely, "Oh, I guess we'll compromise."

Only many years after our divorce did it occur to me that I may have wanted to marry Betty in part because of her Jewishness, rather than in spite of it. Perhaps, I thought, I'd wanted her fa-miliarity with the tradition, and her fluency in Hebrew, as a medi-ating force, a protection of sorts against a Jewish world that frightened me.

The trouble was, it didn't work that way. Trying to make my peace with Betty's Jewishness, I came to feel like an outsider in my own home. We ate according to rules that were irrelevant to me. As a proper father, I was expected to pronounce the prayers on Friday nights, and I did, though feeling more and more a fraud. My children were to learn ideas and practices in which I did not believe. Really, I see in retrospect, I wanted to do as we had always done on Cottage Avenue—celebrate Chanukah and Passover, the festivals of freedom that I loved. All the rest felt false to me.

With this arrangement neither Betty nor I was satisfied; both of us felt deeply compromised. More than this went awry in our marriage, but this was an important part of it. I betrayed myself until I left. Then I found another humiliation lying in wait for me: my having to participate in a traditional Jewish divorce, for Betty's sake. I was a feminist, but as a Jewish husband I alone could set her free; the law did not require Betty's presence or in-vite it. One more time I swallowed back my anger, and swallowed down the stuff I loathed. Before the prescribed three rabbis— three rabbis also had married us—I said my proper lines, and she was free. In accordance with the law of Moses and of Israel.

So, Otts, for me to enter into your kind of Jewishness would require my first dealing with my history of Jewish hurt. If I worked at it, perhaps I could release myself from what is troubling me. Actually, there is much about your "Jewish renewal" that attracts me: I loved the warmth and humor, and the sensitivity to the detail of family experience, of the woman rabbi who officiated at Dad's funeral. But even your new Judaism maintains some of the old forms, and their effects on me would not be readily undone. After the funeral, Grey and I, wanting to honor you, came from Baltimore to Philadelphia to begin the traditional mourning period at your house; but once the prayers began, I felt a familiar sense of hollowness. I had said my goodbye to Dad in Portland, stroking his arm and weeping as he lay in coma, and again when we told stories about him at the funeral service. Saying prayers did not comfort me further or deepen my experience. Again, as so many times so many years before, I was merely going through the motions, stranded outside of my true self.

Your struggle to deal with your family hurt has been a lengthy task. When I contemplate putting myself through an analogous journey, I wonder what the point would be for me. You didn't become Jewish in the way you have just because it seemed a good idea, an opportunity for growth. You did so, it seems to me now, out of political despair. I didn't have your experiences in Washington or Chicago. To start with, I didn't rely so on the identities that you felt shatter; besides, I simply wasn't there, in either place. No Federal troops, no marauding cops, no gas. Different experience.

Also you've had strong motivation to struggle to learn about close-in family relationship. Not only have you wanted more with me; more important yet, you've wanted more with Phyllis and with David and Shoshana too. I've wanted more with you, and I've gone after it—hence the existence of this book—but I don't miss a fuller connection with the larger Jewish family.

The connection that I have feels like enough. I give gifts for Chanukah and light the candles with Ursula each night. As we chant the blessings, I imagine the candles that we used at Cottage Avenue, their soft orange wax melting into crippled shapes that again and again I'd try to straighten. At Pesach I eat matzoh and avoid *chumitz* for the full eight days, cook matzoh balls and matzoh brei and sip on Manischewitz Concord Grape, and I lead a Seder for our family and closest friends, with a

Haggadah *I've* compiled and written (which includes my favorite passages from your Freedom Seder, about the insufficiency of the tradition). And I have a *mezzuzah* on my door post—not for the sake of the Sh'ma tightly rolled inside but for its announcement to the world that I'm a Jew.

In the past ten years I've taught three courses on Jewish-American literature—at Portland's Jewish Community Center, in a private home, and at Evergreen State College, its branch in southwest Washington, where Jews are something of a rarity. The writer I most enjoy, who has delighted and instructed me for over thirty years, is Philip Roth, in all his skeptical, outrageous Jewishness.

My politics are Jewish to their core. When I defend Blacks or gays or lesbians or women or Jews against oppression, or work with some lost or beaten individual struggling to be free, I am fighting for the victims of the concentration camps. Even farther back and deeper down, beneath the layers of the ensuing fifty years—I'm sure this is true; I can see his round, earnest face even as I type this line—I'm Little Joey from my children's book of Jewish history, wielding my sword alongside the Maccabee Brothers.

So while I appreciate your invitation, Otts, I don't believe our situations are as you present them. They're not parallel. I'm content with the belief and practice that I've got. I feel enough connected.

But I am touched that you would like for me to play with you. I understand from my own experience—not only with the stories from Cottage Avenue but with the plays, novels, and poems that I love—how stories and texts can wind in and out of life, delighting and informing it. I understand that you'd like me to talk with you in the language you've adopted.

I've thought, in fact, about coming to your Seder and discoursing with you through the night, the two of us enrapt in thought and words like Hillel and his rabbinic comrades. But my fear is that you won't want just to play; you'll come on like an authority. (Arthur/ Author/ Authority . . .) Is this a version of our old difficulty over Cheyney's *History of England*? Are you inviting me or teaching me, or inviting me *so as* to teach me? Aren't you put off when I confuse the two? Would we be up and down, or straight across? Can we teach each other *and* be straight across?

I like the idea that we could play. Maybe we can find a way.

Now, Otts, about your feeling rejected by my continuing to wonder about your Jewishness. You've told me about it, you say; you've written about it.

I don't think it's so much that I've felt betrayed by your turning, as Tante Freda did. (Maybe a bit. After all, you said you were an atheist when you were in high school. Taking my cue from you as usual, but moderating your position, I called myself agnostic. Then suddenly off you went and changed on me.) But it's more that I haven't *gotten* it; I've never fully understood. To start with, I could never make it fit with the guy I grew up with—that scornful superrationalist who declared that he was an atheist and religion just more bullshit. How could the guy who broke the rules then be living daily now in accordance with so many? Also, I think I never until now have had the sense of your undergoing a conversion; your movement into formal Jewishness has always seemed to me more rational and gradual than that suggests.

Part of this lack of understanding comes from me. You wrote about Passover 1968, I now discover, pulling your books down from the special shelf where they've so long resided, in the first of your Jewish books, *The Bush Is Burning* (which you described in your inscription to me as "the one book I'd never have expected "). I know I didn't read the book right away, but perhaps I never did—its spine is suspiciously uncracked. Or perhaps I read it so hastily that I missed the full import of what you wrote. Or maybe I resisted what I read. It was published only months after I'd extricated myself from the Jewish life with Betty. Now I was supposed to deal with *your* being deeply Jewish too? Also I still was angry at you in those years.

But part of this miss comes from your side as well. I don't think that you *did* fully tell. You wrote about your experience in Washington but didn't *talk* to me about it until long afterward—or, probably, to Honey or Dad or Grandma either. It's as if you expected us to understand your inmost feelings from reading about them in a public document. A large part of those feelings you hadn't yet even written down, much less talked about, until just now. The part about Chicago explains a lot to me, and I'd never heard it before. It completes the picture, makes sense of your conversion.

Political despair answered by a religious/political conversion. Yes. And a search for family—a family large enough to include you, accept you, but small enough for you to be a leader in it. Yes. That sounds to me like you. Not exactly the brother I grew up with, but a brother changed, whom I still recognize.

You be you, Otts; I'll be me. Is it a deal? It wouldn't mean that we can't play.

I love you,
Howard

P.S. Since when do you wink?

ARTHUR

Dear Howard,

Do you mind if I say another word on this (perhaps the last)? I don't know whether you're not quite hearing or I'm not quite saying; but in any case, I want to underline the *joy* that pervaded my explorations of Judaism.

You heard the note of political despair—tears and tear gas in Chicago—but to me that was not the main thread of the melody. Even at the moment when King's death fused for me with the Passover Seder, I heard the Seder as a reminder that "Pharaoh's army was drownded," that even in death Moses had been victorious.

And the joy I felt was not just in this vision of ultimate political victory, or in the sense that in the very struggle for human dignity, no matter how it turns out, there is always a kind of spiritual victory. There was an even deeper joy of feeling some utterly unexpected, profound connections. Connections between an ancient story, a contemporary upheaval, and a mysterious Current that ran through all history and beyond history, a Current of struggle, liberation, transformation—and joy.

Even then, even so early, I might have put a capital letter on this "Current" and seen it as a mysterious spiritual truth, as God.

Indeed, it was probably because of this sense of joyful mystery that when I wrote the Freedom Seder it did not even occur to me that it should not honor God—unlike some other radical Jews, who have honored the Exodus but put God aside.

My "conversion" not only began in joy but has continued in joy, from moments when, in wrestling with Judaism, I felt transformed.

When I wrote you my first word on this, I felt frightened to raise the question—frightened that you would be angry. Now I feel relief and joy that the conversation between us has been deep enough that we can listen to each other, even about this—perhaps the strongest of the ways in which we no longer "resemble."

Love,

Otts

13
Last Word

by Howard

As I write this, it is April 1992, more than five years after Otts and I began.

Dad died in July 1990. "What kind of a fucking world is it," he'd said a week before, "where a member of it can't even push himself up off a toilet seat?"

After a cataract operation two years earlier, he'd gone to Philadelphia to recuperate with Otts and Phyllis. He couldn't put the drops in by himself, couldn't remember when to try to put them in. And he still couldn't even after several weeks.

If he wasn't ready to return to Baltimore by then, he'd come to Portland for a while, the four of us had planned. So out he came. We could build an extra room, Grey and I imagined; maybe eventually he'd live with us. But not a week after his arrival, in the middle of the night he fell. When I picked him up and laid him in his bed, he protested, "But this is what I used to do for you!"

His hip was broken. In the hospital he worked hard to rehabilitate himself, but he couldn't remember the simplest instructions.

Had he had a stroke? Was it the medication? Or the shock? Or was it simply a progressive deterioration of his brain? Whatever the reason, there could be no living by himself ever again, the doctors said.

But then where would he be? Suddenly he seemed beyond the point where Grey and I could care for him at home. He couldn't be left alone for long, and both of us worked full time. The best alternative? An adult foster care home, a small residential facility for five old men and women, managed by a Rumanian woman who cooked stews with familiar smells. Full circle for Dad: from foster home to foster home in seventy years.

"What is my net worth?" he'd ask me when I visited. I'd sit down next to him and write out all the figures on a yellow pad: his teacher's pension, CDs, liquid savings. The next day he'd ask again. Finally I realized it was an unconscious metaphor and told him what he had accomplished in his life. Some of it he was unable to remember. "I registered voters on Cottage Avenue?" he cried, astonished. I summarized: he'd been a force for good. "I already feel much better," he answered, happily. "Tell me more, tell me more!"

Otts thought of immortality already in 1962, when he published his first book. An ambitious young man's desire for recognition. And now, when he's fifty-eight? What drives him now? To teach is to live beyond his death, he says. "What is my net worth?" Is Dad's question now Otts' question too?

It's mine, I know it's mine, and more so the older I get. I want to matter, want to mean.

Always, I realize now, I've had a meaning to fall back on. I knew in my secret heart of hearts that I was the "Good Son." Now I see it was merely a construction, the result of a bias in our family's way of being.

I've written myself out of my original identity. Cut the old ground out from underneath myself. At fifty-five I need new ground to stand on. Otts is working on close-in relationship; I need to earn my own identity, which doesn't depend on my brother as a foil.

What do I want? To help as many people as I can. In what form should I work? I've been a teacher, a restaurateur, briefly a journalist. And for the past fourteen years I've been a therapist; but despite what I said to Dad about that's being perfect for me, in recent years I've thought of becoming a lawyer who defends the poor. Always I hold the options open. What about the unused parts of me? Otts talks of Jewish renewal as his life's work. What is my own best use in the twenty or thirty years remaining to me? Should I begin again in something new?

As I lie in bed awake at 4:00 A.M., the answer comes to me, tingling up my legs into my trunk, flooding my chest, filling it with warmth. Be a father, a therapist, a writer. Do what I already do, be who I already am. I'm good at it.

Yes. The Good Son was a role, but I've filled it up with self. It's made me into, *I've* made me into, a devoted father and a caring therapist. My whole life leads in this direction, who I already am. Let go "well-roundedness." *Define'* yourself, it's later than you think.

I want to be well used. As part of this, I put this portion of my self on record. This is how it was. This matters. Make of it what you will.

Here is a piece of that record—a brief history of the making of this book.

We began it late in 1986. Honey had died in April 1985. Grey and I had married the following March.

Otts' joy at our wedding was important to his and my relationship, and important to our writing. Looking through our photographs a few weeks afterward, I found one of Otts embracing Dad. He is dressed in glistening white silk, a celebratory *kittl*, and he wears a broad black yarmulke, trimmed in gold. His hands are spread across Dad's back, and his face is joyful and sweet— undeniably sweet. I studied that face for many minutes, trying to imprint it on my brain. His eyes were warm, his smile was sweet.

Three months later, on the weekend of the summer solstice of 1986, Otts and Phyllis were married, in the open air, at a farm near Philadelphia all in bloom. Standing next to Otts under the *huppa*, I whispered to him that he smelled to me like Grey. (Really, I suppose, it's that Grey smells to me like Otts.)

The next morning, the four of us—Otts and Phyllis, Grey and I—all that were left of the hundreds who had celebrated, met at a picnic table at the entrance to a corridor of elms. We sipped champagne, munched on leftover wedding food, and talked— about our weddings and our past, how we came from there to here, and about the future too, what the next steps were for Dad.

At one point, sitting across the table from Otts, I looked long at him and then began to cry. Without a word he crossed to my side and held me, held me and rocked me as I wept. Finally he asked why I was crying. "Because I'm trying to see you without the sneer," I said. "And I think I'm getting it."

It was just after this, as we were about to return to our homes three thousand miles apart, that I asked Otts to write a book with me on being brothers. He hesitated, then told me about the political autobiography that he was planning. To that he added, looking troubled: "I read somewhere that Jimmy and Rosalynn Carter almost got divorced when they wrote their book together. You think we could do it? And not turn into enemies?"

"I think we'd make it," I answered, grinning. "We may as well find out." Eventually he agreed to try.

In July 1989, Otts and Phyllis, Grey and I met on a ten-day working vacation in Jamaica, the longest Otts and I have been together in the same space since he left Cottage Avenue in the fall of '54. In Jamaica we bobbed and swam, the four of us, in the warm, jade-green Atlantic, calm as a lake. We talked for hours, through humid evenings that felt like August in Baltimore, on the veranda of our borrowed house. And in the mornings Otts and I worked over the breakfast table on a revision, influencing each other's writing more deeply than we ever had.

"Camerado, I give you my hand!" Walt wrote. "Will you give me yourself? will you come travel with me?" I began this book with Otts wanting him fully in the writing with me. That I haven't quite gotten; for a long time he was a hesitant traveling companion. But since Jamaica, he's been deeply engaged in the reworking of our manuscript. He's been the comrade I wanted from the start.

Before Jamaica, his attention came in electric surges breaking through his wariness; since, it has been warm and steady. So what I *have* gotten is the satisfaction of being with him in a struggle yielding change—Otts coming in. In the comfort of that turn, I can recognize how much he was shaping our book even from his cautious stance as outsider to the process. His own piece on Honey's death, coming as it did before my asking him to write with me, was the *ur*-text that actually began us. His way of cutting to the heart of things and his surprising turns of mind and voice did much to give this book its final form—as much, really, as my gathering and weaving. And now, finally now, as we do our last revisions on the phone, we move easily, with laughter, in and out each other's words—most of the time.

Many memories will stay with me from that vacation in Jamaica—among them, the frightened local couple whom we drove to an impoverished clinic late one night, our visit to a Rastafarian wise-man who gave us a lesson in cooperation, above all the warm and rocking embrace of the Atlantic. Between Otts and me, one moment stands out most vividly.

We are bobbing in the ocean, bathing naked in the tepid, soothing water of that enormous tub, and musingly he asks if Honey ever talked with me of books.

"Not that I remember right off-hand," I say.

"She was really into Poe," he says. "Remember how she was afraid of being buried alive? That was from 'The House of Usher.' And she loved H. Rider Haggard."

"Huh, that was one of Dad's jokes," I remark. "'Ride-her Haggard,' he used to say. Honey would roll her eyes."

"Well, Honey loved Rider Haggard's books. Especially *She*. I've been wondering whether *She* was a kind of model for her—a superwoman."

"No, I don't remember her talking about books to me," I say.

"Really?" he says, giving me a look. "That's interesting. She used to tell me about the books she loved and suggest books to me to read. Political stuff too—she wanted me to read both sides."

"No," I say. "She never talked to me that way. In fact, now that I think about it, I can't even recall her reading to me. She taught me how to read, but I don't think she read *to* me. . . . Well, maybe *The Little Engine That Could*, but not much else. Once I asked her to read me the comic strips, and she said I should ask you instead. I doubt I did."

"That's interesting," he says. "She read to me a lot."

So Otts had a relationship with Honey that I did not. She read to him, she read to him a lot. Perhaps I ended in a special relationship with her, being asked by her to pull the plug. But he began with one, which defined him in a crucial way. His reading was not only the solitary refuge that it became; it had begun as a loving connection to Honey.

Discovering this, I felt something shift inside me. A new fact had dropped into our world, the kaleidoscope had turned. The pieces fall suddenly into a different arrangement; an unfamiliar universe presents itself. True magic; no illusion here.

So it has been all during the progress of this book: new thresholds, new anatomies.

What's in a name? A lot. Avraham and Jules—our names, the names behind our up-front names—began the process of our definition and the shaping of our relationship. We see it the way we call it. What should I call it when the pieces fall into a new reality? When a poem ends just so? Or when a client finds herself?—when the held breath is released? Otts calls it God.

What is happening in this writing that we do? Yes, we are teaching back and forth. We are paying close attention, we are speaking as true as we know how, we are creating a relationship. Also we are showing ourselves, and telling tales outside the family. Call it the making of meaning; call it play; call it rebellion or transformation; call it magic; call it love.

I see Otts differently these days. I've found the Otts who lived behind the sneer. And as I see him new, his warm eyes and soft smile appear more frequently.

Not that he has altogether changed. Sometimes his voice still carries an impatient edge. Sometimes, I recognize when I am honest with myself, I'm still afraid of him. Will he like these last revisions? If he likes them, will he give me praise?

But for all that, the two of us are different from what we were. And as he has changed and my mental picture of him has loosened, I've been able to remember more of what it meant to be his brother.

Forgotten images move in:

Otts laughing with me in the kitchen at Cottage Avenue—at

the caricature of an undertaker, dressed entirely in black, who came gaunt and brooding in the middle of the night to take Pop away after his heart attack.

Otts toasting me and Betty at our wedding—we grinned, he and I, sardonically at one another as he spoke his gracious words—and then driving us to our wedding night hotel, squeezing my shoulder as he said goodbye.

And over the years, Otts giving books to me.

It was not only *Gulliver* he introduced me to. "My big brother told me that . . ." Also *The Catcher in the Rye*. And others—I keep opening books and finding Otts' inscription. For my eighteenth birthday, *The Sound and the Fury*—my first Faulkner. For my engagement to Betty, *Remembrance of Things Past*. For a later birthday, Raymond Williams' *The Long Revolution*. Still later, the *Collected Poems* of Paul Goodman, and then a series of contemporary poets on tape. And it was Otts, I now remember, who taught me about used bookstores and the very notion of a personal library.

Not that I always read these books immediately, or listened to these tapes. But he *did* give them. He did pass along the gift he had from Honey. And though I never learned to love reading itself the way Otts does—cereal boxes, science fiction, detective stories, God the stuff he's read!—I did and do love certain authors, certain books.

I wanted a protector, a brother who would take care of me, and that Otts couldn't do. But he did try, I learned before Dad died; maybe he did try.

(Here, Otts, is a surprise, a gift for you. Think of it as chicken schmaltz on rye with salt. Yes I know you're going light on salt these days, but still . . .)

On one of my visits to Dad in the adult foster home, I read him the passage I'd written about Normy Schuman's breaking Otts' arm. He burst out with, "Arthur was defending you!"

"Defending me?" I answered, stupefied.

"Yeah. Normy had called you a dirty name, or some such thing."

"Really?" I say, the pieces already scattering and falling, beginning to form into another universe.

"Well," Dad says, taking off his Orioles cap, rubbing at his head, "I think so, that's how I remember it."

Dad's memory failed fast, his last two years, but this had the sound of truth. Maybe he was right. Maybe *I* forgot. Anyhow, Otts did try to take care of me by teaching me. That much I do know—now.

So perhaps we were closer all along, somewhat closer, than I've been able to remember.

But not so close as we are now.

Is this a spiral where we find ourselves, or are we arrived upon a gently rolling plain?

Is this a wrestle, or a dance?

Acknowledgments

FOR THEIR helpful responses to part or all of this book in one or another of its manuscript versions, we thank Anne Barrows, Ray Birn, Allan Blackman, Lynn Bonner, Bell Gale Chevigny, Jan Clausen, Mason Drukman, Irene Elkin, Peter Glavin, Susannah Heschel, Steve Lowenstein, Roger Porter, Sandy Ryan (who was also a typist of remarkable dedication and good will), Debra Seals, Rondal Snodgrass, Dan Waskow, David Waskow, Ilan Waskow, Saul Waskow, Shoshana Elkin Waskow, Morgan Wolfe, and Ursula Wolfe-Rocca.

Sydelle Kramer, who was in effect our early editor as well as our persevering agent, and our recent editor, Adam Bellow, whose personal commitment to our project has brought it to fruition, both made very useful suggestions about reshaping the manuscript for publication. Loretta Denner, our production editor, has been patient, good-humored, and precise. We are grateful to them all.

HOWARD. Creating this book has been among other things a lesson in the workings of influence. At the start it was important to me to think of it as original, but I end with the joyful understanding that although it may be that, it is also, in its beginnings as well as in its final form, the work of many minds, hearts, and hands.

In addition to the shapers we have already named, in the book proper as well as here, I want to mention the important contributions of some teachers and companions. Earl R. Wasserman, a professor of English at Johns Hopkins, taught me much about the complex beauty of a literary work. Nan Narboe and Bob Martin, my therapists and teachers of the Gestalt approach, saw me clearly and taught me well. Bell Gale Chevigny, Jan Clausen, Mason Drukman, Roger Porter, and my wife, Grey Wolfe, have over a period of many years encouraged and critiqued my writing. I am indebted also to the writer and musician Anson Wright, whose wonderful book *Jericho*, a novel in the voices of two brothers, was a catalyst to my non-fictive imaginings. It deserves to be more widely known.

For almost thirty years, Mason Drukman has been like an older brother to me; for ten years, Steve Lowenstein was like a younger. Steve died in 1990, much too soon; two weeks before, he'd told me, "Howard, you *must* publish this!" The following year, my good friend Peggy Scherr died, even earlier in her life. I cherished them and miss them.

ARTHUR. The living and writing of this book was intertwined with three other strands of my life that helped me reshape my sense of family:

My marriage to Phyllis Ocean Berman deepened into a bond of body, heart, mind, and spirit. Years of reflection and sharing in a men's group with Jeffrey Dekro, Mordechai Liebling, Jeff Roth, Cy Swartz, and Brian Walt opened up for me new levels of brothering. And the next generation of my family — David Waskow, Shoshana Waskow, Michael Slater, Joshua Sher, and Morissa Sher — have as adults challenged me to reexamine who and how my parents and I were, as children and as parents in our own generations.

For ten years before he died in 1991, Ira Silverman was for me a teacher, guide, friend, supporter, defender: model of courage, grace, and menschlichkeit. Memories of him bless me.